chatGPT를 활용한 영어문제 창작하기

Version 2.0

박지성 지음

도서출판 **오스틴북스**

머리말

chatGPT를 처음 접한 날 그 무한의 잠재력에 감탄을 금하지 못했던 것 같습니다. 제가 처음 chatGPT에 입력한 명령어는 아래와 유사한 내용이었습니다.

> **Prompt** Write an "read between the lines" analysis for the passage below.
> Healthcare workers have been dressing up like clowns to help patients relax and reduce the stress staying in the hospital can cause. Evidence suggests the laughter these medical clowns create is as effective as some medication.

당시 중간고사가 한참 시작하는 시점이어서 다양한 유형의 학습 추가자료를 만드는 중이었습니다. 특히, 추론 문제는 많은 시간이 걸릴 뿐 아니라 문장과 문장 간의 숨은 의미까지 파악해야 하는 고도의 사고력을 요구하는 유형이기에 혹시나 하는 마음에 해당 명령어를 넣어 결과값을 확인했습니다. 아래는 답변의 일부입니다.

 "Read between the lines" analysis:

The passage highlights an interesting phenomenon in healthcare where healthcare workers are adopting unconventional approaches to improve patients' well-being. By dressing up like clowns, these healthcare workers aim to alleviate the stress that often accompanies a hospital stay.

chatGPT의 답변을 응용하면 다양한 양질의 문제를 2차 가공을 통해 제작할 수 있습니다. 특히, 해당 답변의 내용을 바탕으로 추가적인 프롬프트를 넣어 좀 더 세부적인 문제 제작이 가능합니다. 예를 들어, 결어를 넣어 문맥과 어휘력을 파악하는 cloze test를 만들려면 다음과 같은 명령을 넣으면 됩니다.

> **Prompt**) Based on the passage given below, make a cloze test using the provided words.
>
> **Passage**
>
> The passage highlights an interesting phenomenon in healthcare where healthcare workers are adopting unconventional approaches to improve patients' well-being. By dressing up like clowns, these healthcare workers aim to alleviate the stress that often accompanies a hospital stay.
>
> - Words to use: unconventional, alleviate
> - Provide the answer key at the bottom.

결과값은 다음과 같습니다.

> The passage highlights an interesting phenomenon in healthcare where healthcare workers are adopting _____ approaches to improve patients' well-being. By dressing up like clowns, these healthcare workers aim to _____ the stress that often accompanies a hospital stay.
>
> Answer key:
>
> 1. unconventional
> 2. alleviate

머리말

적절한 명령어인 프롬프트를 chatGPT에 넣어주면 문맥에 적절한 "빈칸 채우기 문제"라고 불리는 cloze test를 쉽게 만들 수 있습니다.

영어문제 창작의 영역을 넘어 chatGPT가 사회 전반에 미칠 놀라운 잠재적 능력을 단편적으로 확인하고나서, 인공지능에 대한 정보를 검색하고 그에 대한 다양한 견해를 살펴보았습니다. 하지만, AI의 활용이 시대의 흐름이라면, 우려가 될 만한 부분에 대한 제도적 규제와 함께 인공지능이 우리 사회에 안전하게 자리 잡을 수 있는 지혜가 필요할 것입니다.

콘텐츠 창작의 기폭제로서 chatGPT의 학습적 도구의 기능은 무한합니다. chatGPT를 활용해 다양한 문제를 창작하면서 저자가 느꼈던 점을 한 문장으로 표현하면 다음과 같습니다.

"chatGPT는 도깨비 방망이라기 보다는
프로메테우스가 인간에게 선물해 준 불과 같은 도구이다."

간혹 chatGPT의 가능성에 대한 이야기를 하다보면, 간단한 프롬프트 하나로 원하는 답변을 얻고자 하는 마음에 마치 도깨비 방망이를 내리치면 소원이 이뤄지는 기적을 기대하는 경우가 있습니다. 아쉽게도, 간단한 프롬프트 하나로 모든 것이 해결되지 않습니다. 이는 광물이 곧바로 보석이 되지 않는 이치와 같습니다. 광물을 가공하여 보석으로 만들어 내는 것은 바로 시간과 노력의 산물인듯 chatGPT도 내가 원하는 답변을 얻기 위해선 시간과 노력을 들여 이를 활용하는 능력을 익혀야 합니다. 이는 프롬프트를 잘 짠다는 말과도 같습니다.

"chatGPT를 활용한 영어문제 창작 Version 2.0"은 궁극적으로 양질의 영어문제를 창작하기 위해 단계적으로 프롬프트를 설계할 수 있도록 구성했습니다. 특히, 각 장에서 소개하는 프롬프트를 연습할 수 있도록 "나도 Prompt Engineer"란을 두어 프롬프트를 실습할 수 있도록 구성했습니다.

인공지능 AI를 활용한 콘텐츠 제작은 필수입니다. 그런 의미에서 해당 "chatGPT를 활용한 영어문제 창작 Version 1.0"은 콘텐츠를 제작 하는 영어 선생과 강사에게 a must-have item이 될 것입니다.

저자 박지성

목차

PART 1 Grammar Factory

Prep. 문법 기초 용어와 프롬프트 익히기
- **1** 구와 절 ··· 10
  - 나도 Prompt Engineer ··· 21
- **2** 문장의 종류 ··· 23
  - 나도 Prompt Engineer ··· 28

Chapter 1. 품사
- **1** 명사 noun ·· 30
  - 나도 Prompt Engineer ··· 34

Chapter 2. 동사
- **1** 동사의 종류 ··· 35
  - 나도 Prompt Engineer ··· 41
- **2** 동사의 단복수 singular or plural form of a verb ········ 42
  - 나도 Prompt Engineer ··· 45
- **3** 동사의 시제 Verb Tense ··· 46
  - 나도 Prompt Engineer ··· 68
- **4** 동사의 태 voice of a verb ·· 73
  - 나도 Prompt Engineer ··· 80

Chapter 3. 가정법
  - 나도 Prompt Engineer ··· 94

Chapter 4. to부정사와 동명사
- **1** to 부정사 ·· 97
  - 나도 Prompt Engineer ··· 104
- **2** 동명사 ·· 106
  - 나도 Prompt Engineer ··· 120

PART 2 Reading Comprehension Factory

1. SAT 유형문제
- 문제유형 1. ·· 129
- 문제유형 2. ·· 130
- 문제유형 3. ·· 131
- 문제유형 4. ·· 134
  - 나도 Prompt Engineer ··· 136

2. 수능/내신 유형 문제

문제유형 1. 주제와 응용문제 만들기 ·············· 139
문제유형 2. 요지문제 만들기 ·············· 141
　💬 나도 Prompt Engineer ·············· 141
문제유형 3. 제목문제 만들기 ·············· 145
　💬 나도 Prompt Engineer ·············· 149
문제유형 4. 빈칸 채우기 만들기 ·············· 151
　💬 나도 Prompt Engineer ·············· 160
문제유형 5. 내용일치 / 불일치 / 추론문제 만들기 ·············· 164
　💬 나도 Prompt Engineer ·············· 165
문제유형 6. 밑줄 친 내용의 문맥 추론 / 의도 및 목적 파악문제 ·············· 172
　💬 나도 Prompt Engineer ·············· 174
문제유형 7. 문학 장치를 묻는 문제 ·············· 175
　💬 나도 Prompt Engineer ·············· 180
문제유형 8. 지문의 형태를 변형하여 문제만들기 ·············· 182
　💬 나도 Prompt Engineer ·············· 190
문제유형 9. 사례를 활용한 응용문제 ·············· 194
　💬 나도 Prompt Engineer ·············· 198

PART 3 학교별 특화 내신유형 문제

1️⃣ 문장전환을 활용한 객관식/주관식 문제응용 ·············· 202
2️⃣ 최신 유형의 독해 문제 ·············· 223
3️⃣ 요지 문제의 응용 ·············· 228
4️⃣ 속담을 활용한 문제응용 ·············· 231
5️⃣ "질문–답변" 응용문제 ·············· 232
6️⃣ 외부지문의 활용 ·············· 237
7️⃣ 어휘문제 ·············· 239
　💬 나도 Prompt Engineer ·············· 243

PART 4 chatGPT를 활용한 실전문제 소개

실전문제 ·············· 260

chatGPT를 활용한 영어문제 창작
Version 2.0

PART 1
Grammar Factory

원하는 결과값을 얻어내기 위해선 프롬프트를 잘 작성해야 한다고 들었을 겁니다. 이를 fine-tuning이라고 하는데 제가 생각하는 좋은 프롬프트는 다음과 같습니다.

1. 내용만 바꾸어 반복해서 사용할 수 있는 프롬프트
2. 최소한의 표현으로 원하는 결과값을 얻을 수 있는 프롬프트
3. 누구나 만들 수 있는 프롬프트

chatGPT를 이용한 새로운 세계를 함께 경험해 보도록 하겠습니다.

문법 기초 용어와 프롬프트 익히기

chatGPT를 잘 사용하는 방법은 chatGPT와 소통하는 언어인 프롬프트를 잘 작성하는 것과 같은 말입니다. 간단하고도 명료한 프롬프트는 내가 원하는 결과값을 빠른 시간 안에 얻도록 도와줍니다.

프롬프트를 통해서 원하는 결과값을 얻으려면 먼저 프롬프트에 사용할 문법 용어에 익숙하면 좋습니다. Version 1.0에서는 기본적 문법 용어와 몇 가지 문법을 바탕으로 프롬프트 작성을 익히고, 그 과정에서 자연스럽게 chatGPT의 속성도 살펴보도록 하겠습니다.

1 구와 절

구	phrase	절	clause

구는 아시다시피 phrase라고 하고, 절은 clause라고 합니다. 품사(parts of speech)와 관련하여 꼭 알아야 두어야 할 구와 절이 있습니다. chatGPT에게 물어보도록 하겠습니다.

Prompt *List all types of the English phrases.*

아래와 같은 결과값이 나왔습니다.

> Here are the different types of English phrases:
>
> 1. Noun phrase: a phrase that functions as a noun, such as "the red apple" or "the cat in the hat."
> 2. Verb phrase: a phrase that functions as a verb, such as "is running" or "has been walking."
> 3. Adjective phrase: a phrase that functions as an adjective, such as "very tall" or "full of energy."
> 4. Adverb phrase: a phrase that functions as an adverb, such as "in the morning" or "with great care."
> 5. Prepositional phrase: a phrase that begins with a preposition, such as "in the park" or "with a smile."
> 6. Participial phrase: a phrase that begins with a present or past participle, such as "running down the street" or "broken into pieces."
> 7. Gerund phrase: a phrase that begins with a gerund, such as "swimming in the pool" or "writing a book."
> 8. Infinitive phrase: a phrase that begins with an infinitive, such as "to run" or "to eat."
> 9. Absolute phrase: a phrase that modifies the entire sentence and includes a noun and a participle, such as "her eyes closed, she listened to the music."

동일한 프롬프트를 다시 한 번 넣어 보겠습니다.

 English phrases can be categorized into various types based on their grammatical functions and structures. Here are some common types of English phrases:

1. Noun Phrase (NP): A phrase centered around a noun or pronoun, which functions as a subject, object, or complement in a sentence. Example: "The red car," "My best friend."
2. Verb Phrase (VP): A phrase centered around a verb, which functions as the predicate of a sentence. Example: "Runs quickly," "Has been studying."
3. Adjective Phrase (AdjP): A phrase centered around an adjective, which describes or modifies a noun or pronoun. Example: "Extremely beautiful," "Very talented."
4. Adverb Phrase (AdvP): A phrase centered around an adverb, which describes or modifies a verb, adjective, or another adverb. Example: "Quite slowly," "Very carefully."
5. Prepositional Phrase (PP): A phrase consisting of a preposition followed by a noun or pronoun (the object of the preposition). Example: "In the park," "Under the table."
6. Infinitive Phrase: A phrase that begins with the base form of a verb (infinitive) and may include other elements such as objects or modifiers. Example: "To play soccer," "To visit my grandmother."
7. Gerund Phrase: A phrase that starts with a gerund (verb form ending in -ing) and may include other elements such as objects or modifiers. Example: "Eating ice cream," "Swimming in the pool."
8. Participial Phrase: A phrase that starts with a present participle (-ing form) or past participle (-ed or irregular form) and may include other elements such as objects or modifiers. Example: "Running in the park," "Broken into pieces."
9. Absolute Phrase: A phrase that includes a noun or pronoun accompanied by a participle or adjective, providing additional information about the main clause. Example: "Her arms folded, she stood there," "The sun shining brightly, we went for a walk."
10. Appositive Phrase: A phrase that renames or provides additional information about a noun or pronoun in the sentence. Example: "My friend Jane," "The capital city, London."

These are just a few examples of the types of phrases found in English. There may be other specific types or variations depending on the context and structure of the sentence.

챗GPT 4 Better Questions

간단하고 명료한 프롬프트를 작성하는 것도 중요하지만, 더 잘 사용하기 위해서는 chatGPT의 특성을 아는 것도 중요합니다. 위와 같이 동일한 프롬프트라도 결과값이 달라지고 있습니다. 특히, 두 번째 결과값이 훨씬 더 자세한 내용을 담고 있는데, 이는 사용자가 chatGPT의 앞선 답변에 만족하지 못했을 것이라고 지레짐작하고 제시한 결과라고 볼 수 있습니다.

저는 몇 번 더 동일한 질문을 돌린 후 가장 맘에 드는 결과값을 얻었습니다. 구의 종류를 확인하면서 다양한 프롬프트를 본격적으로 만들어 보도록 하겠습니다.

1) **Noun phrase** : A group of words that functions as a noun in a sentence, typically consisting of a noun and any modifiers, such as adjectives or prepositional phrases. Example: "the big red ball"

먼저 명사구입니다. noun phrase라고 합니다. 위 영영풀이를 활용해서 다음과 같은 프롬프트를 작성해 보았습니다.

Prompt *Make 3 noun phrases containing an adjective modifier.*

*an adjective modifier 형용사 수식어

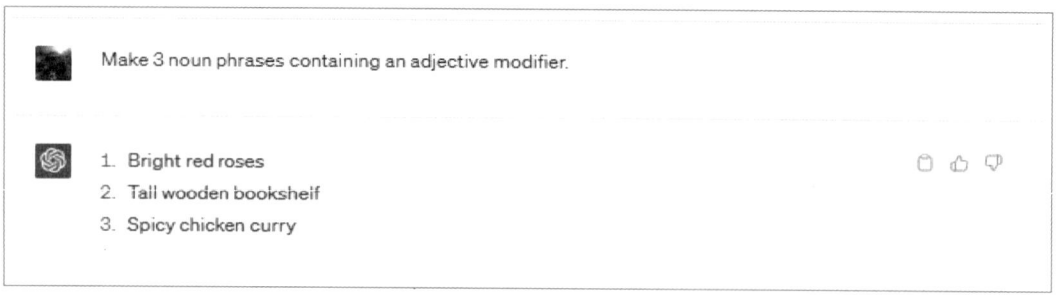

이번에는 형용사 용법의 전치사구의 수식을 받는 명사구를 만들어 달라고 요청해 보겠습니다.

Prompt *Make 3 noun phrases containing an prepositional modifier.*

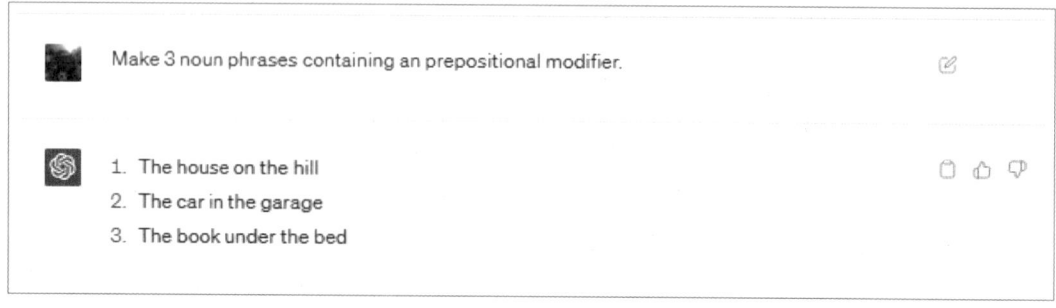

이번에는 프롬프트 내 특정 사이트에서 발췌 또는 참고해 결과값을 이끌어 내 보도록 하겠습니다.

Prompt List 5 noun phrases modified by relative clauses according to the instruction below.

instruction

Refer to the link below. If possible, list 5 noun phrases modified by relative clauses found in the link below. Otherwise, create 5 noun phrases that relate to the content of the link.

🔍 instruction을 주어 좀 더 상세한 결과값을 이끌어 낼 수 있습니다.

https://etc.usf.edu/lit2go/53/anne-of-green-gables/1007/chapter-1-mrs-rachel-lynde-is-surprised/

아래와 같은 결과값을 얻었습니다.

> Here are 5 noun phrases modified by relative clauses found in the link:
>
> 1. The little girl whom Mrs. Rachel Lynde saw walking down the road was talking to herself.
> 2. The big, white farmhouse which the little girl pointed out to Mrs. Rachel Lynde was the Cuthberts'.
> 3. The woman whose house was situated where the lane turned was Mrs. Rachel Lynde.
> 4. The field where the cows were grazing belonged to Mr. Bell.
> 5. The reason why Mrs. Rachel Lynde was surprised was that she expected the Cuthberts to adopt a boy.
>
> Note: The link provided is a chapter from a book, and it contains several sentences with relative clauses that create noun phrases.

아주 근사한 결과값을 얻었습니다. 참고할 사항까지 언급해 놓았네요. 위 링크는 Lucy Maud Montgomery가 쓴 Anne of Green Gables의 Chapter 1의 내용입니다. 결과물을 하나씩 대입해서 원문과 비교해 보니 원문을 그대로 사용하지 않고 좀 더 쉬운 단어를 써서 결과값을 표현하고 있습니다. 프롬프트 내 "Otherwise, create 5 noun phrases that relate to the content of the link." 부분을 반영한 것 같습니다.

아래와 같이 프롬프트를 좀 더 구체화해 보겠습니다.

챗GPT 4 Better Questions

Prompt List as many noun phrases modified by relative clauses as found in the passage below.

Passage

Mrs. Rachel Lynde lived just where the Avonlea main road dipped down into a little hollow, fringed with alders and ladies' eardrops and traversed by a brook that had its source away back in the woods of the old Cuthbert place; it was reputed to be an intricate, headlong brook in its earlier course through those woods, with dark secrets of pool and cascade; but by the time it reached Lynde's Hollow it was a quiet, well-conducted little stream, for not even a brook could run past Mrs. Rachel Lynde's door without due regard for decency and decorum; it probably was conscious that Mrs. Rachel was sitting at her window, keeping a sharp eye on everything that passed, from brooks and children up, and that if she noticed anything odd or out of place she would never rest until she had ferreted out the whys and wherefores thereof.

There are plenty of people in Avonlea and out of it, who can attend closely to their neighbor's business by dint of neglecting their own; but Mrs. Rachel Lynde was one of those capable creatures who can manage their own concerns and those of other folks into the bargain. She was a notable housewife; her work was always done and well done; she "ran" the Sewing Circle, helped run the Sunday-school, and was the strongest prop of the Church Aid Society and Foreign Missions Auxiliary. Yet with all this Mrs. Rachel found abundant time to sit for hours at her kitchen window, knitting "cotton warp" quilts—she had knitted sixteen of them, as Avonlea housekeepers were wont to tell in awed voices—and keeping a sharp eye on the main road that crossed the hollow and wound up the steep red hill beyond. Since Avonlea occupied a little triangular peninsula jutting out into the Gulf of St. Lawrence with water on two sides of it, anybody who went out of it or into it had to pass over that hill road and so run the unseen gauntlet of Mrs. Rachel's all-seeing eye.

결과값은 다음과 같습니다.

> Here are 5 noun phrases modified by relative clauses found in the passage:
>
> 1. The brook that had its source away back in the woods of the old Cuthbert place was traversed by Lynde's Hollow.
> 2. The people who can attend closely to their neighbor's business by dint of neglecting their own are plenty in Avonlea and out of it.
> 3. The creatures who can manage their own concerns and those of other folks into the bargain, of whom Mrs. Rachel Lynde was one, were capable.
> 4. The housekeepers who were wont to tell in awed voices that Mrs. Rachel had knitted sixteen "cotton warp" quilts were from Avonlea.
> 5. The hill road that wound up the steep red hill beyond crossed the hollow and ran the unseen gauntlet of Mrs. Rachel's all-seeing eye.

결과값에 해당하는 문장들은 프롬프트 명령에 맞춰 원문을 약간 바꾸었지만, 원문의 내용에는 변화가 없음을 확인할 수 있습니다.

이번에는 원문을 K-2 수준에 맞춰 다시 재작성해 달라고 해 보겠습니다.

Prompt *Rewrite the passage below into a K-2 level writing.*

> Mrs. Rachel Lynde lived just where the Avonlea main road dipped down into a little hollow, fringed with alders and ladies' eardrops and traversed by a brook that had its source away back in the woods of the old Cuthbert place; it was reputed to be an intricate, headlong brook in its earlier course through those woods, with dark secrets of pool and cascade; but by the time it reached Lynde's Hollow it was a quiet, well-conducted little stream, for not even a brook could run past Mrs. Rachel Lynde's door without due regard for decency and decorum; it probably was conscious that Mrs. Rachel was sitting at her window, keeping a sharp eye on everything that passed, from brooks and children up, and that if she noticed anything odd or out of place she would never rest until she had ferreted out the whys and wherefores thereof.

챗GPT 4 Better Questions

다음과 같은 결과 값을 얻었습니다.

> Mrs. Rachel Lynde lived by a small road in Avonlea that went down into a little hole. There were pretty trees and a brook nearby. The brook started far away in the woods and used to be fast and complicated, but by the time it got to Lynde's Hollow, it was a calm and polite little stream. Even the brook knew to be nice because Mrs. Rachel was watching everything from her window. She saw everything, and if something wasn't right, she wouldn't stop looking until she found out what was going on.

원문보다 부담이 덜한 해당 지문을 바탕으로 앞선 프롬프트를 넣어 보겠습니다.

Prompt List as many noun phrases modified by relative clauses as found in the passage below.

🔍 **Passage**

Mrs. Rachel Lynde lived by a small road in Avonlea that went down into a little hole. There were pretty trees and a brook nearby. The brook started far away in the woods and used to be fast and complicated, but by the time it got to Lynde's Hollow, it was a calm and polite little stream. Even the brook knew to be nice because Mrs. Rachel was watching everything from her window. She saw everything, and if something wasn't right, she wouldn't stop looking until she found out what was going on.

아주 흥미로운 결과값을 주었습니다.

> 1. small road in Avonlea that went down into a little hole
> 2. brook nearby that started far away in the woods
> 3. brook that used to be fast and complicated
> 4. Lynde's Hollow, where the brook was a calm and polite little stream
> 5. Mrs. Rachel who was watching everything from her window
> 6. everything that Mrs. Rachel saw
> 7. something that wasn't right
> 8. what was going on, which Mrs. Rachel wouldn't stop looking until she found out

프롬프트에서 아래 밑줄 친 부분을 고려해 최대한 많은 관계사절의 수식을 받는 명사구를 만들어 주었습니다.

List *as many* noun phrases modified by relative clauses *as* found in the passage below.

아래와 같이 원문에서 관계사절의 수식어구가 달린 명사구를 만든 결과값으로 주고 있습니다.

There were pretty trees and **a brook nearby. The brook started far away in the woods and used to be fast and complicated**....

☑ brook nearby that started far away in the woods
☑ brook that used to be fast and complicated

2) Verb phrase: A group of words that functions as a verb in a sentence, typically consisting of a main verb and any auxiliary verbs or particles. Example: "is going"

이번에는 동사구를 활용한 흥미로운 프롬프트를 작성해 보도록 하겠습니다.

Prompt) List 5 verb phrases with high usage among the impressive expressions in <u>the movie Indiana Jones.</u>

🔍 프롬프트만 잘 짜면, 영화의 대본에 나오는 원하는 표현을 가져올 수도 있습니다.

 Here are five verb phrases with high usage among the impressive expressions in the movie Indiana Jones:

1. "Let's get out of here!" - spoken by Indiana Jones in various situations where he is escaping danger.
2. "Stay behind me!" - spoken by Indiana Jones to his companions when confronting a threat or danger.
3. "Trust me!" - spoken by Indiana Jones when trying to persuade someone to follow his lead or take a risk.
4. "Hold on tight!" - spoken by Indiana Jones when facing a difficult or dangerous situation, usually while riding or driving a vehicle.
5. "Don't look!" - spoken by Indiana Jones to his companions when they are about to witness something dangerous or gruesome.

4 Better Questions

생활 속에서 자주 쓰이는 동사구 표현을 구체적 상황과 함께 설명해 주고 있습니다.

3) Adjective phrase: A group of words that functions as an adjective in a sentence, typically consisting of an adjective and any modifiers, such as adverbs or prepositional phrases. Example: "very happy"

다음은 형용사구와 관련된 표현을 만들어 내는 프롬프트를 만들어 보겠습니다.

> **Prompt** List three sentences containing adjective phrases from the dialogue in the movie Avatar, <u>and</u> create a hypothetical conversation using those expressions.

🔍 단순한 원리지만, 두 가지 이상의 요구사항을 압축적으로 작성하면 한 번에 여러 결과물을 함께 얻을 수 있습니다.

 Sure! Here are three sentences containing adjective phrases from the dialogue in the movie Avatar:

1. "This is a dangerous journey. It's not for the faint of heart." - used to describe someone as weak or timid
2. "This is the most beautiful place I've ever seen." - used to describe something as aesthetically pleasing or breathtaking
3. "You are not the only one with a strong heart." - used to describe someone as brave or determined

Hypothetical conversation:

Person A: "I don't know if I can do this. It's so risky and scary."
Person B: "This is a dangerous journey. It's not for the faint of heart. But I believe in you. You are strong and capable."
Person A: "Wow, look at this view! It's incredible!"
Person B: "I know, right? This is the most beautiful place I've ever seen. It takes your breath away."
Person A: "I'm scared of what's going to happen next. What if we don't make it?"
Person B: "You are not the only one with a strong heart. We will face whatever comes our way, together. And we will overcome it."

아바타 영화에서 뽑은 "형용사구"의 표현이 들어간 세 개의 문장과 해당 문장이 활용된 가상의 대화가 결과값으로 나왔습니다.

이번에는 문법 시험에 빈출되는 부정사구를 이용한 다양한 프롬프트와 그에 따른 결과물을 살펴보는데, 특히 이번에는 조건부를 주어 좀 더 세련된 결과물을 얻어 보도록 하겠습니다.

Prompt) *Construct 3 sentences that contains an infinitive phrase according to the condition below.*

Condition

1. *Extract 3 sentences from the play Trifles by Susan Glaspell.*
2. *The sentences should consist of at least 15 words.*

 프롬프트에 조건부를 넣고, fine-tuning을 통해 더 정밀한 결과값을 얻을 수 있습니다.

Construct 3 sentences that contains an infinitive phrase according to the conditions below.

<Conditions>
1. Extract 3 sentences from the play Trifles by Susan Glaspell.
2. The sentences should consist of at least 15 letters.

1. Mrs. Peters appears to be hesitant to take part in the investigation, preferring to remain on the sidelines and simply observe.
2. The men, however, dismiss the women's concerns as irrelevant and continue their search for evidence to incriminate Mrs. Wright.
3. To their surprise, the women uncover a dead canary hidden in a sewing box, providing the key to solving the mystery of Mr. Wright's murder.

---

to부정사가 활용된 문장을 추출해 달라는 명령어를 만들었는데, 특히 위 프롬프트가 흥미로운 이유는 Trifles라는 작품에서 뽑은 최소 15개 단어가 활용된 문장을 달라고 한 점입니다. chatGPT를 활용하면, 이렇게 특정 문법이 들어간 문장을 원하는 소스에서 발췌가 가능합니다.

챗GPT 4 Better Questions

4) Absolute phrase: A group of words that modifies an entire sentence and typically includes a noun or pronoun and a participle or adjective. Example: "her arms folded, she watched the sunset"

독립분사구문이 포함된 명령어를 주면 어떤 결과값이 나오는지 간단한 프롬프트를 통해서 확인해 보도록 하겠습니다.

Prompt *Create a short dialogue at the restaurant using an absolute phrase.*

> Create a short dialogue at the restaurant using an absolute phrase.
>
> Server: "With the sun setting over the ocean, your table awaits outside."
> Customer: "Excited to dine under the stars, I'll take the seafood linguine, please."
> Server: "Great choice, made with fresh clams and mussels, drizzled with garlic butter sauce."
> Customer: "Having tasted it before, my mouth is already watering."

아래와 같은 대화가 만들어졌습니다.
- Server : "**With the sun setting over the ocean**, your table awaits outside."
- Customer : "**Excited to dine under the stars**, I'll take the seafood linguine, please."
- Server : "Great choice, made with fresh clams and mussels, drizzled with garlic butter sauce."
- Customer : "**Having tasted it before**, my mouth is already watering."

저희가 원하는 "독립분사구문"이 아니라 그냥 분사구문(participle phrase)을 만들어 주었습니다. 독립분사구문이 활용된 문장을 만들기 쉽지 않을 경우 위와 같은 답변이 나오는 경우가 많습니다. chatGPT가 제시하는 결과값이 모두 원하는, 올바른 결과값이 아닐 수도 있다는 것을 알 수 있습니다.

오류도 종종 발생하기에 항상 결과값은 double check을 해야 합니다.

💬 나도 Prompt Engineer

* 아래 프롬프트를 chaGPT에 넣어 결과값을 확인해 보세요.

1. Prompt: List all types of the English phrases.

2. Prompt: Make (개수 넣기) noun phrases containing an adjective modifier.

3. Prompt: Make (개수 넣기) noun phrases containing an prepositional modifier.

4. Prompt: List (개수 넣기) noun phrases modified by relative clauses according to the instruction below.

[instruction]
- Refer to the link below. If possible, list 5 noun phrases modified by relative clauses found in the link below. Otherwise, create 5 noun phrases that relate to the content of the link.

[참조 링크 넣기]

5. Prompt: List as many noun phrases modified by relative clauses as found in the passage below.

[Passage]
지문 넣기

6. Prompt: Rewrite the passage below into a K-2 level writing.

지문 넣기

4 Better Questions

7. Prompt: List 5 verb phrases with high usage among the impressive expressions in the movie (영화 이름).

8. Prompt: List three sentences containing adjective phrases from the dialogue in the movie (영화 이름), and create a hypothetical conversation using those expressions.

9. Prompt: Construct 3 sentences that contains an infinitive phrase according to the condition below.

[Condition]
1. Extract 3 sentences from the play Trifles by Susan Glaspell.
2. The sentences should consist of at least 15 words.

10. Prompt: Create a short dialogue at the restaurant using an absolute phrase.

2 문장의 종류

문장의 종류가 어떤 것이 있는지 ChatGPT에게 물어보도록 하겠습니다.

Prompt *Create a table for types of sentence and their explanation.*

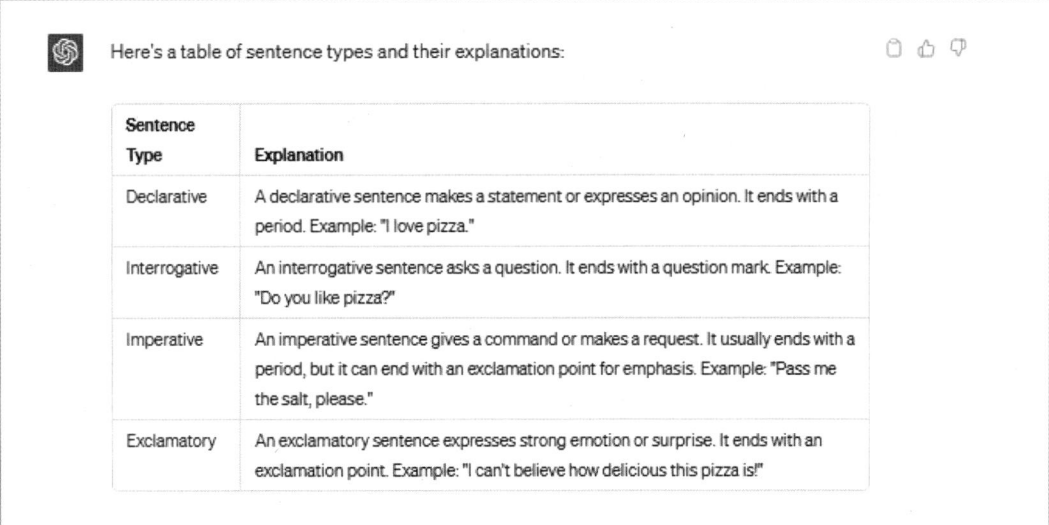

위와 같은 문장의 종류를 만들어 주었는데, 제가 원하는 것은 다른 결과값이어서 구글 결과 값을 활용하도록 하겠습니다.

There are four types of sentences: simple, compound, complex, and compound-complex.

역으로 아래와 같이 프롬프트를 다시 작성하고 넣어 보았습니다.

Prompt *There are four types of sentences: simple, compound, complex, and compound-complex. Create a table outlining each of the four types of sentences, their definitions, and examples.*

챗GPT 4 Better Questions

> Certainly! Here's a table outlining each of the four types of sentences, their definitions, and examples:
>
> | Type of Sentence | Definition | Example Sentence |
> |---|---|---|
> | Simple | A simple sentence contains one independent clause and expresses a complete thought. | "She sings." |
> | Compound | A compound sentence contains two or more independent clauses joined by a coordinating conjunction (such as "and," "but," or "or"). | "She sings, and he dances." |
> | Complex | A complex sentence contains one independent clause and one or more dependent clauses, which cannot stand alone as complete sentences. | "After she sings, he dances." |
> | Compound-Complex | A compound-complex sentence contains two or more independent clauses and at least one dependent clause. | "She sings, and he dances after she finishes, but he doesn't sing." |
>
> Note that in each of these examples, the independent clause is underlined.

제가 원하는 답변을 주었습니다. 문장의 종류에 대한 개념이 정확 잡혀 있어야 프롬프트를 만들 때 원하는 결과값을 얻을 수 있는 fine-tuning이 가능합니다. 한 번씩은 들어봤을 단문, 중문, 복문, 중복문의 영영표현은 다음과 같습니다. 특히, <u>관계대명사나 분사구문과 관련된 문제를 만들 때는 복문에 대한 이해가 중요합니다.</u>

🔍 용어학습은 고급 문제를 만드는 토석과 같습니다.

단문: simple sentence 　　　　　　중문: compound sentence
복문: complex sentence　　　　　　중복문: compound-complex sentence

각 문장의 종류를 바탕으로 다양한 프롬프트를 만드는 연습과 문제도 함께 만들어 보도록 하겠습니다.

Prompt *Make a simple sentence using all the words listed below.*

school, Jeniffer, biology class

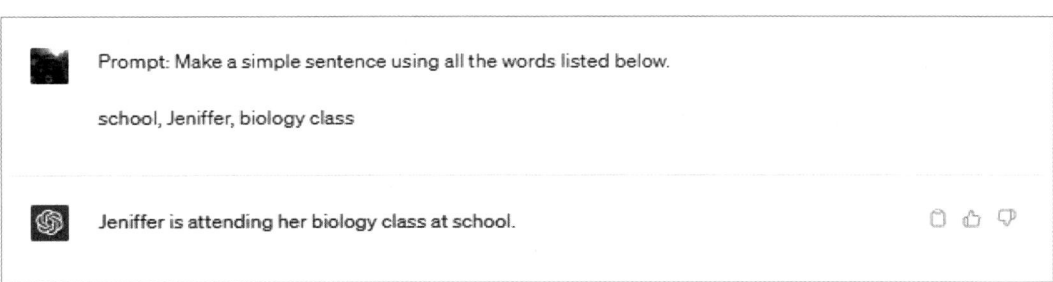

1. 그렇습니다. 이젠 원하는 단어로 원하는 문장을 만들 수 있습니다!

   🔍 프롬프트를 이용해 원하는 단어를 활용한 문장을 만들 수 있습니다.

Prompt) *Create a compound sentence that includes a gerund.*

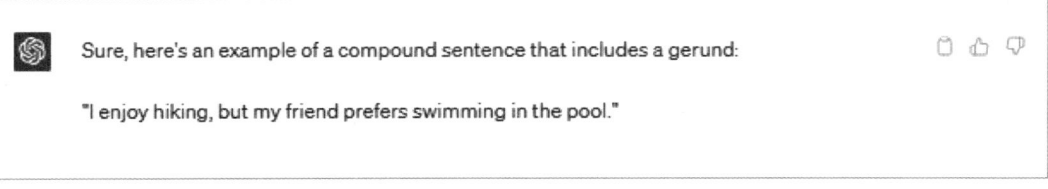

동명사가 활용된 중문을 만들어 달라고 했습니다.

"I enjoy hiking, but my friend prefers swimming in the pool."

등위접속사 but과 동명사가 적절하게 활용된 멋진 문장입니다.

🔍 중문에서 활용되는 등위접속사를 보통 FANBOYS라고 합니다.
for, and, nor, but, or, yet, so
앞 글자를 딴 acronym입니다.

이번에는 관계부사가 활용된 복문을 만들어 달라고 하겠습니다. 흥미를 돋기 위해 프롬프트를 다음과 같이 작성해 보았습니다.

🔍 관계부사를 relative adverb라고 합니다.

Prompt) *List a complex sentence using the relative adverb when that is n relation to the content of Erich Fromm's book "The Art of Loving"*

4 Better Questions

> Here's a complex sentence using the relative adverb "when" related to the book "The Art of Loving" by Erich Fromm:
>
> "When we love, we are free from the fear of loneliness, and when we are not afraid of loneliness, we can find our true self and be with another person in a genuine and loving way," as Erich Fromm writes in "The Art of Loving."

"**When we love, we are free from the fear of loneliness**, and **when we are not afraid of loneliness**, we can find our true self and be with another person in a genuine and loving way," as Erich Fromm writes in "The Art of Loving."

아쉽게도 "사랑의 기술"에서 예문을 가져온 것은 맞지만, 접속사 when의 용례를 보여주고 있습니다. chatGPT의 결과값을 100% 믿어서는 안 된다는 점을 다시 한번 확인할 수 있습니다. 하지만, 특정 책에서 발췌한 문장을 이렇게 빨리 얻을 수 있다는 것만도 chatGPT가 가지는 장점은 대단하다고 말할 수 있을 겁니다. 아래와 같이 프롬프트를 작성해 보면 앞습니다.

이번에는 관계부사 when이 활용된 흥미로운 주제를 다루는 대화를 조건부를 넣어 만들어 달라고 해 보겠습니다.

Prompt *Create a dialogue between the Earthner and an invador from Mars according to the instruction below.*

instruction
— Make it about "Love Beyond."
— No more than 10 lines
— Should contain complex sentences using the relative adverb when.

결과값은 다음과 같습니다.

> Earthner: Greetings, Martian. What brings you to our planet?
>
> Invader: We are in search of Love Beyond our own world.
>
> Earthner: Love Beyond?
>
> Invader: Yes, our planet has long lost the ability to love. We seek to learn from your civilization when love is still a part of life.
>
> Earthner: Love is not just a feeling, it is an art that requires knowledge and effort to cultivate. It takes time and patience to truly love someone.
>
> Invader: We understand that love is not an easy feat. But we are willing to learn and master the art of loving.
>
> Earthner: Then let us show you the way. Love Beyond the boundaries of planets is possible.

chatGPT는 분명 저보다는 상상력이 뛰어난 작가임에는 틀림이 없습니다. 초등과 중등 영어를 가르치는 선생님이나 강사님들은 이런 능력을 가진 chatGPT를 사용하지 않을 이유가 없습니다. 하지만, 아쉬움이 하나 있습니다. 조건부에서 제시한 관계부사 when의 활용에는 오류가 있습니다.

We seek to learn from your civilization **when** love is still a part of life.

위 문장의 when은 관계부사 where이 적절합니다. 특정 주제에 한정하다보니 약간의 억지가 반영되었다고 봐야 할 것 같습니다. 이런 이유에서 매번 이야기 합니다.

"chatGPT는 훌륭한 조교 10명보다 낫지만, 맹신은 금물이다."

4 Better Questions

💬 나도 Prompt Engineer

1. Prompt: Create a table for types of sentence and their explanation.

2. Prompt: There are four types of sentences: simple, compound, complex, and compound-complex. Create a table outlining each of the four types of sentences, their definitions, and examples.

3. Prompt: Make a simple sentence using all the words listed below.

   , , , , (단어 나열)

4. Prompt: Create a compound sentence that includes a gerund.

5. Prompt: List a complex sentence using the relative adverb when that is n relation to the content of (작가와 책 이름)

6. Prompt: Create a complex sentence using the relative adverb when.

7. Prompt: Create a dialogue between the Earthner and an invador from Mars according to the instruction below.

[instruction]
- Make the dialogue about "주제."
- No more than 10 lines
- Should contain complex sentences using the relative adverb when.

품사

chatGPT을 이용해서 좋은 문제를 만들기 위해선 문법 용어를 영어로 알고 있어야 원하는 문제를 지시하는 프롬프트를 만들 수 있습니다. 8품사는 parts of speech라고 하고, 각 품사의 영어표현은 다음과 같습니다.

명사	Noun	부사	adverb
대명사	Pronoun	접속사	conjunction
동사	Verb	전치사	proposition
형용사	adjective	감탄사	Interjection(exclamation)

chatGPT에 다음과 같이 8품사 목록을 만들어 달라고 요청해 보았습니다.

Prompt *Create a table of the parts of speech.*

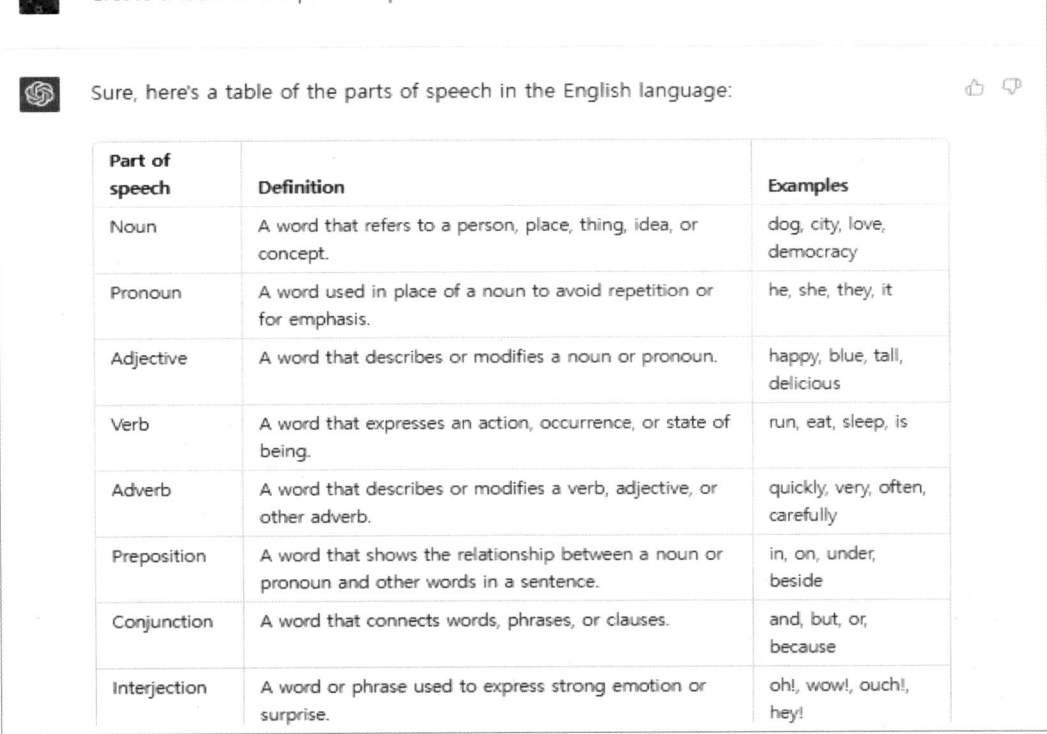

챗GPT 4 Better Questions

1 명사 noun

명사 자체만으로 문제를 만드는 것이 의미가 없는 듯하지만, 먼저 프롬프트에 익숙해진다는 차원에서 아래와 같이 넣어 보았습니다.

Prompt *Make a sentence that contains 3 nouns.*

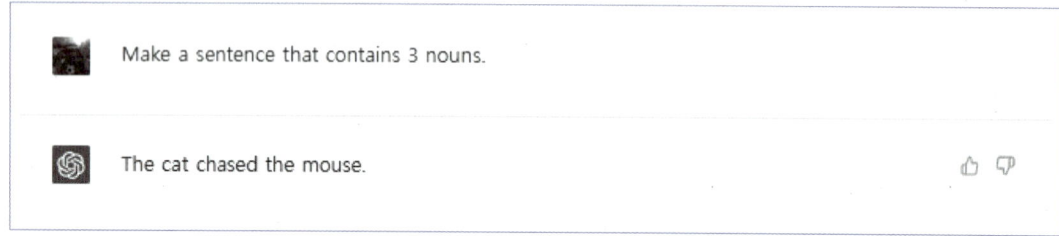

나름 괜찮은 답변이었지만, 답변이 너무 단순하다 싶어 "upgrade the response"라고 명령어를 넣었습니다.

Prompt *upgrade the response.*

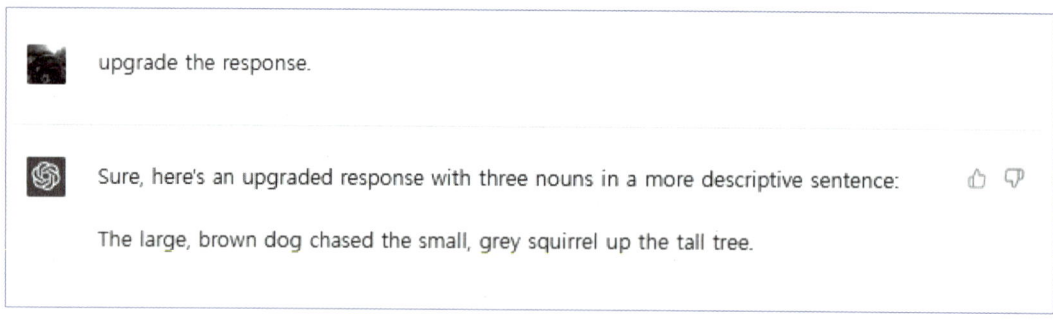

"in a more descriptive sentence"의 표현이 눈에 들어옵니다. 대상에 대한 묘사를 좀 더 상세하게 표현하는 large, brown, small, grey와 같은 형용사와 up the tall tree 부사구 표현이 추가되었습니다.

이번에는 좀 더 흥미로운 프롬프트를 만들어 보겠습니다.

PART 1

Prompt Create a 12 line poem for kids according to the instruction below.

instruction
- Write a poem with about "Inner Beauty."
- Should contain the following words.
- Loss and grief, Relationships, Solitude, Betrayal

다음과 같은 결과값이 나왔습니다

Deep inside of you, there's a light so bright,
An inner beauty that's always shining right.
It's there through loss and grief, to help you cope,
And guides you through relationships, like a rope.

In solitude, it whispers soft and kind,
A light that helps to ease your mind.
And when betrayal comes to call,
Your inner beauty will never fall.

So remember to embrace your inner glow,
And let your beauty shine, for all to know.
For it's a part of who you are,
A shining light, like a twinkling star.

프롬프트에서 요구한 명사를 모두 활용한 12행의 시를 지어 주었습니다.

Deep inside of you, there's a light so bright,
An **inner beauty** that's always shining right.
It's there through loss and grief, to help you cope,
And guides you through relationships, like a rope.

In solitude, it whispers soft and kind,
A light that helps to ease your mind.
And when betrayal comes to call,
Your inner beauty will never fall.

So remember to embrace your inner glow,
And let your beauty shine, for all to know.
For it's a part of who you are,
A shining light, like a twinkling star.

4 Better Questions

특히 각 행의 마지막 단어를 보면 rhyme scheme도 갖추고 있다는 것을 확인할 수 있습니다.

뒤에서 소개하겠지만, chatGPT 활용의 빛나는 기능 중 하나는 특정 지문을 다양한 장르의 글로 바꿀 수 있다는 점입니다. 이 부분은 나중에 좀 더 자세히 다루도록 하겠습니다.

이번에는 명사와 관련된 <u>어법상 어색한 문장</u>을 만들어 달라고 해 보겠습니다.

Prompt *Make a sentence that has a grammatical error related to nouns.*

The childs were playing the park.

명사와 관련된 명사 오류문장을 만들어 주었습니다. 특히, 해당 문장에 어느 부분이 틀렸는지와 그 이유를 상세히 설명해 주는 부분이 감동적이네요.

위 답변에서 보다시피, 명사와 관련된 문장 또는 문제를 만들 때 명사의 단수와 복수에 대한 영어표현을 알고 있으면 원하는 문제를 좀 더 명료하게 만들 수 있습니다.

단수	singular	복수	plural

Prompt *Make a sentence that has a grammatical error related either to singular or plural nouns.*

> PART 1

 Make a sentence that has a grammatical error related either to singular or plural nouns.

 The informations in the report are inaccurate.

The grammatical error in this sentence is that "informations" is not a valid English word. "Information" is an uncountable noun, which means that it is always singular and does not have a plural form. The correct sentence would be "The information in the report is inaccurate."

위와 같이 멋진 오류 문장과 해설을 곁들여 줍니다.

4 Better Questions

 나도 Prompt Engineer

1. Prompt: Make a sentence that contains 3 nouns.

2. Prompt: upgrade the response. (1번 프롬프트에 연속해서)

3. Prompt: Make a sentence that has a grammatical error related to nouns.

4. Prompt: Make a sentence that has a grammatical error related either to singular or plural nouns.

5. Prompt: Create a 12 line poem for kids according to the instruction below.

[Instruction]
- Write a poem with about "시의 주제."
- Should contain the following words.
  , , , , , (포함 시키고 싶은 명사)

CHAPTER 2 동사

동사라는 단어만 보아도 chatGPT를 활용해 얼마나 많은 좋은 문장과 문제를 만들 수 있을지 감도 잡을 수가 없습니다. 앞서 언급했더니 원하는 결과값을 얻어 내기 위해선 프롬프트르 잘 짜야 한다고 했습니다.

1 동사의 종류

동사의 종류에는 다음과 같습니다.

> action verbs(동작동사), Stative verbs(상태동사), Auxiliary verbs(= helping verbs), Modal auxiliary verbs(조동사), Phrasal verbs(구동사), linking verbs(be동사류)

위 동사의 종류를 활용해서 다양한 유형의 문제를 만들어 내는 프롬프트를 입력하고 결과값을 확인해 보도록 하겠습니다.

Prompt Make a sentence using action verb that covers <u>civil rights</u>.

🔍 밑줄 친 부분을 바꾸어 다양한 주제를 다루는 문장을 만들 수 있습니다.

좀 엉뚱하기는 하지만, "인권을 다루는 action verbs를 포함한 문장을 만드시오."라고 입력해 보았습니다.

 Make a sentence using action verb that deals with civil rights.

 The activists marched in the streets, chanting slogans and demanding justice for all people regardless of their race, ethnicity, or background.

문법 뿐 아니라 원하는 내용을 다루는 문장을 만들고 싶을 때도 상당히 유용하게 쓰일 수 있네요.

4 Better Questions

이번에는 phrasal verb와 linking verb를 활용해서 문제를 만들어 보도록 하겠습니다. 먼저 phrasal verb와 관련된 프롬프트를 다음과 같이 주었습니다.

Prompt *Create a stand-up comedy about Fat burgers that consists of 10 sentences using at least 5 phrasal verbs.*

> I'm not one to beat around the bush, so let's get straight to the point. Have you ever been to a fast food joint and ordered one of those fat burgers? You know, the ones that are so big, you need a forklift to lift them? Well, I had one of those burgers the other day and let me tell you, it was a game-changer.
>
> First of all, I had to scarf it down because it was so big. I mean, I didn't want to be caught with my pants down, you know what I mean? So, I just rolled up my sleeves and dug in. And let me tell you, I was sweating bullets by the time I finished that bad boy.
>
> But the best part? The feeling of satisfaction that washed over me. It was like I had just conquered Mount Everest. I mean, I was on cloud nine. I even did a happy dance right there in the restaurant. And let me tell you, I'm not one to cut loose like that.
>
> So, if you're ever feeling down, just remember that there's always a fat burger out there waiting for you. Just be sure to bring your A-game, because those things are not for the faint of heart. And remember, you only live once, so you might as well live it up with a fat burger in hand.

적어도 5개의 구동사가 활용된 10개의 문장으로 구성된 스탠업 코미디 skit을 작성해 달라고 했습니다. 한 소절만 보더라도 꽤나 완성도 높은 원고입니다.

I'm not one to beat around the bush, so let's get straight to the point. Have you ever been to a fast food joint and ordered one of those fat burgers? <u>You know, the ones that are so big, you need a forklift to lift them</u>? Well, I had one of those burgers the other day and let me tell you, it was a game-changer.

바로 이어서 다음과 같은 프롬프트를 입력해 보았습니다.

Prompt) *Explain the meanings and example sentences of the phrasal verbs used in the skit provided.*

> Certainly! Here are the meanings and example sentences for the phrasal verbs used in the skit:
>
> 1. Beat around the bush - to avoid getting to the point or speaking directly
>
> Example: "Can you please stop beating around the bush and tell me what you really mean?"
>
> 2. Scarf down - to eat quickly or hungrily
>
> Example: "I was so hungry that I scarfed down my sandwich in a matter of seconds."
>
> 3. Caught with my pants down - to be caught in an embarrassing or unprepared situation
>
> Example: "I was caught with my pants down when I realized I had forgotten my presentation at home."
>
> 4. Roll up my sleeves - to prepare oneself to work hard or get to work
>
> Example: "I need to roll up my sleeves and get to work on this project."
>
> 5. Dig in - to start eating with enthusiasm or eagerness
>
> Example: "The food looked so good that I couldn't wait to dig in."

이렇게 제공된 지문에서 활용된 구동사의 의미를 예문과 함께 상세히 설명하고 있습니다. 해당 내용을 인터넷에 제공되는 번역기에 돌려 교정을 보면 훌륭한 학습교재도 완성이 됩니다.

4 Better Questions

프롬프트 활용에 좀 더 익숙해지도록 linking verbs를 활용해서 결과값을 만들어 보겠습니다.

 Prompt) *Make 3 K4-level sentences using linking verbs <u>that are inspirational for the depressed</u>.*

 해당 부분을 넣어 원하는 내용을 다루는 문장을 만들도록 했습니다.

> Make 3 K4-level sentences using linking verbs that are inspirational for the depressed.
>
> Sure, here are three K4-level sentences using linking verbs that are inspirational for those who may be feeling down:
>
> 1. You are capable of achieving great things.
> 2. You are important and valued just as you are.
> 3. You have the strength and resilience to overcome any challenges you may face.
>
> These sentences use linking verbs to connect the subject of the sentence (you) to a complement that highlights positive qualities or potential. By emphasizing the individual's abilities and worth, these sentences aim to inspire and uplift those who may be struggling with feelings of depression or self-doubt.

"우울한 사람에게 영감을 줄 수 있도록 연결동사를 활용한 K4 수준의 문장을 세 개 만들어 주세요."라고 했는데, 훌륭한 예문과 설명까지 곁들여 제공하고 있습니다.

이번에는 transitive(타동사), intransitive(자동사), ditransitive(두 개의 목적어를 가지는 동사)와 관련된 다양한 결과값을 도출해 보도록 하겠습니다.

Prompt *Act as a barista at Startbucks. When asked what is the most complicated coffee you make, how would you explain? Make sure to contain in your response at least three sentences using transitive verbs.*

 chatGPT에게 특정 인물이 되어 달라는 프롬프트를 작성할 수 있습니다.

> Customer: What's the most complicated coffee you make here?
>
> Barista: Well, that would be our signature drink, the Caramel Macchiato. It's a layered drink with espresso, steamed milk, and vanilla syrup.
>
> To make it, I first pull a double shot of espresso and add a little vanilla syrup at the bottom of the cup. Then, I steam milk and pour it over the espresso, creating a layer of foam on top. Finally, I drizzle caramel sauce over the foam to give it that delicious caramel flavor.
>
> It's definitely one of our more time-consuming drinks, but it's also one of our most popular!

프롬프트에 담아 놓은 모든 내용을 단 10초도 안 되는 시간 안에 만들어 주네요. 여담으로 미국에서 잠시 델리에서 일할 때 커피 주문받는 게 그렇게도 힘들었는데, 이제는 chatGPT에게 생활 속에서 유용하게 활용된 표현들을 미리 배워가면 삶이 수월할 것 같다는 생각이 듭니다.

미리 이번에는 intransitive(자동사)를 활용하여 프롬프트 작성의 예를 살펴보겠습니다.

Prompt *Make a sentence using an intransitive verb.*

> Make a sentence using an intransitive verb.
>
> I laughed at the silly joke. (laughed is an intransitive verb because it doesn't require a direct object to make sense)

자동사 laugh를 사용한 문장과 친절하게 자동사의 특징을 함께 설명해 주고 있습니다. 이번에는 좀 더 구체적인 내용을 담은 문장을 요구해 보도록 하겠습니다.

Prompt *Make a sentence using an intransitive verb that talks about the current global crisis caused by the corona virus.*

Part 1. Grammar Factory

챗GPT 4 Better Questions

> Make a sentence using an intransitive verb that talks about the current global crisis caused by the corona virus.

> People are panicking due to the pandemic. (panicking is an intransitive verb because it doesn't require a direct object to make sense and talks about the current global crisis caused by the corona virus)

"Pelple are panicking due to the pandemic."라는 예문과 함께 설명이 곁들여 있습니다. 프롬프트를 다음과 같이 입력해서 좀 더 "만족스러운" 답을 얻어내도록 하겠습니다.

Prompt) *Make a short news report using intransitive verbs that talks about the current global crisis caused by the corona virus.*

> Make a short news report using intransitive verbs that talks about the current global crisis caused by the corona virus.

> The number of confirmed COVID-19 cases continues to rise worldwide. Health officials urge people to practice social distancing and stay home to prevent further spread. Many businesses are closing temporarily, and workers are losing their jobs. Governments are taking steps to provide financial aid and medical supplies to those affected. The world watches anxiously as the pandemic unfolds.

continue, rise, close, watch, unfold와 같은 자동사를 활용한 멋진 뉴스를 만들어 주는군요. What a job!

나도 Prompt Engineer

1. Prompt: Make a sentence using action verb that covers civil rights.

2. Prompt: Create a stand-up comedy about Fat burgers that consists of 10 sentences using at least 5 phrasal verbs.

3. Prompt: Explain the meanings and example sentences of the phrasal verbs used in the skit provided.

4. Prompt: Make 3 K4-level sentences using linking verbs that are inspirational for the depressed.

5. Prompt: Act as a barista at Startbucks. When asked what is the most complicated coffee you make, how would you explain? Make sure to contain in your response at least three sentences using transitive verbs.

6. Prompt: Make a sentence using an intransitive verb.

7. Prompt: Make a sentence using an intransitive verb that talks about the current global crisis caused by the corona virus.

8. Prompt: Make a short news report using intransitive verbs that talks about the current global crisis caused by the corona virus.

2 동사의 단복수 singular or plural form of a verb

동사의 단복수는 주어와 동사의 수일치라는 측면에서 이야기를 많이 하죠. 주어와 동사의 수일치는 영어로 Subject-verb agreement라고 합니다. 지금부터 동사의 단복수와 관련된 다양한 프롬프트에 익숙해 보도록 하겠습니다.

🔍 주동의 일치는 subject-verb agreement라 하며, 문제를 만들 때 용어를 알아두면 좋습니다.

Prompt *Extract two inspirational quotes that has a singular verb from the link below.*
https://www.goodreads.com/quotes

🔍 특정 사이트의 내용을 활용하는 프롬프트를 만들 수 있습니다.

 Here are two inspirational quotes with singular verbs that I extracted from Goodreads:

1. "Believe in yourself. You are braver than you think, more talented than you know, and capable of more than you imagine." - Roy T. Bennett
2. "The only way to do great work is to love what you do." - Steve Jobs

단수 동사를 가지는 인용문을 뽑아 달라고 했는데, 두 번째 문장만 단수동사입니다. 결과값에 대해 반드시 double check을 해야 하는 이유입니다. 이번에는 단수동사를 두 개 가지는 문장을 요청해 보도록 하겠습니다.

Prompt *Make another sentence that has two singular verbs.*

 Make another sentence that has two singluar verbs.

 Here's a sentence with two singular verbs:

He studies hard and always attends class.

두 개의 단수 동사를 가진 문장을 만들어 달라고 했더니 등위접속사(coordinated conjunction)로 연결된 단문(simple sentence)을 만들어 주었습니다.
이번에는 조금 복잡한 프롬프트를 만들어 보겠습니다.

Prompt) Make <u>a question with 5 multiple choices</u> that test the knowledge of subject-verb agreement along with other grammatical knowledge listed below.

[list of grammar to test]
- *subject-verb agreement*
- *tense*
- *passive form*
- *relative clause*

Provide the answer and explanation at the bottom.

🔍 5지선다의 명령어는 밑줄 친 표현을 활용하시면 됩니다.

아래와 같은 결과값을 얻었습니다.

 Question: Which of the following sentences has a subject-verb agreement error?

A. The cat climbs up the tree.
B. My parents and my brother is coming to visit me.
C. She has been playing tennis since she was five years old.
D. The novel, which was written by Hemingway, is about the Spanish Civil War.
E. The letter was written by her yesterday.

Answer: B. "My parents and my brother is coming to visit me" has a subject-verb agreement error. The subject of the sentence is "My parents and my brother," which is plural, so the verb should also be plural ("are" instead of "is").

Explanation of other grammatical knowledge:

- A: Present simple tense in the active voice.
- C: Present perfect continuous tense in the active voice.
- D: Past simple tense in the passive voice with a relative clause.
- E: Past simple tense in the passive voice.

　주동의 수일치 뿐 아니라 조건부에서 언급한 모든 사항을 간접적으로 평가할 수 있도록 문제를 만들어 주었습니다. 물론, 답과 함께 해설도 제공하고 있습니다.

　chatGPT의 특징 중 하나는 일정 시간 후에 동일한 프롬프트를 넣는다고 해도 같은 내용을 반복해서 제시해 주지 않는 경우가 있습니다. 위의 프롬프트를 그대로 다시 넣어 보도록 하겠습니다.

챗GPT 4 Better Questions

이번에는 다음과 같은 결과값을 얻었습니다.

> Question: Choose the sentence that demonstrates correct subject-verb agreement, uses the present progressive tense, includes the passive form, and contains a relative clause.
>
> A) The book was being read by me, who enjoys mysteries.
> B) The books was being read by me, who enjoy mysteries.
> C) The book was being read by me, who enjoy mysteries.
> D) The books was being read by me, who enjoys mysteries.
> E) The book is being read by me, who enjoys mysteries.
>
> Answer: E) The book is being read by me, who enjoys mysteries.
>
> Explanation:
>
> * Correct subject-verb agreement: "The book" (singular subject) is paired with the singular verb "is."
> * Present progressive tense: "is being read" indicates an ongoing action in the present.
> * Passive form: "is being read" employs the passive voice, with the subject receiving the action.
> * Relative clause: "who enjoys mysteries" serves as a relative clause, providing additional information about the subject "me" within the sentence.

프롬프트에서 요구한 문법을 모두 활용하였지만, 구조 문제를 만들어 주었습니다. 이는 두 가지 측면에서 이해할 수 있을 것 같습니다. 하나는 앞서 한 번 언급했듯이 chatGPT는 사용자와의 대화를 기억하기에 사용자가 결과값에 만족하지 못했다고 판단하거나 다른 결과값을 기대한 것으로 스스로 판단하는 경향을 보이는 것 같습니다. 두 번째는 작성한 프롬프트가 그만큼 fine-tuning이 되어 있지 않다는 말이기도 할 것입니다. 프롬프트에 대한 끊임없는 연구가 필요한 이유이기도 합니다.

나도 Prompt Engineer

1. Prompt: Extract two inspirational quotes that has a singular verb from the link below.

2. Prompt: Make another sentence that has two singular verbs.

3. Prompt: Make a question with 5 multiple choices that test the knowledge of subject-verb agreement along with other grammatical knowledge listed below.

[list of grammar to test]
- subject-verb agreement
- tense
- passive form
- relative clause

Provide the answer and explanation at the bottom.

챗GPT 4 Better Questions

3 동사의 시제 Verb Tense

동사의 시제에는 보통 12개가 있다고 하죠. 해당 시제의 영어표현을 알고, 이를 활용한 명령어를 사용하면 멋진 문제를 만들어 낼 수 있습니다.

Simple present 단순현재	Past continuous 과거진행
Present perfect 현재완료	Past perfect continuous 과거완료진행
Present continuous 진행시제	Simple future 단순미래
Present perfect continuous 현재완료시제	Future perfect 미래완료
Simple past 단순과거	Future continuous 미래진행
Past perfect 과거완료	Future perfect continuous 미래완료진행

12시제 중 현재와 관련된 시제를 중심으로 프롬프트의 종류 살펴보고, 적용해 보도록 하겠습니다. 특히, 이번에는 시제와 관련된 프롬프트를 짤 때, 다양한 주제를 다루는 글을 함께 도출해 보겠습니다.

Prompt *List three latest issues using three different verb tenses.*

🔍 특정 시제를 반영한 문장을 만들 때 무작위 내용이 아니라 특정 주제를 다루는 문장을 만들 수 있습니다.

 List three latest issues using three different verb tenses.

1. COVID-19 cases are surging in many countries around the world.
2. Yesterday, a major earthquake struck the coast of Japan.
3. By next year, scientists hope to have developed a more effective vaccine against the flu.

현재, 과거, 미래 시제 동사를 활용한 최신 이슈에 관련된 문장을 만들어 주었습니다.

이번에는 2차 세계대전의 원인을 논하는 글을 현재형 시제로 쓰는 프롬프트를 만들어 보겠습니다.

Prompt *Write a passage that talks about the cause of WWII in the simple present tense.*

> Write a passage that talks about the cause of WWII in the simple present tense.

> The cause of World War II is rooted in the aftermath of World War I. The Treaty of Versailles, which was signed after World War I, imposed strict penalties on Germany, forcing them to accept responsibility for the war and pay for the damage caused by the conflict. These strict penalties, combined with economic turmoil, led to the rise of the Nazi party in Germany, led by Adolf Hitler. Hitler's expansionist ambitions and desire for German hegemony in Europe eventually led to his invasion of Poland in 1939, which marked the beginning of World War II. In the present day, historians still debate the complex factors that contributed to the outbreak of war, but the consequences of this conflict have shaped the world we live in today.

현재시제 동사가 활용된 2차 세계대전의 원인을 설명하는 깔끔한 지문을 만들어 주었습니다. 이번에는 해당 지문을 바탕으로 3개의 문법 문제를 만들어 달라고 요청해 보려고 하는데, 시험에 주로 출제되는 문법 사항을 정리하면 다음과 같습니다.

Singular and Plural Nouns	Correlative Conjunctions
Possessive Nouns	Parallel Ideas
Cases of Personal Pronouns	Conjunctive Adverbs
Reflexive and Intensive Pronouns	Subordinating Conjunctions
Interrogative Pronouns	Participles and Participial Phrases
Action Verbs	Restrictive and Nonrestrictive Participial Phrases
Linking Verbs	Misplaced Participial Phrases
Helping Verbs	Gerunds and Gerund Phrases
Types of Verbs	To-infinitive and To-infinitive Phrase
Transitive vs. Intransitive Verb	Adjective Clauses
Active vs. Passive Voice	Restrictive and Nonrestrictive Adjective Clauses
Moods of Verbs	Adverb Clauses
Agreement of Verbs	Noun Clauses
Structure of sentence	Classifying Dependent Clauses
Adverbs Modifying Verbs	Run-On Sentences and Fragments
Adverbs Modifying Adjectives	
Coordinate Conjunctions	

챗GPT 4 Better Questions

시제와 함께 위에서 몇 가지를 골라 3개의 문법 문제를 만들어 달라는 프롬프트를 만들어 보겠습니다.

Prompt) Make 3 questions question with 5 multiple choices that test the grammar knowledge with the instruction below.

instruction

* list of grammar to test
— subject-verb agreement
— Gerunds and Gerund Phrases
— Active/Passive Voice
— Run-On Sentences and Fragments

🔍 평가하고자 하는 문법 사항을 넣으면 됩니다.

* Types of Stem

Question 1. Choose one that is NOT grammatically correct?
Question 2. Which of the following best fills in the blanks (A) and (B) in the sentence given below?
Question 3. Which of the following is NOT a run-on sentence?

🔍 문제를 3개 만들어 달라고 했으므로 각각의 문제를 입력해 주면 됩니다.

* Type of Alternative
①
②
③
④
⑤

[Provide the answer and explanation at the bottom.]

아래는 첫 번째 문제에 대한 결과값입니다.

> Question 1. Choose one that is NOT grammatically correct?
> ① The dogs barks loudly at night.
> ② He like to swim in the ocean.
> ③ She enjoys reading books and watching movies.
> ④ They was late for the meeting.
> ⑤ We have been waiting for hours.

5지선다로 구성된 주동의 수일치 문제를 만들어 주었습니다. 아래 답 설명을 보면 알 수 있지만, 오류가 발생했습니다.

다음은 두 번째 문제에 대한 결과값입니다.

> Question 2. Which of the following best fills in the blanks (A) and (B) in the sentence given below?
> (A) _____ in the park is my favorite pastime. (B) _____ makes me feel calm and relaxed.
> ① Running / It
> ② Run / Running
> ③ Ran / Run
> ④ To run / It
> ⑤ Run / It

5지선다의 two-blank 문제를 만들어주었습니다. 답에도 오류가 없습니다. 아래는 세 번째 문장에 대한 결과값입니다.

> Question 3. Which of the following is NOT a run-on sentence?
> ① I went to the store to buy some milk, I also bought some bread.
> ② She likes to dance, he likes to sing.
> ③ We went to the beach, swam in the ocean, and sunbathed on the sand.
> ④ After I finished my homework, I went to bed early.
> ⑤ They went to the movies, had dinner, and went bowling.

④번 보기를 제외하고는 모두 run-on sentence에 해당합니다. 정답과 설명도 깔끔합니다. 두 번째 문제에 오류가 발생하긴 했지만, 이는 2차 가공을 통해서 난이도까지 조절이 가능합니다.

챗GPT 4 Better Questions

이번에는 원하는 문장을 활용한 프롬프트를 만들어 보겠습니다. 특히, 문항수와 보기에 활용한 문장의 수도 줄이고, 문제수도 두 개로 줄여 보겠습니다.

Prompt) Based on the passage below, make 2 questions question with 5 multiple choices that test the grammar knowledge according to the instruction below.

Passage

One cause of disease is dirt. Dirt is full of germs. These germs are too small to see. You need a microscope to see them. They may be small, but they are alive. They can get inside our bodies and make us sick. They enter through our mouths more easily than through our noses. So we should try to keep our mouths closed and breathe through our noses.

instruction

* list of grammar to test
− subject-verb agreement
− Gerunds and Gerund Phrases
− Active/Passive Voice

* Types of Stem

Question 1. Choose one that is NOT grammatically correct?
Question 2. Which of the following best fills in the blanks (A) and (B) in the sentence given below?

🔍 문제의 질을 높이려는 의도에서 문항 수를 줄여 보았습니다.

* Contents of the options

When making options, use the sentences in the passage as they are.

🔍 앞선 프롬프트와 달리 "선지의 내용"이라는 말을 넣고, 본문의 문장을 변형하지 말고 그대로 사용해 달라고 요청했습니다.

[Type of Alternative]
①

②
③
④
⑤

* *Provide the answer and explanation at the bottom.*

아래와 같은 결과값을 얻었습니다.

Question 1: Which of the following sentences contains an error in subject-verb agreement?
① Dirt is full of germs that can make us sick.
② Germs are too small to see without a microscope.
③ Closing our mouths can help prevent germs from entering our bodies.
④ Breathing through our noses is recommended in order to reduce the risk of getting sick.
⑤ Keeping our bodies clean is an effective way to prevent disease.

Question 2: Which of the following best fills in the blanks (A) and (B) in the sentence given below?
"They may be small, but they are alive. They can get inside our bodies and make us sick. They enter through our mouths more easily than through our noses. So we should try to keep our (A)_____ and (B)_____."
① (A) noses closed (B) mouths open
② (A) noses open (B) mouths closed
③ (A) ears closed (B) eyes open
④ (A) noses closed (B) eyes closed
⑤ (A) ears open (B) mouths open

요청한 유형의 5지선다 문제를 만들어 주었습니다. 하지만, 아래 해설에서 확인할 수 있듯이 오류가 발생했습니다. 약간의 수정이 필요한 상황입니다. 두 번째 문제의 경우에도 대명사 they를 germs로 표현했으면 더 좋았을 겁니다.

🔍 결과값에 대한 검수가 항상 필요한 이유입니다.

4 Better Questions

> Answer:
> Question 1: ⑤ Keeping our bodies clean is an effective way to prevent disease. (Subject-verb agreement error)
> Explanation: The subject of the sentence is "keeping our bodies clean," which is singular, but the verb "are" is plural. The correct sentence would be "Keeping our bodies clean is an effective way to prevent disease."
>
> Question 2: ② (A) noses open (B) mouths closed
> Explanation: The passage states that germs enter our bodies more easily through our mouths than through our noses, so the best option for (B) is "mouths closed" to reduce the risk of getting sick. For (A), the opposite of "mouths closed" is "noses open," which is the best option as it fits the context. The other options are not mentioned or are not suitable in the context.

이번에는 다양한 시제가 활용된 감동적인 영화대사를 찾아 달라는 프롬프트를 넣어 보도록 하겠습니다.

Prompt *Find an impressive dialogue from the movie Mulan that uses the present perfect verb.*

> Here is a dialogue from the movie Mulan that uses the present perfect verb:
>
> Mulan: "Maybe I didn't go for my father. Maybe what I really wanted was to prove I could do things right. So when I looked in the mirror, I'd see someone worthwhile. But I was wrong. I see nothing."
>
> Li Shang: "You risked your life to save this dumb... flower?!"
>
> Mulan: "To save a friend."
>
> Li Shang: "Ping... you're the craziest man I've ever met. And for that, I owe you my life. From now on, you have my trust."
>
> In this dialogue, Li Shang uses the present perfect verb "have met" to describe the past action of meeting Mulan, emphasizing the ongoing relevance of the experience to the present moment.

이번에는 문제까지 만들어 달라고 해 보겠습니다.
현재완료가 들어갈 대화와 그에 대한 해설까지 해 주고 있습니다.

> **Prompt**) Write a short but touching story that makes use of the present perfect sentences, and based on the story, make a <u>cloze test</u> with as many blanks as possible to test the grammar knowledge listed below.

🔍 빈칸을 뚫어 만드는 문제를 cloze test라고 합니다.

*list of grammar to test
— Active vs. Passive Voice
— Participles and Participial Phrases
— Gerunds and Gerund Phrases
— To-infinitive and To-infinitive Phrase
— Prompt: Extract two inspirational quotes

Provide the answer at the bottom.

아래와 같은 결과값을 얻었습니다.

 [Story]
Emily has always loved animals. Since she was a child, she would spend hours at the local animal shelter, volunteering and helping the abandoned and mistreated animals find new homes. She has adopted several dogs and cats over the years, providing them with a loving and caring environment. Her dedication and compassion have made a significant impact on the lives of these animals. Many of them have been given a second chance at life because of Emily's selfless actions. She continues to advocate for animal rights and encourages others to do the same. Emily's love for animals has not only changed their lives but has also changed her own, filling her heart with joy and purpose.

[Cloze Text]
Emily ____ always ____ animals. Since she ____ a child, she ____ hours at the local animal shelter, volunteering and helping the abandoned and mistreated animals ____ new homes. She ____ adopted several dogs and cats over the years, providing them with a loving and caring environment. Her dedication and compassion ____ made a significant impact on the lives of these animals. Many of them ____ ____ a second chance at life because of Emily's selfless actions. She continues to advocate for animal rights and encourages others ____ ____ the same. Emily's love for animals ____ not only changed their lives but ____ also changed her own, filling her heart with joy and purpose.

원하는 형태에 맞춰 결과값을 주었습니다.

> [Answer]
>
> - Present Perfect Tense: has loved, has spent, has adopted, have found, has made, have been given, have encouraged, has not only changed, has also changed.
> - Active vs. Passive Voice: None.
> - Participles and Participial Phrases: helping the abandoned and mistreated animals find new homes.
> - Gerunds and Gerund Phrases: volunteering, providing them with a loving and caring environment, advocating for animal rights.
> - To-infinitive and To-infinitive Phrase: to do the same.

이야기도 감동적이지만 각각의 항목에 따른 답을 제시해 주는 점이 맘에 듭니다. 동일한 프롬프트를 한 번 더 넣어 보았더니 아래와 같은 결과값이 나왔습니다.

> Story: The Gift of Life
>
> Mary has always wanted to be a mother. She and her husband have been trying for years to conceive a child, but to no avail. After many failed attempts, they decided to explore other options. They started looking into adoption and found a beautiful baby girl who needed a loving home. They were overjoyed and immediately started the process to bring her home. It was a long and difficult process, but finally, they received the call they had been waiting for. The adoption had been approved, and their daughter was waiting for them at the agency.
>
> When they arrived, they were filled with excitement and nerves. They couldn't believe that they were finally going to be parents. As they held their daughter for the first time, tears filled their eyes. They knew that this was the start of a beautiful journey, and they were grateful for the gift of life that had been given to them.

Cloze Test:

Mary and her husband (1) _____ for years to conceive a child. After many failed attempts, they decided (2) _____ other options. They started (3) _____ adoption and found a beautiful baby girl who (4) _____ a loving home. They were overjoyed and immediately started the process to bring her home. It (5) _____ a long and difficult process, but finally, they (6) _____ the call they (7) _____ waiting for. The adoption (8) _____ approved, and their daughter was waiting for them at the agency.

When they arrived, they were filled with excitement and nerves. They (9) _____ believe that they (10) _____ finally going to be parents. As they held their daughter for the first time, tears (11) _____ their eyes. They (12) _____ that this (13) _____ the start of a beautiful journey, and they (14) _____ grateful for the gift of life that had (15) _____ given to them.

이야기의 내용과 cloze test의 빈칸 수는 맘에 들 정도로 잘 만들어 주었습니다. 그런데, 아쉽게도 동일한 프롬프트임에도 답만 제시하고 있습니다. 물론, 답안의 특성상 해설을 제공하는 것이 큰 의미가 없기는 합니다.

Answer:

1. have been trying
2. to explore
3. looking into
4. needed
5. was
6. received
7. had been
8. had been
9. couldn't
10. were
11. filled
12. knew
13. was
14. were
15. been

챗GPT 4 Better Questions

챗GPT를 활용한 다양한 장점 중 특히 눈에 띄는 것은 입력한 글의 유형을 다른 형태로 바꾸어 주는 능력입니다. 아래와 같이 프롬프트를 입력해 보도록 하겠습니다.

Prompt Turn the passage below into a dialogue between the characters in it.

Passage

Mary has always wanted to be a mother. She and her husband have been trying for years to conceive a child, but to no avail. After many failed attempts, they decided to explore other options. They started looking into adoption and found a beautiful baby girl who needed a loving home. They were overjoyed and immediately started the process to bring her home. It was a long and difficult process, but finally, they received the call they had been waiting for. The adoption had been approved, and their daughter was waiting for them at the agency.

When they arrived, they were filled with excitement and nerves. They couldn't believe that they were finally going to be parents. As they held their daughter for the first time, tears filled their eyes. They knew that this was the start of a beautiful journey, and they were grateful for the gift of life that had been given to them.

결과값은 다음과 같습니다.

> Mary: (sighs) It's just not fair. Why can't we have a child?
>
> Husband: I know, Mary. It's been tough, but we have to keep trying.
>
> Mary: (tearfully) We've been trying for years. I don't know if I can keep going through this.
>
> Husband: (comfortingly) We don't have to. There are other options out there.
>
> Mary: (hopeful) Like what?
>
> Husband: (smiling) Adoption, for one. We can give a child a loving home, even if they're not biologically ours.
>
> Mary: (excitedly) You're right! Let's look into it.
>
> (After months of searching and paperwork...)
>
> Husband: (answering phone) Hello?
>
> Agency: Hi, Mr. and Mrs. Johnson. We have good news. The adoption has been approved, and your daughter is waiting for you at the agency.
>
> Mary: (gasps) Oh my god, this is it! We're finally going to be parents!
>
> Husband: (grinning) Let's go get our daughter.
>
> (After arriving at the agency...)
>
> Mary: (tearfully) Hi, sweetheart. We've been waiting so long for you.
>
> Husband: (overwhelmed) I can't believe this is happening. We're parents!
>
> Mary: (smiling through tears) This is the start of a beautiful journey. We're so grateful for the gift of life that's been given to us.

입력한 글을 대화체로 바꾼 것입니다. 약간의 수작업이 들어간다면, 시제와 관련된 다양한 문제를 창작할 수 있습니다. 학교 내신과 같은 구체적 형태의 문제까지 구현하지는 못하지만, chatGPT를 활용하여 훌륭한 문제를 만들 수 있습니다. 필자는 올해 초 chatGPT의 이런 능력을 보고, chatGPT가 나온 이래 치르는 첫 내신 시험에서 지문 유형을 변경한 문제가 나올 것이 생각했는데, 제가 담당한 고등학교에서 chatGPT를 활용한 것 같은 지문 변형 문제가 나왔습니다.

4 Better Questions

이번에는 현재완료를 평가하는 조금 복잡한 프롬프트를 넣어 결과값을 얻어 보도록 하겠습니다.

Prompt) *Make a "fill-in-the-blank" question with 5 multiple choices that evaluates the students' understanding of present perfect tense, and provide the answer and the explanation for it. Use the touching lines that appear in the movie Dead Poets Society for the options.*

Refer to the link: https://www.dailyscript.com/scripts/dead_poets_final.html You can find the whole script.

 프롬프트에 링크를 잘 활용하시면 무한의 자료를 활용할 수 있는 장점이 있습니다.

아래 같은 놀라운 결과값을 얻었습니다. I am just speechless.

Question: Which of the following sentences is in the present perfect tense?

(A) "Seize the day, boys. Make your lives extraordinary."
(B) "We don't read and write poetry because it's cute. We read and write poetry because we are members of the human race."
(C) "We are food for worms, lads."
(D) "No matter what anybody tells you, words and ideas can change the world."
(E) "I've seen you. You're not that man. Wait until you see it."

Answer: (E) "I've seen you. You're not that man. Wait until you see it."

Explanation:
The present perfect tense is formed by using "have" or "has" with the past participle of the verb. In this sentence, "I've seen" is the present perfect tense of the verb "see". The use of "have" ("I have seen you") shows that the action of seeing occurred at an indefinite time in the past, and it is still relevant or has an effect on the present moment.

문제는 단순하지만, "죽은 시인의 사회" 대본에서 문장을 가져와 보기의 내용을 만들어 주었습니다.

PART 1

이번에는 현재 진행형 시제와 관련된 문제를 만드는 프롬프트를 연습해 보도록 하겠습니다.

Prompt *Make 5 fill-in-the-blank questions that ask students to complete the sentence using the present continuous tense along with the answer and explanation.*

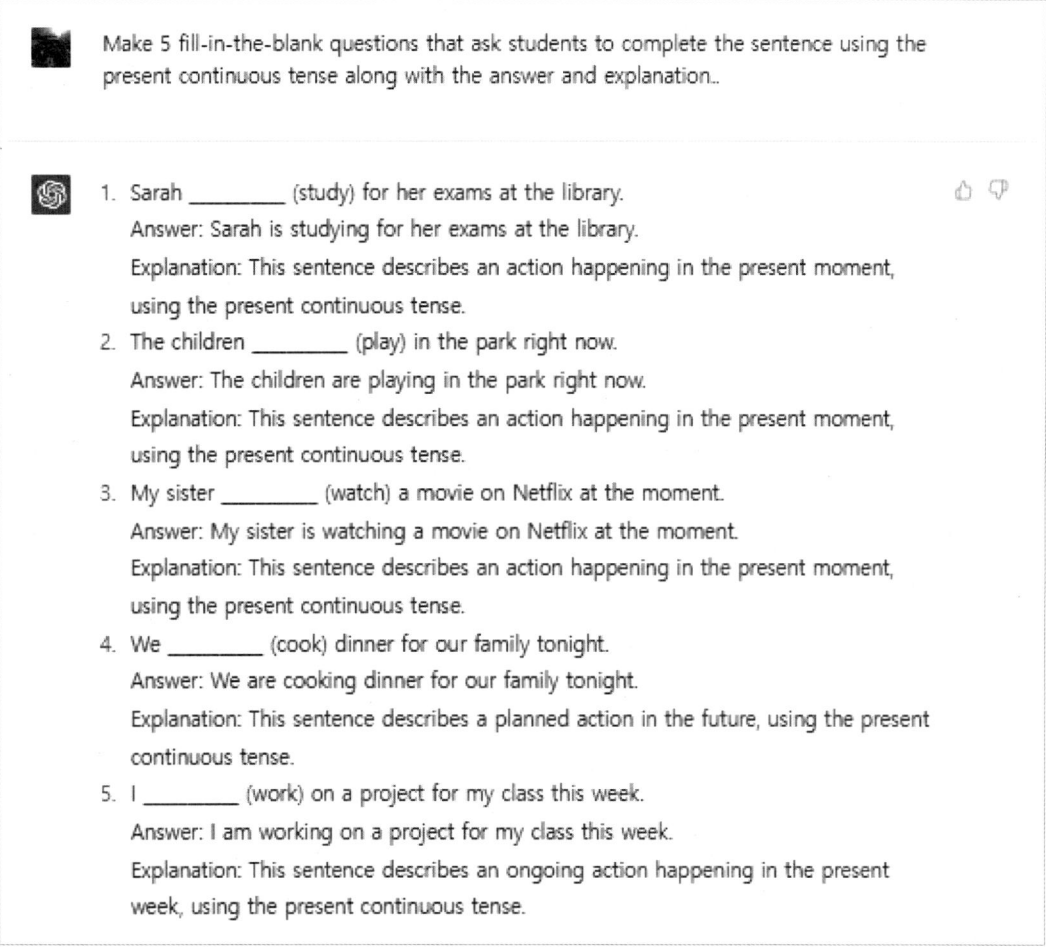

예문, 문제, 그리고 해설까지 깔끔하게 제공되고 있습니다. 만약 객관식 문제로 만들고 싶다면, 초기 프롬프트를 다음과 같이 입력하면 됩니다.

Prompt *Make 5 fill-in-the-blank questions with 5 multiple choices that ask students to complete the sentence using the present continuous tense along with the answer and explanation.*

챗GPT 4 Better Questions

> Make 5 fill-in-the-blank questions with 5 multiple choices that ask students to complete the sentence using the present continuous tense along with the answer and explanation.

Sure, here are 5 fill-in-the-blank questions with multiple choices that ask students to complete the sentence using the present continuous tense:

1. What _____ (you, do) this weekend?
    a) are you doing
    b) were you doing
    c) have you done
    d) did you do

   Answer: a) are you doing

   Explanation: This question is asking about an action that is happening in the present, specifically the upcoming weekend. The correct answer is the present continuous tense, which is formed with the auxiliary verb "are" and the present participle "doing."

2. Why _____ (you, laugh) so much?
    a) do you laugh
    b) did you laugh
    c) are you laughing
    d) have you laughed

   Answer: c) are you laughing

   Explanation: This question is asking about a present action, specifically the reason why the person is laughing so much. The present continuous tense is used to describe an action that is currently in progres... is "are you laughing."

현재진행형 시제를 활용하여, 앞서 만들어 보았던 지문 창작과 창작한 글의 유형을 바꾸는 연습도 다시 해 보도록 하겠습니다.

Prompt *Make a short dialogue between two people making use of present continuous tense.*

PART 1

> Make a short dialogue between two people making use of Present continuous tenses.

Sarah: What are you doing this weekend?

John: I'm playing in a tennis tournament on Saturday.

Sarah: Wow, that sounds exciting. Are you practicing a lot?

John: Yes, I've been practicing every day this week to prepare for the tournament.

Sarah: That's great. I'm sure you'll do really well.

John: Thanks! After the tournament, I'm going out to dinner with some friends.

Sarah: Nice! Where are you going?

John: We're going to a new Italian restaurant downtown. I've heard it's really good.

Sarah: Sounds delicious. Have fun!

현재진행 시제가 활용된 대화를 만들어 주었습니다. 역으로 해당 대화를 일반적 글로 바꾸어 달라고 요청해 보도록 하겠습니다.

Prompt *Change the above dialogue into the narrative.*

챗GPT 4 Better Questions

> Sarah: What are you doing this weekend?
> John: I'm playing in a tennis tournament on Saturday.
> Sarah: Wow, that sounds exciting. Are you practicing a lot?
> John: Yes, I've been practicing every day this week to prepare for the tournament.
> Sarah: That's great. I'm sure you'll do really well.
> John: Thanks! After the tournament, I'm going out to dinner with some friends.
> Sarah: Nice! Where are you going?
> John: We're going to a new Italian restaurant downtown. I've heard it's really good.
> Sarah: Sounds delicious. Have fun!
>
> Change the above dialouge into the narrative.

> Sarah asked John about his plans for the upcoming weekend. John replied that he was scheduled to participate in a tennis tournament on Saturday. Sarah expressed her excitement and asked if John was practicing enough for the tournament. John informed her that he had been practicing every day of the week to ensure he was well-prepared. Sarah encouraged him and told him that she was sure he would do really well in the tournament. John thanked her and shared his plans for after the tournament. He mentioned that he would be going out for dinner with some friends at a new Italian restaurant located downtown, which he had heard was really good. Sarah said that it sounded delicious and wished him a great time.

이렇게 대화를 이야기체로 바꾸어 주었습니다. 대화체에서 주로 사용된 시제는 현재진행, 현재완료진행이고, 이야기체의 글에서 과거시제를 기준으로 과거진행, 과거완료 진행 시제가 눈에 들어 눈에 띕니다. 그럼 이렇게 챗GPT를 활용해 창작(?)한 두 지문을 바탕으로 시제 관련된 수작업이 들어간 문제로 만들어 보겠습니다.

| 문제 ▶

지문 B는 지문 A의 대화체를 이야기체의 글로 바꾼 것이다. 시제에 유의하여 괄호 안의 제시된 단어의 바른 형태를 ㉠과 ㉡에 각각 써넣으시오.

PART 1

〈지문 A〉

Sarah: What are you doing this weekend?
John: I ㉠_____ _____(play) in a tennis tournament on Saturday.
Sarah: Wow, that sounds exciting. Are you practicing a lot?
John: Yes, I ㉡____ _____ _____(practice) every day this week to prepare for the tournament.
Sarah: That's great. I'm sure you'll do really well.
John: Thanks! After the tournament, I'm going out to dinner with some friends.
Sarah: Nice! Where are you going?
John: We're going to a new Italian restaurant downtown. I've heard it's really good.
Sarah: Sounds delicious. Have fun!

〈지문 B〉

Sarah asked John about his plans for the upcoming weekend. John replied that he was scheduled to participate in a tennis tournament on Saturday. Sarah expressed her excitement and asked if John ㉢_____ _____(practice) enough for the tournament. John informed her that he ㉣____ _____ _____(practice) every day of the week to ensure he was well-prepared. Sarah encouraged him and told him that she was sure he would do really well in the tournament. John thanked her and shared his plans for after the tournament. He mentioned that he would be going out for dinner with some friends at a new Italian restaurant located downtown, which he had heard was really good. Sarah said that it sounded delicious and wished him a great time.

답▶ ㉠ am playing ㉡ have been practicing ㉢ was practicing ㉣ had been practicing

위와 같이 약간의 수작업이 들어가면 현재진행, 현재완료진행, 과거진행, 과거완료진행 시제의 활용을 문제로 만들 수 있습니다.

현재완료시제를 묻는 아래와 같은 프롬프트를 만들어 보았습니다.

Prompt) *Make two multiple-choice questions that ask students to choose out of the three kinds of tense: present perfect, present continuous, and present perfect continuous using specific example sentences.*

챗GPT 4 Better Questions

> Make two multiple-choice questions that ask students to choose out of the three tenses: present perfect, present continuous, and present perfect continuous using specific example sentences.

1. Which tense is used in the following sentence to describe an action that began in the past and is still ongoing at the present moment?
   "I have been studying for my exam all week."
   a) Present perfect
   b) Present continuous
   c) Present perfect continuous
2. Which tense is used in the following sentence to describe an action that was completed in the recent past and has a connection to the present?
   "I have just finished reading this book."
   a) Present perfect
   b) Present continuous
   c) Present perfect continuous

이번에는 단계적으로 문제를 만드는 방법을 한 번 익혀보겠습니다. 물론, 아래 해당하는 여러 프롬프트의 내용을 하나로 담아 편리성을 구현할 수 있겠지만, chatGPT의 성격을 익힌다는 점에서 chatGPT와는 어울리지 않는 "아날로그" 방식으로 접근해 보겠습니다. 현재완료 진행형의 문제를 만들기 위한 적절한 수준의 지문을 만들어 달라고 요청하고, 그다음 해당 지문을 통해서 실전 유형의 5지선다 문제를 만들어 보도록 하겠습니다.

Prompt *create a K2 level story that is of use in understanding the knowledge of verb tense.*

🔍 이야기나 문제의 난이도에 대한 입력값을 추가하고 싶을 때 level of difficulty를 K1 ~ K12로 설정해 주면 됩니다.

PART 1

 create a K2 level story that is of use in understanding the knowledge of verb tense.

 Once upon a time, there is a little girl named Lily. She loves playing outside and spending time with her friends. One day, Lily went to the park with her friends. They were having so much fun on the swings and slides.

Suddenly, Lily's mom called her on the phone and said, "Lily, it's time to come home for dinner."

Lily said goodbye to her friends and started walking home. As she walked, she saw a butterfly fluttering by. She tried to catch it, but it flew away.

When Lily got home, her mom asked her, "What did you do at the park?"

Lily replied, "I played on the swings and slides with my friends, and I tried to catch a butterfly on my way home."

Her mom smiled and said, "It sounds like you had a fun day."

In this story, children can learn about different verb tenses, such as the past tense ("Lily went to the park"), present tense ("Lily loves playing outside"), and past participle ("Lily had a fun day"). Teachers can also highlight the use of the simple past tense ("Lily played on the swings and slides") and the past continuous tense ("Lily tried to catch a butterfly on her way home"). This simple story can help young children understand verb tenses and how they are used in everyday language.

K2 수준의 이야기를 만들어 달라고 했는데, 다소 지문의 길이가 길어 아래와 같은 프롬프트를 넣었습니다.

Prompt *Please make the story a little shorter.*

 Please make the story a little shorter.

 Once upon a time, there was a little girl named Lily who loved playing outside with her friends. One day, Lily went to the park and played on the swings and slides with her friends. Later, she saw a butterfly on her way home and tried to catch it. When she got home, her mom asked her what she did, and Lily said she had a fun day. In this story, children can learn about different verb tenses, such as the past tense and the past continuous tense.

챗GPT 4 Better Questions

추가적으로 해당 지문을 바탕으로 아래와 같은 프롬프트를 넣어 문제를 뽑아 보았습니다.

Prompt *Based on the passage above, make a question with 5 multiple-choices like "Among (a) ~ (e), which of the underlined sentences is NOT grammatically correct?" along with the answer and explanation at the end.*

> Based on the passage above, make a 5 multiple-choice question like "Among (a) ~ (e), which of the underlined sentences is NOT grammatically correct?" with the answer and explanation.
>
> Here's a multiple-choice question based on the passage:
>
> Which of the following underlined sentences is NOT grammatically correct?
>
> a) "Lily loved playing outside with her friends."
> b) "Lily went to the park and played on the swings and slides."
> c) "Later, she saw a butterfly and tried to catch it."
> d) "When she got home, her mom asked her what she did."
> e) "Lily says she had a fun day."
>
> Answer: e) "Lily says she had a fun day."
>
> Explanation: The sentence in option e) is not in the correct verb tense. The sentence is written in the present tense, while the story is written in the past tense. The correct sentence should be "Lily said she had a fun day," which is in the past tense to match the rest of the story. The other options are all written in the past tense and are grammatically correct.

문제, 정답, 해설이 제공되고 있습니다. 아쉽게도 밑줄 어법 문제를 의도한 것이지만, 현재 chatGPT의 기본형으로 구현이 되지 않고 있습니다. 하지만 여기서 주목할 점은 앞서 언급했지만 chatGPT는 지금까지 거쳐온 일련의 질문과 답변의 내용을 기억하고, 이를 바탕으로 다음 프롬프트에 대한 답변을 준다는 점입니다. 예를 들어, 해당 원고를 작성하는 과정에서 chatGPT와 주고 받는 대화가 "동사의 시제" 관련 내용이다 보니 아래와 같이 프롬프트를 지시했을 때 같은 맥락의 결과값을 제시해 줍니다.

Prompt *Make an "arrow connecting" grammar question using two columns.*

🔍 밑줄 친 표현은 보통 화살표를 이용해 매칭하는 문제를 만들 때 사용하는 용어입니다.

PART 1

 Make an "arrow connecting" grammar question using two columns.

 Here's an "arrow connecting" grammar question using two columns:

Column A:

1. Simple Present
2. Present Continuous
3. Simple Past
4. Past Continuous
5. Present Perfect

Column B:
a) An action that was completed before another action in the past.
b) An action that started in the past and continues up to the present.
c) An action that happens regularly or repeatedly.
d) An action that is happening now.
e) An action that happened at a specific time in the past.

Match the tense on the left in Column A with the correct description on the right in Column B by drawing an arrow between the two.

Answer Key:

1. Simple Present - An action that happens regularly or repeatedly (c)
2. Present Continuous - An action that is happening now (d)
3. Simple Past - An action that happened at a specific time in the past (e)
4. Past Continuous - An action that started in the past and continued up to another

프롬프트의 명령값은 an "arrow connecting" grammar question이라고 했지만, 시제 관련 문제로 만들어 주고 있습니다.

챗GPT 4 Better Questions

💬 나도 Prompt Engineer

1. Prompt: List three latest issues using three different verb tenses.

2. Prompt: Write a passage that talks about the cause of WWII in the simple present tense.

3. Prompt: Make 3 questions question with 5 multiple choices that test the grammar knowledge with the instruction below.

[Instruction]
 * list of grammar to test

  - subject-verb agreement
  - Gerunds and Gerund Phrases
  - Active/Passive Voice
  - Run-On Sentences and Fragments

* Types of Stem
Question 1. Choose one that is NOT grammatically correct?
Question 2. Which of the following best fills in the blanks (A) and (B) in the sentence given below?
Question 3. Which of the following is NOT a run-on sentence?

* Type of Alternative
①
②
③
④
⑤
* Provide the answer and explanation at the bottom.

4. Prompt: Based on the passage below, make 2 questions question with 5 multiple choices that test the grammar knowledge according to the instruction below.

[Passage]
One cause of disease is dirt. Dirt is full of germs. These germs are too small to see. You need a microscope to see them. They may be small, but they are alive. They can get inside our bodies and make us sick. They enter through our mouths more easily than through our noses. So we should try to keep our mouths closed and breathe through our noses.

[Instruction]
* list of grammar to test
    - subject-verb agreement
    - Gerunds and Gerund Phrases
    - Active/Passive Voice

* Types of Stem
    Question 1. Choose one that is NOT grammatically correct?
    Question 2. Which of the following best fills in the blanks (A) and (B) in the sentence given below?

Contents of the options
When making options, use the sentences in the passage as they are.

* Type of Alternative]
①
②
③
④
⑤

* Provide the answer and explanation at the bottom.

4 Better Questions

5. Prompt: Find an impressive dialogue from the movie Mulan that uses the present perfect verb.

6. Prompt: Write a short but touching story that makes use of the present perfect sentences, and based on the story, make a cloze test with as many blanks as possible to test the grammar knowledge listed below.

[list of grammar to test]
 - Active vs. Passive Voice
 - Participles and Participial Phrases
 - Gerunds and Gerund Phrases
 - To-infinitive and To-infinitive Phrase
 - Prompt: Extract two inspirational quotes

* Provide the answer at the bottom.

7. Prompt: Turn the passage below into a dialogue between the characters in it.

[Passage]
Mary has always wanted to be a mother. She and her husband have been trying for years to conceive a child, but to no avail. After many failed attempts, they decided to explore other options. They started looking into adoption and found a beautiful baby girl who needed a loving home. They were overjoyed and immediately started the process to bring her home. It was a long and difficult process, but finally, they received the call they had been waiting for. The adoption had been approved, and their daughter was waiting for them at the agency.
When they arrived, they were filled with excitement and nerves. They couldn't believe that they were finally going to be parents. As they held their daughter for the first time, tears filled their eyes. They knew that this was the start of a beautiful journey, and they were grateful for the gift of life that had been given to them.

8. Prompt: Make a "fill-in-the-blank" question with 5 multiple choices that evaluates the students' understanding of present perfect tense, and provide the answer and the explanation for it. Use the touching lines that appear in the movie Dead Poets Society for the options.

Refer to the link:
https://www.dailyscript.com/scripts/dead_poets_final.html
You can find the whole script.

9. Prompt: Make 5 fill-in-the-blank questions that ask students to complete the sentence using the present continuous tense along with the answer and explanation.

10. Prompt: Make 5 fill-in-the-blank questions that ask students to complete the sentence using the present continuous tense along with the answer and explanation.

11. Prompt: Make 5 fill-in-the-blank questions with 5 multiple choices that ask students to complete the sentence using the present continuous tense along with the answer and explanation.

12. Prompt: Make a short dialogue between two people making use of present continuous tense.

13. Prompt: Change the above dialogue into the narrative.

14. Prompt: Make two multiple-choice questions that ask students to choose out of the three kinds of tense: present perfect, present continuous, and present perfect continuous using specific example sentences.

4 Better Questions

15. Prompt: create a K2 level story that is of use in understanding the knowledge of verb tense.

16. Prompt: Please make the story a little shorter.

17. Prompt: Based on the passage above, make a question with 5 multiple-choices like "Among (a) ~ (e), which of the underlined sentences is NOT grammatically correct?" along with the answer and explanation at the end.

18. Prompt: Make an "arrow connecting" grammar question using two columns.

4 동사의 태 voice of a verb

동사의 태를 voice라고 하고, 능동태를 active voice, 수동태를 passive voice라고 각각 말합니다. 일반적으로 문장전환 문제와 함께 다양한 유형의 문제 출제가 가능합니다.

우선, 평서문의 능동문을 수동문으로 바꾸어 달라는 요청해 보도록 하겠습니다. 저희가 하는 게 아니라 "슈퍼컴퓨터"가 하는 것이니 조금 긴 문장을 아래의 프롬프트와 함께 명령해 보도록 하겠습니다.

Prompt *Make the following sentence into a passive sentence.*

Robots and astronauts use much of the same equipment in space.

 Make the following sentence into a passive sentence.
Robots and astronauts use much of the same equipment in space.

 Much of the same equipment in space is used by robots and astronauts.

서술형 출제를 위한 다소 복잡한 문장에 대한 문장전환이 이제는 아주 쉬운 작업이 되었습니다. 물론, 오류도 줄일 수 있습니다.

참고로, 문법 용어와 용례에 대한 표현을 영어로 알아보고자 한다면 아래 사이트도 좋습니다.
https://www.englishgrammar101.com/

이번에는 5지선다 문제를 통해서 동사의 태(verb voice)에 대한 지식을 묻는 문제를 만들어 보도록 하겠습니다.

이번에는 조금 어려운 지문을 바탕으로 5지선다의 태와 관련된 문법 문제를 만들어 달라고 해 보겠습니다.

챗GPT 4 Better Questions

Prompt) *Create 2 grammar questions with 5 multiple-choices that test the knowledge of the verb voice according to the instruction below.*

instruction

* When making the options, refer to the link below.
https://www.pagebypagebooks.com/Thomas_Paine/Common_Sense/Of_The_Origin_And_Design_Of_Government_In_General_With_Concise_Remarks_On_The_English_Constitution_p1.html

[Stem]
Question 1. Which of the following best fills in the blank?
Question 2. When transforming the sentence into a passive one, which is CORRECT?

[Type of Alternative]
①
②
③
④
⑤

* <u>Show the contents of the alternatives.</u>

> 🔍 때로 보기의 내용이 나오지 않을 경우가 있습니다. 그럴 땐 해당 문구를 마지막에 넣어 두시면 됩니다.

참고로 링크는 토머스 페인의 "Common sense"입니다. 다음과 같은 결과값이 나왔습니다.

> Question 1. Which of the following best fills in the blank?
> According to Thomas Paine, "Society is _____ for the sake of happiness."
> ① formed
> ② forming
> ③ form
> ④ to form
> ⑤ was formed
>
> Answer: ① formed
>
> Explanation: The sentence is in the passive voice, and the correct option is in the past participle form.

수동태의 이해를 묻는 빈칸 문제를 잘 만들어 주었습니다. 다음 두 번째 문제에 대한 결과값입니다.

> Question 2. When transforming the sentence into a passive one, which is CORRECT?
> "The principle of hereditary succession has no just basis in nature, but stands as an affront to the human understanding."
>
> ① No correction needed.
> ② The principle of hereditary succession has no basis in nature which is just and stands as an affront to the human understanding.
> ③ There is no just basis in nature for the principle of hereditary succession, but it is stood as an affront to the human understanding.
> ④ The principle of hereditary succession is stood as an affront to the human understanding without just basis in nature.
> ⑤ The principle of hereditary succession is not based on nature, but an affront to the human understanding.
>
> Answer: ⑤ The principle of hereditary succession is not based on nature, but an affront to the human understanding.
>
> Explanation: This question is testing the student's ability to transform an active sentence into a passive one. In the original sentence, "stands" is the active verb. To transform this sentence into a passive one, we need to make "principle of hereditary succession" the subject and change "stands" to the passive form of the verb "to be" (is). Among the options, only ⑤ correctly transforms the sentence into the passive voice.

제시문이 나오고 해당 문장을 수동태로 바르게 바꾼 것을 고르는 문제인데, 첫 번째 선지가

챗GPT 4 Better Questions

큰 의미가 없어 보입니다. 얼핏보기에는 결과물에 만족하지 못할 수도 있습니다. 아래 해설을 잘 살펴보면, chatGPT의 능력이 엄청나다는 것을 알 수 있습니다. 정답으로 제시한 내용을 보면, 제시문에 다시 눈이 갑니다.

"The principle of hereditary succession **has no just basis** in nature, but **stands** as an affront to the human understanding."

▶ The principle of hereditary succession **is not based** on nature, but an affront to the human understanding.

원문의 위에 밑줄 친 표현과 같이 등위접속사 but으로 병치되는 3형식 능동표현과 자동사가 함께 쓰인 문장이기 때문에 학교에서 학습하는 1차적 변형으로 접근이 불가능합니다. 이를 응용해서 be based on의 수동표현을 활용한 것임을 파악할 수 있습니다. 프롬프트 하나로 내가 원하는 높은 수준의 결과값을 얻지는 못하지만, 이를 2차 가공할 경우 상당한 수준의 문제를 만들어 낼 수 있습니다.

> 🔍 chatGPT 명령어 하나로 모든 것을 해결할 수 없습니다. 하지만, 2차 가공이 들어가면 상상만 했던, 상상하지도 못했던 결과값을 얻어낼 수 있습니다.

이번에는 수동태를 포함한 다양한 문법을 활용한 프롬프트 짜 보도록 하겠습니다.

Prompt) Create a 5 multiple-choice question that tests the knowledge of grammar according to the instruction.

🚩 **instruction**

[List of Grammar to test]
― Verb voice
― Subject-verb agreement
― Modal verb
― Relative clause

* When making the options, use only complex sentences that talk about stock market debacle.

> 🔍 학습에 흥미를 유발하는 내용을 단시간에 문제화 할 수 있다는 점에서 chatGPT를 활용하지 않을 이유가 1도 없음을 느낍니다.

PART 1

* *Stem*

Which of the following sentences is NOT grammatically correct?

* *Type of Alternative*
①
②
③
④
⑤

다음과 같은 결과값이 나왔습니다.

 Question: Which of the following sentences is NOT grammatically correct?

① Despite the stock market debacle, many investors are still optimistic that the market will rebound soon.
② If the stock market had not experienced such a debacle, we would not have implemented new risk management strategies.
③ The stock market debacle, which was caused by a combination of factors, has had a significant impact on the global economy.
④ Many experts believe that the stock market debacle could have been avoided if regulators had taken a more proactive approach.
⑤ Measuring the full extent of the damage caused by the stock market debacle will take time and careful analysis.

Answer: ② If the stock market had not experienced such a debacle, we would not have implemented new risk management strategies.

Explanation: The sentence uses the past perfect verb tense "had not experienced," but the main clause is in the present tense "we would not have implemented." This is a mismatch in tense and results in a grammatically incorrect sentence. The correct way to write this sentence in a complex form would be: "If the stock market had not experienced such a debacle, we would not be implementing new risk management strategies."

해설에 다소 오류가 있지만, 프롬프트에서 요구한 문법사항을 적용해서 멋진 문제를 만들어 주었습니다. 2차 가공 시, 특정 주제를 바탕으로 좋은 문법 문제를 만들어 낼 수 있습니다.

챗GPT 4 Better Questions

이번에는 죠지 오웰의 소설 "동물농장"에서 예문을 추출해서 문법 문제를 만들어 달라고 해 보겠습니다. 좀 더 compact한 프롬프트에 익숙해진다는 측면에서 프롬프트를 조금 단순하게 작성해 보겠습니다.

Prompt *Create a question with 5 multiple-choices like "Which of the following sentences is NOT grammatically correct?" with the conditions below.*

💡 **Condition**

1. Extract the contents of the options from the novel Animal Farm.
2. Extracted sentences should contain any one or more of these grammatical items: gerund, a relative clause that, to-infinitive, and subject-verb agreement.
3. Explain the answer and explanation at the bottom.

아래와 같은 결과값이 나왔습니다.

> Question: Which of the following sentences is NOT grammatically correct?
>
> ① The animals on the farm, working tirelessly to overthrow their human oppressors, succeeded in establishing a new order.
> ② Snowball, who had been driven out by Napoleon, continued to be a symbol of resistance for the animals.
> ③ To build a windmill that would generate electricity for the farm was the animals' ambitious goal.
> ④ Boxer, the loyal and hardworking horse, was admired by all the animals for his dedication.
> ⑤ The pigs, who had taken control of the farm, enacted a series of oppressive rules.
>
> Answer: ③ To build a windmill that would generate electricity for the farm was the animals' ambitious goal.
>
> Explanation: This sentence is not grammatically correct. The subject-verb agreement is incorrect. The subject "To build a windmill that would generate electricity for the farm" is singular, but the verb "was" is in the plural form. To make the sentence grammatically correct, it should be rephrased as "Building a windmill that would generate electricity for the farm was the animals' ambitious goal." This way, the subject and verb agree in number, making the sentence grammatically correct.

정답 설명에는 오류가 발생하고 있습니다. 항상 double-check을 해야 할 이유입니다. 그 외 다른 조건은 너무도 훌륭하게 만족하고 있습니다. 2차 가공을 통해 흥미롭고, 질 좋은 문제를 만들 수 있습니다.

챗GPT 4 Better Questions

나도 Prompt Engineer

1. Prompt: Make the following sentence into a passive sentence.

Robots and astronauts use much of the same equipment in space.

2. Prompt: Create 2 grammar questions with 5 multiple-choices that test the knowledge of the verb voice according to the instruction below.

[Instruction]
* When making the options, refer to the link below.
https://www.pagebypagebooks.com/Thomas_Paine/Common_Sense/Of_The_Origin_And_Design_Of_Government_In_General_With_Concise_Remarks_On_The_English_Constitution_p1.html

[Stem]
Question 1. Which of the following best fills in the blank?
Question 2. When transforming the sentence into a passive one, which is CORRECT?

[Type of Alternative]
①
②
③
④
⑤

3. Prompt: Create a 5 multiple-choice question that tests the knowledge of grammar according to the instruction.

[Instruction]
* List of Grammar to test
- Verb voice
- Subject-verb agreement
- Modal verb
- Relative clause

* When making the options, use only complex sentences that talks about stock market debacle.

* Stem
Which of the following sentences is NOT grammatically correct?

* Type of Alternative
①
②
③
④
⑤

4. Prompt: Create a question with 5 multiple-choices like "Which of the following sentences is NOT grammatically correct?" with the conditions below.

[Conditions]
1. Extract the contents of the options from the novel Animal Farm.
2. Extracted sentences should contain any one or more of these grammatical items: gerund, a relative clause that, to-infinitive, and subject-verb agreement.
3. Explain the answer and explanation at the bottom.

CHAPTER 3 가정법

chatGPT를 활용하는데 있어 가정법만큼 즐거운 문법 파트가 있을지 싶을 정도네요. 무한의 상상력을 발휘해 보도록 해요.

가정법을 시작하기 전에 문장의 종류와 문장 내 주절과 종속절에 대한 영어 표현을 알아야 하는데, 본 책의 앞쪽 "용어 설명"을 통해서 함께 살펴보았습니다. 해당 부분을 다시 살펴보고 계속 이어 나가는 것도 좋을 것 같습니다.

학교에서 이런 내용을 배운 적이 있습니다.

"있는 사실을 그대로 말하는 직설법(Indicative mood), 명령조로 말하는 명령법(Imperative mood), 그리고 존재하지 않거나 사실이 아닌 것을 말하는 가정법(Subjunctive mood)이라 한다."

문장을 만들 때 의도하는 바에 따라 직설법, 명령법, 가정법의 문장으로 표현을 하죠. 이 중 가정법에 해당하는 영어 표현은 subjunctive mood 또는 conditional sentence라고 말합니다.

Prompt *Make five sentences in the subjunctive mood*

 Sure, here are five examples of sentences in the subjunctive mood:

1. If I were rich, I would travel the world.
2. I suggest that he study harder if he wants to pass the exam.
3. It's important that she be on time for the meeting.
4. I wish I could speak French fluently.
5. The teacher requested that the students not use their phones during class.

PART 1

어렵지 않게 5개의 가정법 문장을 만들었습니다. 아래와 같이 멋진 문장을 만들어 주었습니다.

If I were rich, I would travel the world.
I suggest that he study harder if he wants to pass the exam.
It's important that she be on time for the meeting.
I wish I could speak French fluently.
The teacher requested that the students not use their phones during class.

위 문장을 응용해서 주어진 문장을 가지고 아래와 같은 문법 문제를 한 번 만들어 보겠습니다.

프롬프트를 아래와 같이 주었습니다.

Prompt) *Make a grammar question with 5 multiple choices with the answer and explanation under the condition below.*

* *Use the sentences below for the options.*

If I were rich, I would travel the world.
I suggest that he study harder if he wants to pass the exam.
It's important that she be on time for the meeting.
I wish I could speak French fluently.
The teacher requested that the students not use their phones during class.

* *Stem*
Which of the following is NOT grammatically correct?

* *Type of alternative*
①
②
③
④
⑤

* *Display all the alternatives.*

4 Better Questions

결과값은 다음과 같습니다.

> Which of the following is NOT grammatically correct?
>
> ① If I was rich, I would travel the world.
> ② I suggest that he studies harder if he wants to pass the exam.
> ③ It's important that she is on time for the meeting.
> ④ I wish I could fluently speak French.
> ⑤ The teacher requested that the students don't use their phones during class.
>
> Answer:
>
> The sentence that is NOT grammatically correct is option ②: "I suggest that he studies harder if he wants to pass the exam."
>
> Explanation:
>
> The sentence contains a subjunctive mood, and the verb "study" should be in its base form, which is "study." Therefore, the correct form of the sentence should be "I suggest that he study harder if he wants to pass the exam."
>
> Option ① uses the incorrect past tense form "was" instead of the subjunctive mood "were." Option ③ correctly uses the subjunctive mood "be." Option ④ has the correct word order for an adverb "fluently," but the adjective "French" should come before the verb "speak." Option ⑤ uses the correct form of the subjunctive "don't" to indicate a negative request.

모든 점에서 완벽하네요. 원하는 문장을 바탕으로 가정법 문제와 함께 해설까지 깔끔하게 제공하고 있습니다.

PART 1

복습차원에서 위에서 사용한 프롬프트를 조금 자세히 살펴보도록 하겠습니다.

Prompt *Make a grammar question with 5 multiple choices with the answer and explanation under the condition below.*

🔍 프롬프트의 개괄적 목적을 적는 곳입니다.

💡 **Condition**

* *Use the sentences below for the options.*

If I were rich, I would travel the world.
I suggest that he study harder if he wants to pass the exam.
It's important that she be on time for the meeting.
I wish I could speak French fluently.
The teacher requested that the students not use their phones during class.

🔍 명령어의 조건부를 넣은 곳입니다. Instruction을 사용해도 무방합니다.

* *Stem*
Which of the following is NOT grammatically correct?

🔍 문제를 입력하는 곳입니다.

* *Type of alternative*
①
②
③
④
⑤

* *Display all the alternatives.*

🔍 보기의 유형을 작성하는 곳입니다.

Part 1. Grammar Factory 85

4 Better Questions

학교에서 가정법의 종류를 가정법 현재, 과거, 과거완료, 혼합가정법등 다양한 형태를 배웁니다. 해당 내용에 대한 설명을 표로 작성해 달라고 해보겠습니다.

Prompt) Create a table that show different types of sentences in the subjunctive mood.

> Sure! Here is a table that shows different types of sentences in the subjunctive mood:
>
> | Type of Subjunctive Sentence | Example |
> |---|---|
> | Present Subjunctive (Wish, Doubt, Necessity) | I suggest that he study harder if he wants to pass the exam. |
> | Past Subjunctive (Contrary-to-Fact or Hypothetical Situations) | If I were rich, I would travel the world. |
> | Subjunctive in Adjective Clauses (Expressing Uncertainty or Doubt) | I'm looking for a book that is interesting. |
> | Subjunctive in Noun Clauses (Expressing Emotion or Opinion) | It's important that she be on time for the meeting. |
> | Subjunctive in Requests, Suggestions, Demands, and Proposals | The teacher requested that the students not use their phones during class. |
>
> Note that the subjunctive mood is used less frequently in modern English, and in many cases, the indicative mood (regular verb forms) is used instead.

위와 같은 결과값을 얻었습니다. 가정법 과거완료나 가정법 미래에 대한 설명이 없어 아쉬워 그 대안으로 구글에서 정보를 가져왔습니다.

- 가정법 현재: Present subjunctive
- 가정법 과거: Past subjunctive
- 가정법 과거완료: Present perfect subjunctive
- 가정법 미래: Future subjunctive

참고로 영어에서 도치는 inversion이라고 합니다.

위 용어를 활용해서 아래의 흥미로운 프롬프트와 그에 따른 결과값을 바탕으로 문제까지 만들어 보겠습니다.

✓ 가정법 현재: Present subjunctive

Prompt) *Make a K2-level conversation between two kids waiting for the long Summer vacation which is just around the corner under the condition below.*

> 프롬프트의 내용을 좀 더 다채롭게 구성해 보았습니다. 학생들이 즐거워 할 수 있는 내용을 바탕으로 문제를 만들 수 있으니 출제자의 상상력을 무한으로 발휘해 보세요.

💡 Condition

- No more 10 lines.
- Make sure to include at least one sentence that contains the present subjunctive.

 Kid 1: "I can't wait for Summer vacation! What are you going to do?"

Kid 2: "I wish we could go on a big trip, but I don't think my parents will let us."

Kid 1: "If we ask nicely, maybe they'll say yes. It's important that we have fun before school starts again."

Kid 2: "You're right. Let's make a plan and suggest it to our parents. Maybe they'll be willing to let us go on a fun adventure."

Kid 1: "I hope they'll agree. It's important that we have a great Summer together."

아래와 같은 대화의 결과값을 얻었습니다. 특히, 명사절 내 should의 생략 구문이 눈에 들어옵니다.

Kid 1: "I can't wait for Summer vacation! What are you going to do?"
Kid 2: "I wish we could go on a big trip, but I don't think my parents will let us."
Kid 1: "If we ask nicely, maybe they'll say yes. **It's important that we have fun before school**

4 Better Questions

starts again."
Kid 2: "You're right. Let's make a plan and suggest it to our parents. Maybe they'll be willing to let us go on a fun adventure."
Kid 1: "I hope they'll agree. It's important that we have a great Summer together."

해당 대화를 바탕으로 아래와 같은 문제를 한 번 만들어 보겠습니다.

Make 2 questions with 5 multiple choices along with the answer and explanation using the dialogue below.

<Dialogue>
Kid 1: "I can't wait for Summer vacation! What are you going to do?"
Kid 2: "I wish we could go on a big trip, but I don't think my parents will let us."
Kid 1: "If we ask nicely, maybe they'll say yes. It's important that we have fun before school starts again."
Kid 2: "You're right. Let's make a plan and suggest it to our parents. Maybe they'll be willing to let us go on a fun adventure."
Kid 1: "I hope they'll agree. It's important that we have a great Summer together."

<Stem>
Question 1. Which of the following is the topic of the conversion?
Question 2. Which of the following is NOT correct about the conversation?

<Type of Alternative>
①
②
③
④
⑤

아래와 같은 결과값을 얻었습니다.

🔍 해당 결과값에서는 오류가 없지만, AI를 100% 믿어서는 안 된다는 점은 다시 한 번 강조드립니다.

Question 1:
Which of the following is the topic of the conversation?
① Summer vacation
② School assignments
③ Winter break
④ Sports activities
⑤ Music lessons

Answer: ① Summer vacation
Explanation: The conversation between the two kids is about their upcoming Summer vacation and their plans for it.

Question 2:
Which of the following is NOT correct about the conversation?
① Kid 2 wishes they could go on a big trip.
② Kid 1 suggests asking nicely to persuade their parents.
③ Kid 2 thinks their parents will agree to their plan.
④ Kid 1 and Kid 2 agree that having fun is important.
⑤ Kid 1 hopes they will have a great Summer together.

Answer: ③ Kid 2 thinks their parents will agree to their plan.
Explanation: Kid 2 is hopeful that their parents will be willing to let them go on a fun adventure, but they do not express certainty that their parents will agree.

∨ 가정법 과거: Past subjunctive

이번에는 chatGPT에게 조금 challenging한 프롬프트를 만들어 보겠습니다.

Prompt) *Write 5 tips for surviving on Mars. Use sentences starting with "If" in the past subjunctive mood.*

🔍 화성에서 생존하는 5가지 팁에 대한 흥미로운 프롬프트를 요청했습니다.

4 Better Questions

> Sure, here are 5 tips for surviving on Mars using sentences starting with "If" in the past subjunctive mood:
>
> 1. If there were a dust storm, it would be important to seek shelter immediately.
> 2. If I were to plant crops on Mars, I would make sure to use soil that has been specially engineered for the planet's harsh conditions.
> 3. If there were a malfunction in the life support systems, it would be crucial to have backup systems in place to ensure survival.
> 4. If I were exploring the planet's surface, I would take care to avoid areas with high levels of radiation.
> 5. If there were an emergency, it would be important to have a well-stocked medical kit and a plan in place for communicating with Earth for assistance.

이번에는 스탠드업 코미디를 위한 skit을 작성해 달라고 했는데 아래와 같은 조건을 달았습니다. 가능할지 한 번 살펴보겠습니다.

Prompt) *Write a skit for stand-up comedy according to the condition below.*

💡 **Condition**

- *No more than 10 lines.*
- *Compact but super fun story*
- *Make sure to use at least one sentence in the subjunctive mood.*

PART 1

Title: "Lost in Translation"

Comedian: Hi, guys! You know what's the worst thing that can happen when traveling abroad? It's not getting lost. It's not running out of money. It's being lost in translation.
Audience: *laughs*
Comedian: So, I was in Japan, trying to order some sushi. I thought I did everything right, I bowed and said "Arigatou gozaimashita," but the chef just stared at me.
Audience: *laughs*
Comedian: Then I remembered, "If I were a Japanese chef and someone butchered my language, I'd probably stare too."
Audience: *laughs*
Comedian: I then used my phone to show the translation app and said, "Kore o kudasai." The chef finally got it and handed me a plate of sashimi.
Audience: *applauses*
Comedian: It's amazing how a simple change in language can make a world of difference, right? I mean, if only it were that easy to translate my jokes into Japanese.
Audience: *laughs*

위와 같은 멋진 스탠업 코미디 원고를 만들어 주었습니다. 아래와 같은 가정법 문장이 들어간 대본을 만들어 주었습니다. 좀 더 compact한 것을 원해서 아래 Regenerate response를 눌렀습니다.

Here's a potential skit:

"Have you ever wanted to time-travel? I have. But I don't want to end up like Marty McFly. So, if I were to time-travel, I'd make sure to find out the winning lottery numbers before I go back. I mean, I wouldn't want to alter the course of history, but a little bit of extra cash in the present wouldn't hurt, right? If only the present perfect subjunctive could take me back in time and make that happen."

[audience laughs]

이번에는 가정법 과거와 미래(Future subjunctive)를 모두 활용한 너무 맘에 드는 skit을 만들어 주었네요. 해당 표현에서 가정법 문장이 많이 사용되었고, 무엇보다 마지막 문장에서 센스가

챗GPT 4 Better Questions

넘칩니다.

"Have you ever wanted to time-travel? I have. But I don't want to end up like Marty McFly. So, if I were to time-travel, I'd make sure to find out the winning lottery numbers before I go back. I mean, I wouldn't want to alter the course of history, but a little bit of extra cash in the present wouldn't hurt, right? If only the present perfect subjunctive could take me back in time and make that happen."

위 지문을 바탕으로 다음과 같은 문제를 한 번 만들어 보겠습니다.

Prompt) Make a cloze test using the passage below. Use the words listed below for the answers for the blanks.

🔍 빈칸을 채우는 문제의 유형을 cloze test 또는 cloze quiz라고 부릅니다.

🔍 **Passage**

"Have you ever wanted to time-travel? I have. But I don't want to end up like Marty McFly. So, if I were to time-travel, I'd make sure to find out the winning lottery numbers before I go back. I mean, I wouldn't want to alter the course of history, but a little bit of extra cash in the present wouldn't hurt, right? If only the present perfect subjunctive could take me back in time and make that happen."

[Words to fill in the blanks]
were to, find out, wouldn't, alter, back in time

위의 Prompt를 넣어 얻은 값은 다음과 같습니다.

PART 1

"Have you ever wanted to time-travel? I have. But I don't want to end up like Marty McFly. So, if I _____ time-travel, I'd make sure to _____ the winning lottery numbers before I go back. I mean, I _____ want to _____ the course of history, but a little bit of extra cash in the present _____ hurt, right? If only the present perfect subjunctive could take me _____ and make that happen."

[Answers]
were to, find out, wouldn't, alter, wouldn't, back in time

원하는 곳에 빈칸을 뚫어 주고, 아래에 답을 제시해 줍니다. Way to go, chatGPT!

*"선생님들, chatGPT와 함께
무한의 상상력을 바탕으로 다양한 문제를 창작해 보세요!"*

4 Better Questions

💬 나도 Prompt Engineer

1. Prompt: Make five sentences in the subjunctive mood

2. Prompt: Make a grammar question with 5 multiple choices with the answer and explanation under the condition below.

* Use the sentences below for the options.

If I were rich, I would travel the world.
I suggest that he study harder if he wants to pass the exam.
It's important that she be on time for the meeting.
I wish I could speak French fluently.
The teacher requested that the students not use their phones during class.

* Stem
Which of the following is NOT grammatically correct?

* Type of alternative
①
②
③
④
⑤

* Display all the alternatives.

3. Prompt: Create a table that show different types of sentences in the subjunctive mood.

4. Prompt: Make a K2-level conversation between two kids waiting for the long Summer vacation which is just around the corner under the condition below.

⟨Condition⟩
- No more 10 lines.
- Make sure to include at least one sentence that contains the present subjunctive.

5. Make 2 questions with 5 multiple choices along with the answer and explanation using the dialogue below.

⟨Dialogue⟩
Kid 1: "I can't wait for Summer vacation! What are you going to do?"
Kid 2: "I wish we could go on a big trip, but I don't think my parents will let us."
Kid 1: "If we ask nicely, maybe they'll say yes. It's important that we have fun before school starts again."
Kid 2: "You're right. Let's make a plan and suggest it to our parents. Maybe they'll be willing to let us go on a fun adventure."
Kid 1: "I hope they'll agree. It's important that we have a great Summer together."

⟨Stem⟩
Question 1. Which of the following is the topic of the conversion?
Question 2. Which of the following is NOT correct about the conversation?

⟨Type of Alternative⟩
①
②
③
④
⑤

6. Prompt: Write 5 tips for surviving on Mars. Use sentences starting with "If" in the past subjunctive mood.

7. Prompt: Write a skit for stand-up comedy according to the condition below.

⟨Condition⟩
- No more than 10 lines.
- Compact but super fun story
- Make sure to use at least one sentence in the subjunctive mood

8. Prompt: Make a
cloze test using the passage below. Use the words listed below for the answers for the blanks.

[Passage]
"Have you ever wanted to time-travel? I have. But I don't want to end up like Marty McFly. So, if I were to time-travel, I'd make sure to find out the winning lottery numbers before I go back. I mean, I wouldn't want to alter the course of history, but a little bit of extra cash in the present wouldn't hurt, right? If only the present perfect subjunctive could take me back in time and make that happen."

[Words to fill in the blanks]
were to, find out, wouldn't, alter, back in time

to부정사와 동명사

1 to 부정사

영어시험에서 to부정사와 동명사만큼 중요한 파트도 없겠죠. 그만큼 영어 문장에서 자주 활용된다는 의미도 되겠습니다. to부정사는 to-infinitive이라고 하고, 동명사는 gerund라고 합니다.

Prompt *Create a table summarizing the definition and usage of to-infinite and gerund.*

 Sure, here's a table summarizing the definition and usage of the to-infinitive and gerund:

	To-infinitive	Gerund
Definition	A verb form that begins with "to" (e.g., to go, to eat)	A verb form that ends in "-ing" (e.g., going, eating)
Function	Often used to express purpose, intent, or future action (e.g., "I want to go to the store", "She plans to start a new job")	Often used to express ongoing or continuous action (e.g., "He enjoys skiing", "I'm tired of waiting")
Verb Patterns	Can be used after certain verbs (e.g., want, need, hope) or as the subject or object of a sentence (e.g., "To travel is my dream", "I need to eat breakfast")	Can be used after certain verbs (e.g., enjoy, avoid, suggest) or as the subject or object of a sentence (e.g., "Skiing is his favorite hobby", "I'm tired of waiting for the bus")
Passive Forms	Can be used in the passive voice (e.g., "The book was difficult to read")	Can be used in the passive voice (e.g., "Skiing is enjoyed by many people")

Note: The usage and functions of the to-infinitive and gerund can vary and are not always interchangeable.

위와 같이 to부정사와 동명사의 정의와 용례를 잘 설명한 표를 만들어 주었습니다. 그럼 to부정사를 활용한 다양한 프롬프트를 통해서 결과값을 만들어 보겠습니다. 특히, 이번 장에서는 좀 더 고급스러운 프롬프트를 만드는 작업도 시도해 보겠습니다.

챗GPT 4 Better Questions

to부정사를 활용한 기본적인 프롬프트로 시작해 보겠습니다.

Prompt) *Summarize the novel The Lord of the Flies.*
- *Use sentences containing to-infinitive.*

To escape from a war, a group of British boys are stranded on an uninhabited island, where they struggle to survive and establish order while dealing with their innermost desires and fears. As they begin to unravel and succumb to their primal instincts, some of the boys turn to a false idol known as the "Lord of the Flies" to appease their superstitions, leading to the ultimate collapse of their society. To be rescued, the remaining boys must overcome their own demons and work together to signal for help, but not all of them will make it out alive.

Prompt) *Explain the concept of panopticon in language easy enough for the K-6 to understand and include a test at the end with the answers.*
- *When explaining the concept, use as many sentences as possible containing to-infinitive.*

🔍 to부정사 문장을 사용해서 특정 주제에 대한 내용을 설명하고, 마지막에 내용 파악을 위한 독해 문제를 곁들여 달라는 프롬프트를 짰습니다.

Panopticon is a word that describes a type of building or system that allows people to see everything, even if they can't see everyone at the same time. It was invented by a man named Jeremy Bentham a long time ago.

Imagine a big building with a watchtower in the middle. From the watchtower, you can see into every room, but the people in the rooms can't see you. This means that you could be watching them at any time, and they wouldn't know.

The idea behind the panopticon is that if people know they could be watched at any time, they will be more likely to behave well. This is because they won't know when they are being watched, so they will always have to be on their best behavior.

For example, if you were in a classroom with a panopticon system, you would always have to behave well because the teacher could be watching you at any time, even if they were not in the room with you. If you were in a park with a panopticon system, you would always have to throw your garbage in the trash can because you wouldn't know if someone was watching you or not.

to부정사가 적절히 활용된 K-6아이들이 이해하기 쉬운 언어로 작성해 주었습니다. 그리고, 아래와 같이 이해 정도를 파악할 수 있는 문제를 만들어 주었습니다.

Test:

1. Who invented the panopticon system?
    A) Jeremy Bentham
    B) Albert Einstein
    C) Thomas Edison
2. What is a panopticon building?
    A) A building with a watchtower in the middle.
    B) A building with a swimming pool on the roof.
    C) A building with a playground in the basement.
3. Why do people behave well in a panopticon system?
    A) Because they know they could be watched at any time.
    B) Because they can do whatever they want.
    C) Because they know nobody is watching them.

Answers:

1. A) Jeremy Bentham
2. A) A building with a watchtower in the middle.
3. A) Because they know they could be watched at any time.

이번에는 조금 더 복잡한, 고급스러운 프롬프트를 작성해 보겠습니다.

Prompt) *Write a persuasive email to convince potential customers to try our service "Bug Extermination" under the condition below.*

💡 Condition

- *Make sure to include at least two "to-infinitive" sentences.*
- *Make the email kids' friendly.*

아래의 결과값을 얻었습니다.

챗GPT 4 Better Questions

> Subject: Got bugs bugging you? Let us help!
>
> Hi there,
>
> Do you have pesky bugs invading your home? Do they make you feel itchy and scratchy? No worries, our Bug Extermination service is here to save the day!
>
> Our team of friendly experts will help get rid of all the bugs in your home, leaving you with a clean and cozy space. We use safe and eco-friendly methods to make sure the bugs won't come back, so you can enjoy your home without any creepy crawlies.
>
> To get started, just ask your grown-up to give us a call and we'll take care of the rest. We promise to make the process quick and easy, so you can get back to having fun and playing with your toys.
>
> So don't let bugs bug you anymore! Give us a call and we'll take care of everything. We can't wait to help make your home a bug-free zone!
>
> Best regards,
>
> [Your Name]
>
> P.S. Remember, bugs aren't your friends. Let us help you get rid of them!

위 지문을 바탕으로 아래와 같은 문제를 만들어 보도록 하겠습니다. 아래와 같은 프롬프트를 만들어 보았습니다.

Prompt) *Make 3 questions with 5 multiple choices along with the answer and explanation using the passage below.*

💡 Condition

- Use the passage below.
- Make 3 questions listed below.

Question 1. Which of the following would be the subject that goes in the blank (A)?
The answer: Got bugs bugging you? Let us help!
Questions 2. Which of the followig is NOT correct about the emil?
Question 3. Which of the following best fills in the blank (B) in the passage?
The answer: won't come back

PART 1

🔍 Passage

Prompt) Make 5 questions that test the student's knowledge of to-infinitive using the passage below.

Subject: (A)_____

Hi there,

Do you have pesky bugs invading your home? Do they make you feel itchy and scratchy? No worries, our Bug Extermination service is here to save the day!

Our team of friendly experts will help get rid of all the bugs in your home, leaving you with a clean and cozy space. We use safe and eco-friendly methods to make sure the bugs (B)_____, so you can enjoy your home without any creepy crawlies.

To get started, just ask your grown-up to give us a call and we'll take care of the rest. We promise to make the process quick and easy, so you can get back to having fun and playing with your toys.

So don't let bugs bug you anymore! Give us a call and we'll take care of everything. We can't wait to help make your home a bug-free zone!

Best regards,
James

P.S. Remember, bugs aren't your friends. Let us help you get rid of them!

<Stem>
Question 1. Which of the following would be the subject that goes in the blank (A)?
Questions 2. Which of the followig is NOT correct about the emil?
Question 3. Which of the following best fills in the blank (B) in the passage?

<Type of Alternative>
①

챗GPT 4 Better Questions

②
③
④
⑤

*Show the contents of the alternatives.

위와 같은 프롬프트를 넣어 얻은 결과값은 다음과 같습니다.

 Question 1. Which of the following would be the subject that goes in the blank (A)?
A. Got bugs bugging you? Let us help!
B. Our team of experts is here to serve you.
C. We use safe and eco-friendly methods.
D. Bugs are a common problem in many homes.
E. A clean and cozy space is essential for your home.

Answer: A. Got bugs bugging you? Let us help!

Explanation: The subject that goes in the blank (A) is the sentence "Got bugs bugging you? Let us help!" This sentence is a question that serves as the main topic of the email.

Question 2. Which of the following is NOT correct about the email?
A. The email offers a bug extermination service.
B. The team of experts uses safe and eco-friendly methods.
C. The email is intended for adults only.
D. The process is quick and easy.
E. The email promises to make your home a bug-free zone.

Answer: C. The email is intended for adults only.

Explanation: The email does not explicitly state that it is intended for adults only, so this statement is not correct. In fact, the email is likely intended for parents or guardians to read and consider on behalf of their children.

첫 번째와 두 번째 문제, 정답, 해설까지 꼼꼼하게 만들어 주었습니다.

Question 3. Which of the following best fills in the blank (B) in the passage?
A. will keep coming back
B. might return
C. are a necessary part of nature
D. are harmful to humans
E. won't come back

Answer: E. won't come back

Explanation: The blank (B) refers to what will happen to the bugs after the Bug Extermination service has been performed. The best answer is "won't come back," which implies that the bugs will be fully eliminated and will not return to the home. This aligns with the promise made in the email to create a bug-free zone.

세 번째 문제도 원하는 결과물이 나왔습니다.

챗GPT 4 Better Questions

💬 나도 Prompt Engineer

1. Prompt: Create a table summarizing the definition and usage of to-infinite and gerund.

2. Prompt: Summarize the novel The Lord of the Flies.
   - Use sentences containing to-infinitive.

3. Prompt: Explain the concept of panopticon in language easy enough for the K-6 to understand and include a test at the end with the answers.
   - When explaining the concept, use as many sentences as possible containing to-infinitive.

4. Prompt: Write a persuasive email to convince potential customers to try our service "Bug Extermination" under the condition below.

[Condition]
- Make sure to include at least two "to-infinitive" sentences.
- Make the email kids' friendly.

5. Prompt: Make 3 questions with 5 multiple choices along with the answer and explanation using the passage below.

[Conditions]
- Use the passage below.
- Make 3 questions listed below.
Question 1. Which of the following would be the subject that goes in the blank (A)?
The answer: Got bugs bugging you? Let us help!
Questions 2. Which of the followig is NOT correct about the emil?
Question 3. Which of the following best fills in the blank (B) in the passage?
The answer: won't come back

⟨Passage⟩
Prompt: Make 5 questions that test the student's knowledge of to-infinitive using the passage below.

Subject: (A)_____

Hi there,

Do you have pesky bugs invading your home? Do they make you feel itchy and scratchy? No worries, our Bug Extermination service is here to save the day!

Our team of friendly experts will help get rid of all the bugs in your home, leaving you with a clean and cozy space. We use safe and eco-friendly methods to make sure the bugs (B)_____, so you can enjoy your home without any creepy crawlies.

To get started, just ask your grown-up to give us a call and we'll take care of the rest. We promise to make the process quick and easy, so you can get back to having fun and playing with your toys.

So don't let bugs bug you anymore! Give us a call and we'll take care of everything. We can't wait to help make your home a bug-free zone!

Best regards,
James
P.S. Remember, bugs aren't your friends. Let us help you get rid of them!

<Stem>

Question 1. Which of the following would be the subject that goes in the blank (A)?

Questions 2. Which of the followig is NOT correct about the emil?

Question 3. Which of the following best fills in the blank (B) in the passage?

<Type of Alternative>

①
②
③
④
⑤

Part 1. Grammar Factory

챗GPT 4 Better Questions

2 동명사

동명사는 영어로 gerund라고 합니다.

아래와 같은 프롬프트를 넣어 보겠습니다.

Prompt *Create a table for the definition of gerund and its example usage.*

 Here's a table for the definition of gerund and its example usage:

Definition	Example
A verb form that ends in "-ing" and functions as a noun in a sentence.	Swimming is my favorite activity.
It can be used as the subject of a sentence.	Reading helps me relax.
It can be used as the object of a verb.	I enjoy swimming in the ocean.
It can be used as the object of a preposition.	She is afraid of flying.
It can be used as the complement of a linking verb.	My favorite hobby is playing the guitar.

다양한 용례와 함께 동명사의 정의를 깔끔하게 설명한 표를 만들어 주었습니다. 이번에는 조건부를 조금 더 깐깐하게 만들어 좀 더 세부적인 결과값을 얻어보도록 하겠습니다.

Prompt *Create a K-5 level short skit for the school talent show. Make sure to use sentences that contain the words and the grammar as listed below.*

<Words to use>
<Grammar to use>
gerund
to-infinitive
relative clause

위 프롬프트에서 words to use에 해당하는 단어가 생각이 나지 않아 아래와 같은 명령을 넣어 보았습니다.

Prompt Show me some sample words that can be used to create a skit for a school talent show.

Sure, here are some sample words that you can use to create a skit for a school talent show:

1. Superhero
2. Time traveler
3. Aliens
4. Famous historical figures
5. Animal characters
6. Fairy tale characters
7. Sports personalities
8. Celebrity impersonations
9. Mythical creatures
10. Robots

With these words as a starting point, you can create a variety of skits that showcase different talents such as acting, dancing, singing, comedy, or even magic tricks. Good luck with your talent show!

chatGPT가 제시한 단어의 예를 활용해서 만들어 보겠습니다.

Prompt Create a K-5 level, 1 minute skit for <u>the school talent show</u>. Make sure to use sentences that contain the words and the grammar as listed below.

🔍 chatGPT의 무한한 능력에 선생님들의 상상력이 더해지면 최고의 수업 자료가 탄생할 수 있습니다.

<Words to use>
Superhero
Time traveler
Aliens
Famous historical figures
Animal characters
Fairy tale characters
Sports personalities
Celebrity impersonations
Mythical creatures

챗GPT 4 Better Questions

Robots

<Grammar to use>
gerund
to-infinitive
relative clause

위 내용에 대한 결과값은 다음과 같습니다.

> Mr. Einstein: (enters, looking around curiously) "Excuse me, young ones. Have you seen a strange device lying around? It's a time machine, you know."
>
> Sally: "Wait, you're Mr. Einstein? The famous physicist who came up with the theory of relativity?"
>
> Mr. Einstein: "Yes, that's me."
>
> Sally: "Wow, this is amazing! We have a superhero, an alien, a sports enthusiast, and a famous historical figure all in one place!"
>
> Max: "Hey, can you show us some of your superhero moves, Sally?"
>
> Sally: (starts doing some karate moves) "Sure thing, Max. I've been practicing my moves for a while now."
>
> Alice: "I can also do some cool alien moves. Watch this!" (starts doing a funny dance)
>
> Mr. Einstein: "And as for me, I can explain the theory of relativity to you. It's all about the concept of time."
>
> Max: "Wow, this is so cool! I wish we could stay like this forever."
>
> Sally: "Well, I have to get back to my own time, but it was great meeting all of you. Let's do this again sometime!"
>
> (All characters wave goodbye as they exit the stage)
>
> The End.
>
> ↻ Regenerate response

해당 결과값에서 아래 내용이 반영됐는지 확인해 보도록 하겠습니다.

∨ **gerund**

"**Traveling** through time can be so disorienting. I never know where or when I'll end up."

PART 1

☑ **to-infinitive**

"Hello there! I am Alice from Planet Zog. I have traveled a long way **to meet** you, Sally!"

☑ **relative clause**

"Wait, you're Mr. Einstein? The famous physicist **who** came up with the theory of relativity?"

명령에서 요구한 모든 사항을 충족하고 있습니다. 이번에는 동명사의 활용을 평가하는 고등학교 수준의 문법 문제를 만들어 보도록 하겠습니다. 조금 복잡하지만, 더 정교한 값을 얻어낼 수 있는 프롬프트를 작성해 보도록 하겠습니다.

Prompt) *Come up with 3 grammar questions that test the student's knowledge of gerund. Follow the instruction.*

instruction

Number of questions: 3
Target Student: Students preparing the SAT verbal test
Grammatical item to be evaluated: Gerund
Level of difficulty: Hard
Provide the answer and explanation at the bottom.

[Types of Stem]
Question 1: Which of the following sentences is grammatically CORRECT?
Question 2: Which of the following best fills in the blank of the given sentence?
Question 3: Which of the following best paraphrase the given sentence?

아래와 같은 결과값을 얻었습니다.

챗GPT 4 Better Questions

> **Question 1:**
> Which of the following sentences is grammatically CORRECT?
>
> A. "Swimming in the ocean all day can lead to dehydration."
> B. "The teacher asked her students reading the assigned book before class."
> C. "To running in the park is what I prefer for exercise."
> D. "Writing poems can be a fun hobby for many people."
>
> Answer: A. "Swimming in the ocean all day can lead to dehydration." (This sentence uses the gerund "swimming" as the subject of the sentence.)
>
> **Question 2:**
> Which of the following best fills in the blank of the given sentence?
>
> "She was interested in _____ a new language, so she decided to enroll in a language school."
>
> A. to learn
> B. learn
> C. learning
> D. learned
>
> Answer: C. learning (This sentence requires a gerund as the object of the preposition "in," so "learning" is the correct choice.)

정답과 해설까지 각 문제 아래에 제공하고 있습니다. 빈칸 문제도 동명사의 활용 능력을 묻는 정교한 문제를 만들어 주었습니다.

> Question 3:
> Which of the following best paraphrases the given sentence?
>
> "He loves playing the piano more than anything else."
>
> A. His love of playing the piano is greater than anything else.
> B. He loves nothing else as much as playing the piano.
> C. He prefers playing the piano to anything else.
> D. All of the above.
>
> Answer: D. All of the above. (All three paraphrases accurately convey the meaning of the original sentence, which uses the gerund "playing" as the object of the verb "loves.")

동명사와 연계된 패러프레이징 문제를 요구했는데, 멋지게 만들어주었네요. 제대로 된 명령어를 넣으면 기대 이상의 결과값이 나옵니다.

이번에는 선지에서 활용할 문장까지 명령어에 넣어 보도록 하겠습니다.

Prompt) Come up with 3 grammar questions that test the student's knowledge of gerund. Follow the instruction.

instruction

Number of questions: 3
Target Student: Students preparing the SAT verbal testG
Grammatical item to be evaluated: Gerund
Level of difficulty: Hard
Provide the answer and explanation at the bottom.

Use sentences excerpted from the book Sapiens, Yuval Noah Harari as sample sentences for alternatives. Refers to the website, https://www.goodreads.com/work/quotes/18962767-itsur-toldot-ha-enoshut for_excerpts.

[Types of Stem]
Question 1: Which of the following sentences is grammatically CORRECT?
Question 2: Which of the following best fills in the blank of the given sentence?
Question 3: Which of the following best paraphrase the given sentence?

4 Better Questions

아래와 같은 내용을 위 프롬프트에 추가했습니다.

Use sentences excerpted from the book Sapiens, Yuval Noah Harari as sample sentences for alternatives. Refers to the website, https://www.goodreads.com/work/quotes/18962767-itsur-toldot-ha-enoshut for excerpts.

아래와 같은 결과값을 얻었습니다.

> Sure, here are the revised questions:
>
> [Types of Stem]
>
> Question 1:
> Which of the following sentences from the book Sapiens uses the gerund phrase correctly?
>
> A. "But why should it be obvious that intelligence will enable humans to conquer the planet?"
> B. "At first, their impact on the natural world was negligible even foraging bands were responsible for extinguishing some of the larger mammals."
> C. "Their daily life cycle, social life, and even their sexual life remained largely the same as those of the foragers."
>
> Answer: B. "At first, their impact on the natural world was negligible even foraging bands were responsible for extinguishing some of the larger mammals." (This sentence correctly uses the gerund "foraging" as an adjective modifying the noun "bands.")

유발 하라리의 책 '사피엔스'에서에서 발췌한 문장을 가지고 선지를 만들어 주었습니다. 원하는 선지의 문장이 있는 사이트를 제시해 주기만 하면 됩니다.

> Question 2:
> Which sentence correctly uses the gerund as the subject of the sentence to convey the idea of preference?
>
> A. "I prefer to hike in the mountains than to swim in the ocean."
> B. "Hiking in the mountains is my preferred outdoor activity."
> C. "To hike in the mountains is more preferable than to swim in the ocean."
> D. "My preference is to hike in the mountains rather than swimming in the ocean."
>
> Answer: B. "Hiking in the mountains is my preferred outdoor activity." (This sentence correctly uses the gerund "hiking" as the subject of the sentence to convey the idea of preference.)

두 번째 결과값은 프롬프트에서 요구한 사항과는 다소 거리가 있습니다.

> Question 3:
> Which of the following paraphrases accurately conveys the meaning of the sentence "The foragers had a profound impact on the planet, despite their relatively simple technology and social organization"?
>
> A. "The foragers changed the planet significantly, even though they had limited technology and social organization."
> B. "The planet was deeply affected by the foragers, who used only basic technology and had a simple social structure."
> C. "Although the foragers had simple technology and social organization, they still made a significant impact on the planet."
> D. "All of the above."
>
> Answer: D. "All of the above." (All three paraphrases accurately convey the meaning of the original sentence, which uses the gerund "changing" as the object of the verb "had.")

세 번째 문제는 해당 책에서 발췌한 문장을 바탕으로 패러프레이징을 만들어 주었습니다. 다소 뻔한 문제이긴 하지만, 프롬프트를 좀 더 정교하게 2차 가공을 한다면 훨씬 높은 수준의 문제를 만들 수 있을 겁니다.

챗GPT 4 Better Questions

이번에는 조금 다른 조건부로 일반적인 유형의 문법 문제를 한 번 만들어 보겠습니다.

아래 문장은 Sandel, Michael J의 "Justice: What's the Right Thing to Do?"에서 발췌한 문장입니다.

"Markets are useful instruments for organizing productive activity. But unless we want to let the market rewrite the norms that govern social institutions, we need a public debate about the moral limits of markets."

"Self-knowledge is like lost innocence; however unsettling you find it, it can never be 'unthought' or 'unknown'."

"The mere fact that a group of people in the past agreed to a constitution is not enough to make that constitution just."

"The more we regard our success as our own doing, the less responsibility we feel for those who fall behind."

"To achieve a just society we have to reason together about the meaning of the good life, and to create a public culture hospitable to the disagreements that will inevitably arise."

— Michael J. Sandel, Justice: What's the Right Thing to Do?

앞선 5문장을 바탕으로 아래와 같은 프롬프트를 넣어 보겠습니다.

> 🔍 자연어를 사용하여 AI가 이해할 수 있는 간단하면서 세부적인 프롬프트를 만드는 것이 핵심입니다.

Prompt Make 3 grammar questions along with the answer and explanation with the instruction below.

[Sentences to use]
"Markets are useful instruments for organizing productive activity. But unless we want to let the market rewrite the norms that govern social institutions, we need a public debate about the moral limits of markets.
"Self-knowledge is like lost innocence; however unsettling you find it, it can never be

'unthought' or 'unknown'."

"The mere fact that a group of people in the past agreed to a constitution is not enough to make that constitution just."

"The more we regard our success as our own doing, the less responsibility we feel for those who fall behind."

"To achieve a just society we have to reason together about the meaning of the good life, and to create a public culture hospitable to the disagreements that will inevitably arise."

instruction

- Make questions using the sentences given above.
- Test the student's <u>OVERALL</u> knowledge of grammar
- Assess students' use of language in terms of the list below.

Parts of speech
Sentence structure
Verb forms
Pronouns
Adjectives and adverbs
Conjunctions
Prepositions
Passive voice

[Types of Stem]
Question 1 & 2: Which of the following is NOT grammatically correct?
Question 3: In order to complete the grammatically correct sentence, which of the following best fills in the blank in the given sentence?

첫 번째 문제에 대한 명령어의 결과값을 살펴보겠습니다.

챗GPT 4 Better Questions

> Question 1: Which of the following is NOT grammatically correct?
> a) "Markets are useful instruments for organizing productive activity."
> b) "Unless we want to let the market rewrite the norms that govern social institutions, we need a public debate about the moral limits of markets."
> c) "We needs a public debate about the moral limits of markets, unless we want to let the market rewrite the norms that govern social institutions."
> d) "But unless we want to let the market rewrite the norms that govern social institutions, markets are useful instruments for organizing productive activity."
>
> Answer: c) "We needs a public debate about the moral limits of markets, unless we want to let the market rewrite the norms that govern social institutions." This sentence is not grammatically correct because the subject "we" and the verb "needs" do not agree in number. "We" is a plural subject, so it requires the plural form of the verb "need."
>
> Explanation: This question tests the student's knowledge of subject-verb agreement in a sentence. In option c), the subject "we" is plural, and it should take the plural form of the verb "need." The correct sentence would be, "We need a public debate about the moral limits of markets, unless we want to let the market rewrite the norms that govern social institutions."

우선, 제시된 문장을 활용해 어법 문제를 만들어줬습니다. 프롬프트를 잘 작성하면 원하는 결과값을 얻을 수 있다는 것을 다시 확인할 수 있습니다. 물론 정답과 해설 또한 꼼꼼하게 작성되어 있습니다. 아래에서는 조건부에서 문법 사항이 얼마나 적용되었는지 보도록 하겠습니다.

Answer: c) "We needs a public debate about the moral limits of markets, unless we want to let the market rewrite the norms that govern social institutions." This sentence is not grammatically correct because <u>the subject "we" and the verb "needs" do not agree in number</u>. "We" is a plural subject, so it requires the plural form of the verb "need."

🔍 Subject-verb agreement에 해당하는 문법을 묻는 문제였습니다.

Explanation: This question tests the student's knowledge of subject-verb agreement in a sentence. In option c), the subject "we" is plural, and it should take the plural form of the verb "need." The correct sentence would be, "We need a public debate about the moral limits of markets, unless we want to let the market rewrite the norms that govern social institutions."

🔍 나머지 보기 항에 대한 설명도 곁들여 있습니다.

두 번째 문제에 대한 결과값입니다.

> Question 2: Which of the following is NOT grammatically correct?
> a) "Self-knowledge is like lost innocence; however unsettling you find it, it can never be 'unthought' or 'unknown'."
> b) "However unsettling you find it, self-knowledge can never be 'unthought' or 'unknown'."
> c) "Self-knowledge can never be 'unthought' or 'unknown'; however unsettling you find it."
> d) "Self-knowledge, however unsettling you find it, can never be 'unthought' or 'unknown'."
>
> Answer: a) "Self-knowledge is like lost innocence; however unsettling you find it, it can never be 'unthought' or 'unknown'." This sentence is not grammatically correct because it uses a semicolon to separate two independent clauses without a coordinating conjunction.
>
> Explanation: This question tests the student's knowledge of punctuation and sentence structure. In option a), the semicolon should be replaced with a comma and a coordinating conjunction (e.g., "and," "but," or "or") to connect the two independent clauses. The correct sentence would be, "Self-knowledge is like lost innocence, however unsettling you find it, it can never be 'unthought' or 'unknown'."

해설 부분을 통해서 어떤 유형의 문제를 만들었는지 알아보겠습니다.

Answer: a) "Self-knowledge is like lost innocence; however unsettling you find it, it can never be 'unthought' or 'unknown'." This sentence is not grammatically correct because it uses a semicolon to separate two independent clauses without a coordinating conjunction.

> 해당 결과값에 오류가 있습니다. 세 번째 문제를 살펴본 후 chatGPT에게 문제를 수정해 달라고 요청해 보겠습니다.

Explanation: This question tests the student's knowledge of punctuation and sentence structure. In option a), the semicolon should be replaced with a comma and a coordinating conjunction (e.g., "and," "but," or "or") to connect the two independent clauses. The correct sentence would be, "Self-knowledge is like lost innocence, however unsettling you find it, it can never be 'unthought' or 'unknown'."

챗GPT 4 Better Questions

빈칸 유형의 세 번째 문제에 대한 결과값입니다.

> Question 3: In order to complete the grammatically correct sentence, which of the following best fills in the blank in the given sentence?
> "The mere fact that a group of people in the past agreed to a constitution is not enough to make that constitution _____."
>
> a) fair
> b) fairly
> c) fairness
> d) fairer
>
> Answer: a) fair. The sentence should read, "The mere fact that a group of people in the past agreed to a constitution is not enough to make that constitution fair."
>
> Explanation: This question tests the student's knowledge of adjective forms and sentence structure. In the sentence, the blank needs an adjective to describe the constitution. The most appropriate adjective is "fair," which describes a just or impartial constitution. The other options are not appropriate because they are either adverbs (b) "fairly") or nouns (c) "fairness") that do not describe the constitution directly. Option d) "fairer" would be incorrect because it suggests that the constitution is being compared to another constitution, and this comparison is not implied in the original sentence.

사용을 요청한 문장을 바탕으로 5형식 목적보어 자리에 들어갈 품사를 묻는 문제를 만들어 주었습니다. 아래 두 항목을 활용한 문제임을 파악할 수 있습니다.

Sentence structure
Adjectives and adverbs

첫 번째와 세 번째 문제의 경우 원하는 결과값을 얻었지만, 두 번째 구두점을 활용한 문제에서는 오류가 발생했습니다. 문장의 구조를 파악하는 부분에서 punctuation과 관련된 문제를 만들어 준 것인데 다음과 같은 프롬프트를 주어 수정해 보도록 하겠습니다.

Prompt *There is a logical error in the second question. Correct the question.*

There is a logical error in the second question. Correct the question.

I apologize for the error in the second question. Here is the corrected question:

Question 2 (revised): Which of the following sentences uses incorrect punctuation to separate two independent clauses?
a) "Self-knowledge is like lost innocence; however unsettling you find it, it can never be 'unthought' or 'unknown'."
b) "However unsettling you find it, self-knowledge can never be 'unthought' or 'unknown'."
c) "Self-knowledge can never be 'unthought' or 'unknown'; however unsettling you find it."
d) "Self-knowledge, however unsettling you find it, can never be 'unthought' or 'unknown'."

Thank you for bringing this to my attention.

이번에는 주어진 문장을 가지고, 구두점의 활용을 묻는 오류가 없는 문제를 만들어 주었습니다. 이렇게 chatGPT도 오류가 발생할 수 있기에 결과물에 대해선 반복적인 검수가 필요하며, 무엇보다 사용자가 해당 부분에 대한 지식을 알고 있는 것이 중요합니다.

4 Better Questions

 나도 Prompt Engineer

1. Prompt: Create a table for the definition of gerund and its example usage.

2. Prompt: Show me some sample words that can be used to create a skit for a school talent show.

3. Prompt: Create a K-5 level, 1 minute skit for the school talent show. Make sure to use sentences that contain the words and the grammar as listed below.

〈Words to use〉
Superhero
Time traveler
Aliens
Famous historical figures
Animal characters
Fairy tale characters
Sports personalities
Celebrity impersonations
Mythical creatures
Robots

〈Grammar to use〉
- gerund
- to-infinitive
- relative clause

4. Prompt: Come up with 3 grammar questions that test the student's knowledge of gerund. Follow the instruction.

[Instruction]
Number of questions: 3
Target Student: Students preparing the SAT verbal test
Grammatical item to be evaluated: Gerund
Level of difficulty: Hard
Provide the answer and explanation at the bottom.

[Types of Stem]
Question 1: Which of the following sentences is grammatically CORRECT?
Question 2: Which of the following best fills in the blank of the given sentence?
Question 3: Which of the following best paraphrase the given sentence?

5. Prompt: Come up with 3 grammar questions that test the student's knowledge of gerund. Follow the instruction.

[Instruction]
Number of questions: 3
Target Student: Students preparing the SAT verbal testG
Grammatical item to be evaluated: Gerund
Level of difficulty: Hard
Provide the answer and explanation at the bottom.

Use sentences excerpted from the book Sapiens, Yuval Noah Harari as sample sentences for alternatives. Refers to the website, https://www.goodreads.com/work/quotes/18962767-itsur-toldot-ha-enoshut for excerpts.

[Types of Stem]
Question 1: Which of the following sentences is grammatically CORRECT?
Question 2: Which of the following best fills in the blank of the given sentence?
Question 3: Which of the following best paraphrase the given sentence?

4 Better Questions

6. Prompt: Make 3 grammar questions along with the answer and explanation with the instruction below.

[Sentences to use]
"Markets are useful instruments for organizing productive activity. But unless we want to let the market rewrite the norms that govern social institutions, we need a public debate about the moral limits of markets.
"Self-knowledge is like lost innocence; however unsettling you find it, it can never be 'unthought' or 'unknown'."
"The mere fact that a group of people in the past agreed to a constitution is not enough to make that constitution just."
"The more we regard our success as our own doing, the less responsibility we feel for those who fall behind."
"To achieve a just society we have to reason together about the meaning of the good life, and to create a public culture hospitable to the disagreements that will inevitably arise."

[Instruction]
- Make questions using the sentences given above.
- Test the student's OVERALL knowledge of grammar
- Assess students' use of language in terms of the list below.
Parts of speech
Sentence structure
Verb forms
Pronouns
Adjectives and adverbs
Conjunctions
Prepositions
Passive voice

[Types of Stem]
Question 1 & 2: Which of the following is NOT grammatically correct?
Question 3: In order to complete the grammatically correct sentence, which of the following best fills in the blank in the given sentence?

M·E·M·O

chatGPT를 활용한 영어문제 창작

Version 2.0

PART 2
Reading Comprehension Factory

4 Better Questions

1 SAT 유형 문제

chatGPT를 활용한 문제창작은 독해파트에서 그 빛을 발한다고 볼 수 있을 겁니다. 먼저, 수능유형과 중고등 내신용 독해 문제를 만드는 프롬프트 연습 이전에 일반적인 독해 문제를 만드는 연습을 해 보도록 하겠습니다.

먼저, chatGPT에게 아래와 같은 프롬프트를 넣어 보겠습니다.

> **Prompt**) *What types of reading comprehension questions I can make with the help of chatGPT?*

아래와 같은 결과값이 나왔습니다.

As an AI language model, I can help you create various types of reading comprehension questions. Here are a few examples:

1. Literal comprehension questions: These types of questions require the reader to find explicit information from the text. For example:

- Who is the main character in the story?
- Where does the story take place?
- What happened to the protagonist at the end of the story?

2. Inferential comprehension questions: These types of questions require the reader to make educated guesses based on the information given in the text. For example:

- What do you think will happen next in the story?
- Why did the main character behave that way?
- What message is the author trying to convey through the text?

3. Critical comprehension questions: These types of questions require the reader to analyze and evaluate the text. For example:

- Do you agree with the protagonist's decision? Why or why not?
- How does the author use symbolism in the text to support the theme?
- What is your opinion about the issue discussed in the text?

These are just a few examples, but there are many more types of reading comprehension questions that you can create depending on the text and the level of understanding you want to evaluate.

↻ Regenerate response

다음과 같은 프롬프트를 넣어 보겠습니다.

Prompt) *Let me know all types of SAT Reading Comprehension questions.*

아래와 같은 결과값을 얻었습니다.

 SAT Reading Comprehension questions can be broadly classified into three categories:

1. Vocabulary-in-Context Questions: These questions ask you to determine the meaning of a word or phrase as it is used in the context of the passage. They may ask you to identify the definition of a word or to select a synonym or antonym based on the passage.
2. Information and Ideas Questions: These questions ask you to identify main ideas, themes, and arguments presented in the passage. They may ask you to summarize the passage or to draw inferences from the information presented.
3. Rhetoric Questions: These questions ask you to analyze the author's use of language, tone, and structure. They may ask you to identify the purpose of a particular passage or to determine the author's attitude toward a particular subject.

Here are some examples of the types of SAT Reading Comprehension questions you may encounter:

- Vocabulary-in-Context Question: "What does the word 'pervasive' mean in the context of the passage?"
- Information and Ideas Question: "What is the main idea of the passage?"
- Rhetoric Question: "What is the author's tone toward the subject of the passage?"

좀 더 많은 질문의 형태를 보고 싶으면, 아래와 같이 제시하면 됩니다.

Prompt) *Let me know at least 10 types of SAT Reading Comprehension questions along with examples.*

4 Better Questions

아래와 같이 다양한 유형의 문제를 소개해 주고 있습니다.

> Sure, here are 10 types of SAT Reading Comprehension questions along with examples:
>
> 1. Vocabulary-in-Context Questions: "What is the meaning of the word 'alacrity' as it is used in the passage?"
> 2. Information and Ideas Questions: "What is the main idea of the passage?"
> 3. Rhetoric Questions: "What is the author's purpose in using a metaphor in the third paragraph?"
> 4. Inference Questions: "What can be inferred from the author's description of the character's behavior?"
> 5. Function Questions: "What is the function of the second paragraph in the overall structure of the passage?"
> 6. Detail Questions: "According to the passage, what is the name of the character's father?"
> 7. Purpose Questions: "What is the purpose of the character's dialogue in the third paragraph?"
> 8. Tone Questions: "What is the author's tone towards the protagonist in the passage?"
> 9. Style Questions: "How does the author's use of imagery contribute to the overall style of the passage?"
> 10. Comparison Questions: "How does the author compare and contrast the two characters in the passage?"

아래 동물농장(Animal Farm)에서 발췌한 내용을 바탕으로 위에서 제시한 문제를 한 번 만들어 보겠습니다.

Mr. Jones, of the Manor Farm, had locked the hen-houses for the night, but was too drunk to remember to shut the popholes. With the ring of light from his lantern dancing from side to side, he lurched across the yard, kicked off his boots at the back door, drew himself a last glass of beer from the barrel in the scullery, and made his way up to bed, where Mrs. Jones was already snoring.

As soon as the light in the bedroom went out there was a stirring and a fluttering all through the farm buildings. Word had gone round during the day that old Major, the prize Middle White boar, had had a strange dream on the previous night and wished to communicate it to the other animals. It had been agreed that they should all meet in the big barn as soon as Mr. Jones was safely out of the way. Old Major (so he was always called, though the name under which he had been exhibited was Willingdon Beauty) was so highly regarded on the farm that everyone was quite ready to lose an hour's sleep in order to hear what he had to say.

from Animal Farm by George Orwell

PART 2

문제유형 ①

Vocabulary-in-Context Questions: "What is the meaning of the word 'alacrity' as it is used in the passage?"

Prompt) *Make a vocabulary-in-context question with 5 multiple choices along with the instruction listed below.*

Passage of use

Mr. Jones, of the Manor Farm, had locked the hen-houses for the night, but was too drunk to remember to shut the popholes. With the ring of light from his lantern dancing from side to side, he lurched across the yard, kicked off his boots at the back door, drew himself a last glass of beer from the barrel in the scullery, and made his way up to bed, where Mrs. Jones was already snoring.

∨ Stem

What is the meaning of the phrase 'lurched across' as it is used in the passage?

∨ Type of Alternative

①
②
③
④
⑤

챗GPT 4 Better Questions

아래와 같은 결과값을 얻었습니다.

> Sure, here's a vocabulary-in-context question with five multiple-choice options based on the given passage:
>
> [Stem]
> What is the meaning of the phrase 'lurched across' as it is used in the passage?
>
> [Types of Alternatives]
> ① staggered clumsily
> ② skipped joyfully
> ③ tiptoed silently
> ④ sprinted quickly
> ⑤ danced elegantly
>
> Answer: ① staggered clumsily
>
> Explanation: The word "lurched" implies a sudden, unsteady movement, which is associated with clumsiness or lack of balance. Therefore, option ①, staggered clumsily, is the correct answer. The other options are unrelated or opposite in meaning to the given phrase.

문제유형 ② ▶

Information and Ideas Questions: "What is the main idea of the passage?"

Prompt) *Make a question with 5 multiple choices along with the instruction listed below.*

[Passage to use]
Mr. Jones, of the Manor Farm, had locked the hen-houses for the night, but was too drunk to remember to shut the popholes. With the ring of light from his lantern dancing from side to side, he lurched across the yard, kicked off his boots at the back door, drew himself a last glass of beer from the barrel in the scullery, and made his way up to bed, where Mrs. Jones was already snoring.

[Stem]
What is the main idea of the passage?

PART 2

[Type of Alternative]
①
②
③
④
⑤

🔍 보기의 내용이 보이지 않을 경우 Show the contents of the alternatives.라고 입력하면 됩니다.

> Sure, here's a question about the main idea of the given passage:
>
> [Stem]
> What is the main idea of the passage?
>
> [Types of Alternatives]
> ① Mr. Jones's farm has many hen-houses.
> ② Mr. Jones's wife snores loudly.
> ③ Mr. Jones is a heavy drinker.
> ④ Mr. Jones forgets to close the popholes.
> ⑤ Mr. Jones is going to bed.
>
> Answer: ③ Mr. Jones is a heavy drinker.
>
> Explanation: The main idea of the passage is the portrayal of Mr. Jones as a drunkard who forgets to close the popholes of the hen-houses. This is evident from the description of Mr. Jones's actions, such as "was too drunk to remember to shut the popholes," "drew himself a last glass of beer," and "made his way up to bed, where Mrs. Jones was already snoring." Option ③, Mr. Jones is a heavy drinker, best summarizes the main idea of the passage.

문제유형 ▶

Rhetoric Questions: "What is the author's purpose in using a metaphor in the third paragraph?"

위 문제에서 문학장치(literary device)에 대한 문제를 추가해서 함께 만들어 보도록 하겠습니다.

Prompt *Make TWO questions with 5 multiple choices along with the instruction listed below.*

챗GPT 4 Better Questions

[Passage to use]

Mr. Jones, of the Manor Farm, had locked the hen-houses for the night, but was too drunk to remember to shut the popholes. <u>With the ring of light from his lantern dancing from side to side</u>, he lurched across the yard, kicked off his boots at the back door, drew himself a last glass of beer from the barrel in the scullery, and made his way up to bed, where Mrs. Jones was already snoring.

[Stem]

Question 1: What literary device is used in the expression "With the ring of light from his lantern dancing from side to side" in the passage?

Question 2: What is the author's purpose of the expression "With the ring of light from his lantern dancing from side to side" in the passage?

[Type of Alternative]

①
②
③
④
⑤

다음과 같은 결과값을 얻었습니다.

Sure, here are two questions with five multiple-choice options based on the given passage:

Question 1:
[Stem]
What literary device is used in the expression "With the ring of light from his lantern dancing from side to side" in the passage?

[Types of Alternatives]
① metaphor
② personification
③ alliteration
④ simile
⑤ onomatopoeia

Answer: ② personification

Explanation: Personification is a literary device that gives human qualities or actions to non-human objects. In the given expression, the author uses personification to describe the way the light from the lantern moves, as if it were a person dancing from side to side. The other options are not applicable as there is no comparison, repetition, or sound in the given expression.

첫 번째 문제에 대한 만족스런 결과값을 얻었습니다.
두 번째 문제에 대한 결과값은 다음과 같습니다.

Question 2:
[Stem]
What is the author's purpose of the expression "With the ring of light from his lantern dancing from side to side" in the passage?

[Types of Alternatives]
① to illustrate Mr. Jones's drunkenness
② to describe the night sky
③ to highlight the beauty of the lantern
④ to emphasize the importance of locking the hen-houses
⑤ to suggest the presence of ghosts in the yard

Answer: ① to illustrate Mr. Jones's drunkenness

Explanation: The expression "With the ring of light from his lantern dancing from side to side" is used to show how Mr. Jones is unsteady on his feet due to his drunkenness, and the movement of the lantern light is used to emphasize this. Therefore, option ①, to illustrate Mr. Jones's drunkenness, is the correct answer. The other options are not relevant to the given expression.

정답과 해설까지 깔끔하게 만들어 주었습니다.

위에 문제 출제에서 눈치를 챈 독자도 있겠지만, 출제하고자 하는 지문에 대한 깊은 이해가 바탕이 되어야 좋은 문제를 만들 수가 있습니다. 만약, 지문 분석에 도움을 얻고자 한다면 아래와 같이 chatGPT를 활용하시면 됩니다.

Prompt *Offer a line-by-line analysis for the passage above.*

챗GPT 4 Better Questions

문제유형 ④

Inference Questions: "What can be inferred from the author's description of the character's behavior?"

Prompt) Make a question with 5 multiple choices along with the instruction listed below.

[Passage to use]
Mr. Jones, of the Manor Farm, had locked the hen-houses for the night, but was too drunk to remember to shut the popholes. With the ring of light from his lantern dancing from side to side, he lurched across the yard, kicked off his boots at the back door, drew himself a last glass of beer from the barrel in the scullery, and made his way up to bed, where Mrs. Jones was already snoring.

[Stem]
What can be inferred from the author's description of the character's behavior?

[Type of Alternative]
①
②
③
④
⑤

아래와 같은 만족스러운 결과값을 얻었습니다.

> Sure, here's a question with five multiple-choice options based on the given passage:
>
> [Stem]
> What can be inferred from the author's description of the character's behavior?
>
> [Types of Alternatives]
> ① Mr. Jones is a responsible and trustworthy individual.
> ② Mr. Jones has a history of neglecting his duties.
> ③ Mr. Jones is a teetotaler who never drinks alcohol.
> ④ Mrs. Jones is the one who usually takes care of the hen-houses.
> ⑤ Mr. Jones forgot to lock the hen-houses on purpose.
>
> Answer: ② Mr. Jones has a history of neglecting his duties.
>
> Explanation: The author's description of Mr. Jones's behavior in the passage suggests that he has a history of neglecting his duties. He is too drunk to remember to shut the popholes, and he appears unsteady on his feet as he makes his way to bed. The fact that Mrs. Jones is already snoring when he arrives also implies that he is not taking care of his responsibilities as a husband. The other options are not supported by the given passage.

지금까지 SAT과 같은 시험에서 볼 수 있는 몇 가지 간략한 문제 제작을 살펴보았습니다. 이제 수능 영어와 학교 내신 영어시험에 맞는 문제를 chatGPT를 활용해서 만들어 보겠습니다. 먼저, 기억할 내용은 간단한 프롬프트 명령어 하나만으로 원하는 결과값을 얻을 수 없다는 점입니다. chatGPT는 도깨비 방망이라기보다는 프로메테우스가 인간에게 선물해 준 불과 같은 존재입니다.

챗GPT **4 Better Questions**

💬 나도 Prompt Engineer

1. Prompt: What types of reading comprehension questions can I make with the help of chatGPT?

2. Prompt: Let me know all types of SAT Reading Comprehension questions.

3. Prompt: Let me know at least 10 types of SAT Reading Comprehension questions along with examples.

4. Prompt: Make a vocabulary-in-context question with 5 multiple choices along with the instruction listed below.

[Passage to use]
Mr. Jones, of the Manor Farm, had locked the hen-houses for the night, but was too drunk to remember to shut the popholes. With the ring of light from his lantern dancing from side to side, he lurched across the yard, kicked off his boots at the back door, drew himself a last glass of beer from the barrel in the scullery, and made his way up to bed, where Mrs. Jones was already snoring.

[Stem]
What is the meaning of the phrase 'lurched across' as it is used in the passage?

[Type of Alternative]
①
②
③
④
⑤

5. Prompt: Make a question with 5 multiple choices along with the instruction listed below.

PART 2

[Passage to use]
Mr. Jones, of the Manor Farm, had locked the hen-houses for the night, but was too drunk to remember to shut the popholes. With the ring of light from his lantern dancing from side to side, he lurched across the yard, kicked off his boots at the back door, drew himself a last glass of beer from the barrel in the scullery, and made his way up to bed, where Mrs. Jones was already snoring.

[Stem]
What is the main idea of the passage?

[Type of Alternative]
①
②
③
④
⑤

6. Prompt: Make TWO questions with 5 multiple choices along with the instruction listed below.

[Passage to use]
Mr. Jones, of the Manor Farm, had locked the hen-houses for the night, but was too drunk to remember to shut the popholes. With the ring of light from his lantern dancing from side to side, he lurched across the yard, kicked off his boots at the back door, drew himself a last glass of beer from the barrel in the scullery, and made his way up to bed, where Mrs. Jones was already snoring.

[Stem]
Question 1: What literary device is used in the expression "With the ring of light from his lantern dancing from side to side" in the passage?
Question 2: What is the author's purpose of the expression "With the ring of light from his lantern dancing from side to side" in the passage?

4 Better Questions

[Type of Alternative]
①
②
③
④
⑤

7. Prompt: Make a question with 5 multiple choices along with the instruction listed below.

[Passage to use]
Mr. Jones, of the Manor Farm, had locked the hen-houses for the night, but was too drunk to remember to shut the popholes. With the ring of light from his lantern dancing from side to side, he lurched across the yard, kicked off his boots at the back door, drew himself a last glass of beer from the barrel in the scullery, and made his way up to bed, where Mrs. Jones was already snoring.

[Stem]
What can be inferred from the author's description of the character's behavior?

[Type of Alternative]
①
②
③
④
⑤

2 수능/내신 유형 문제

문제유형 ① ▶ 주제와 응용문제 만들기

주제를 묻는 문제를 만드는 프롬프트는 간단합니다.

Prompt) *Create the topic of the passage given below.*

> **Passage**
>
> *Shakespeare had been recreated in the image of desire of his biographers who had been reared in the strict code of 19th century gentility, and they accepted two ideas without question. One was that there are few things more important than an English lord; the other was that there are few things less important than a mere actor. For them the notion that Shakespeare had spent all these years as the working member of a company of London actors was so abhorrent that it was never seriously considered. It could not be so; therefore it was not.*

아래와 같은 결과값을 주었습니다.

 Shakespeare's image in the eyes of his biographers.

해당 유형의 문제를 만드는 프롬프트를 작성해 보겠습니다.

Prompt) *Make a question with 5 multiple choices along with the answer and explanation using the passage below.*

> **Passage**
>
> *Shakespeare had been recreated in the image of desire of his biographers who had been reared in the strict code of 19th century gentility, and they accepted two ideas without question. One was that there are few things more important than an English lord; the other was that there are few things less important than a mere actor. For them the notion that Shakespeare had spent all these years as the working member of a company of London actors was so abhorrent that it was*

4 Better Questions

never seriously considered. It could not be so; therefore it was not.

[Stem]
Which of the following is the topic of the passage?

[Types of Alternative]
①
②
③
④
⑤

- *Show all the alternatives.*

 보기의 내용을 보여주지 않은 경우가 있어 해당 문구를 넣습니다.

아래와 같이 정답 및 해설과 함께 멋진 주제 문제를 만들어 주었습니다.

> Which of the following is the topic of the passage?
>
> ① Shakespeare's background and upbringing.
> ② The importance of English lords in 19th century society.
> ③ The low status of actors in 19th century society.
> ④ Shakespeare's image in the eyes of his biographers.
> ⑤ The role of London theater companies in Shakespeare's career.
>
> Answer: ④ Shakespeare's image in the eyes of his biographers.
>
> Explanation: The passage discusses how Shakespeare was perceived by his biographers, who were influenced by the social norms and values of their time, which led them to view actors as unimportant and incompatible with Shakespeare's supposed status. The passage does not delve into Shakespeare's background or upbringing, the importance of English lords, the low status of actors in general, or the role of London theater companies in his career.

문제유형 2 ▶ 요지 문제 만들기

이번에는 요지를 묻는 문제를 만들어 보겠습니다.

Prompt *Make a question with 5 multiple choices along with the answer and explanation using the passage below.*

Passage

Shakespeare had been recreated in the image of desire of his biographers who had been reared in the strict code of 19th century gentility, and they accepted two ideas without question. One was that there are few things more important than an English lord; the other was that there are few things less important than a mere actor. For them the notion that Shakespeare had spent all these years as the working member of a company of London actors was so abhorrent that it was never seriously considered. It could not be so; therefore it was not.

[Stem]
Which of the following is the main idea of the passage?

[Types of Alternative]
①
②
③
④
⑤

- Show all the alternatives.

4 Better Questions

아래와 같은 결과값을 얻었습니다.

>
> ① Shakespeare's biographers were reared in the strict code of 19th century gentility.
> ② The importance of an English lord was unquestioned by Shakespeare's biographers.
> ③ Shakespeare's biographers did not consider the notion of him being a member of a London acting company.
> ④ The notion of Shakespeare being a mere actor was abhorrent to his biographers.
> ⑤ Shakespeare's image was recreated in the desire of his biographers.
>
> Answer:
> ⑤ Shakespeare's image was recreated in the desire of his biographers.
>
> Explanation:
> The passage discusses how Shakespeare was perceived by his biographers who were influenced by the social norms of their time, specifically the idea that being a mere actor was less important than being an English lord. The main idea of the passage is that Shakespeare's image was recreated by his biographers to fit the desires of their social norms, which included the notion that a mere actor could not have written such great works. The passage highlights how Shakespeare's biographers were unable to see beyond their own social biases, and how this influenced their perception of the playwright.

오류 없이 정답과 해설까지 깔끔하게 제시하고 있습니다.

나도 Prompt Engineer

1. Prompt: Create the topic of the passage given below.

[Passage]
Shakespeare had been recreated in the image of desire of his biographers who had been reared in the strict code of 19th century gentility, and they accepted two ideas without question. One was that there are few things more important than an English lord; the other was that there are few things less important than a mere actor. For them the notion that Shakespeare had spent all these years as the working member of a company of London actors was so abhorrent that it was never seriously considered. It could not be so; therefore it was not.

2. Prompt: Make a question with 5 multiple choices along with the answer and explanation using the passage below.

[Passage]
Shakespeare had been recreated in the image of desire of his biographers who had been reared in the strict code of 19th century gentility, and they accepted two ideas without question. One was that there are few things more important than an English lord; the other was that there are few things less important than a mere actor. For them the notion that Shakespeare had spent all these years as the working member of a company of London actors was so abhorrent that it was never seriously considered. It could not be so; therefore it was not.

[Stem]
Which of the following is the topic of the passage?

[Types of Alternative]
①
②
③
④
⑤

- Show all the alternatives.

챗GPT **4 Better Questions**

3. Prompt: Make a question with 5 multiple choices along with the answer and explanation using the passage below.

[Passage]
Shakespeare had been recreated in the image of desire of his biographers who had been reared in the strict code of 19th century gentility, and they accepted two ideas without question. One was that there are few things more important than an English lord; the other was that there are few things less important than a mere actor. For them the notion that Shakespeare had spent all these years as the working member of a company of London actors was so abhorrent that it was never seriously considered. It could not be so; therefore it was not.

[Stem]
Which of the following is the main idea of the passage?

[Types of Alternative]
①
②
③
④
⑤

- Show all the alternatives.

문제유형 ③ ▶ 제목 문제 만들기

Prompt) *Make a question with 5 multiple choices along with the answer and explanation using the passage below.*

Passage

The fading of this mythology is the result of Americans' gradual realization that science and technology's dreamy wonders sometimes turn out to be nightmarish blunders. Detergents that make dishes gleam may kill rivers. Dyes that prettify the food may cause cancer. Pills that make sex safe may dangerously complicate health. DDT, cyclamates, thalidomide and estrogen are but a few of the mixed blessings that, all together, have taught the layman a singular lesson: the promising fruits of science and technology often come with hidden worms.

[Stem]
Which of the following is the best title of the passage?

[Types of Alternative]
①
②
③
④
⑤

- Show all the alternatives.

4 **Better Questions**

아래와 같은 결과값이 나왔습니다.

① The Benefits and Drawbacks of Science and Technology
② The Evolution of American Mythology
③ The Nightmarish Consequences of Dish Detergents
④ The Hidden Worms in Dyes and Pills
⑤ The Mixed Blessings of DDT, Cyclamates, Thalidomide, and Estrogen

The correct answer is ① The Benefits and Drawbacks of Science and Technology.

Explanation: The passage discusses how Americans are realizing the drawbacks of science and technology, despite its promising benefits. The author gives examples of products like detergents, dyes, and pills that can have negative consequences such as killing rivers or causing cancer. The passage also mentions specific examples like DDT, cyclamates, thalidomide, and estrogen as "mixed blessings" that come with hidden worms. The best title that summarizes the passage is "The Benefits and Drawbacks of Science and Technology." Therefore, option ① is the correct answer. The other options focus on specific details mentioned in the passage but do not capture the overall message of the passage.

제목의 경우에는 주제나 요지를 묻는 문제와는 달리 보기의 내용을 구성할 때 본문의 요지를 전달하는 다양한 표현이 가능합니다. 단락 속 주제와 요지는 전달하는 내용이 정해져 있으므로, 동의표현을 제외하고는 다양한 표현이 나오기 힘들지만, 제목의 경우 요지를 반영한 다양한 표현이 가능하므로 아래와 같이 동일한 내용을 바탕으로 다음과 같이 프롬프트를 작성해 보도록 하겠습니다.

Prompt) Make a question with 5 multiple choices with the answer and explanation. Follow the Instruction.

instruction

* *Passage to use*

The fading of this mythology is the result of Americans' gradual realization that science and technology's dreamy wonders sometimes turn out to be nightmarish blunders. Detergents that make dishes gleam may kill rivers. Dyes that prettify the food may cause cancer. Pills that make sex safe may dangerously complicate health. DDT, cyclamates, thalidomide and estrogen are but a few of the mixed blessings that, all together, have taught the layman a singular lesson: the promising fruits of science and technology often come with hidden worms.

* Stem
Which of the following is the best title of the passage?

When making the option, make sure to include idioms or symbolic expressions related to the passage, and explain them in the answer.

* Type of Alternative
①
②
③
④
⑤

- Show all the alternatives.

아래와 같은 결과값을 얻었습니다.

> Which of the following is the best title of the passage, which discusses the potential dangers of scientific and technological advancements?
>
> ① The Bitter Fruits of Progress
> ② Science and Technology: A Double-Edged Sword
> ③ The Worms in the Apple of Innovation
> ④ From Myth to Reality: The Risks of Technological Advancement
> ⑤ The Nightmarish Blunders of Modern Science
>
> Answer: The best title of the passage is (②) Science and Technology: A Double-Edged Sword.
>
> Explanation: The phrase "double-edged sword" is an idiom that means something that has both beneficial and harmful effects. In the passage, the author uses examples to demonstrate that while science and technology have produced many benefits, they have also led to unintended negative consequences. The phrase "double-edged sword" captures this idea well, as it implies that science and technology have both a positive and negative side. Therefore, option (②) is the most appropriate title for the passage.

4 Better Questions

제시된 답변을 조금 자세히 들여다 보도록 하겠습니다. 먼저, 보기를 보면, 아래 밑줄 친 부분에서 관용적 표현과 상징적 표현이 반영되었다는 것을 볼 수 있습니다.

① The **Bitter Fruits** of Progress
② Science and Technology: **A Double-Edged Sword**
③ **The Worms in the Apple** of Innovation

그리고, 프롬프트에서 요구한 것처럼 해설에 자세한 설명을 곁들이고 있습니다.

The phrase "double-edged sword" is an idiom that means something that has both beneficial and harmful effects. In the passage, the author uses examples to demonstrate that while science and technology have produced many benefits, they have also led to unintended negative consequences. The phrase "double-edged sword" captures this idea well, as it implies that science and technology have both a positive and negative side. Therefore, option (②) is the most appropriate title for the passage.

감동이네요. 약간의 2차 가공을 한다면 높은 수준의 문제까지 제작이 가능합니다. Way to go, chatGPT!

나도 Prompt Engineer

1. Prompt: Make a question with 5 multiple choices along with the answer and explanation using the passage below.

[Passage]
The fading of this mythology is the result of Americans' gradual realization that science and technology's dreamy wonders sometimes turn out to be nightmarish blunders. Detergents that make dishes gleam may kill rivers. Dyes that prettify the food may cause cancer. Pills that make sex safe may dangerously complicate health. DDT, cyclamates, thalidomide and estrogen are but a few of the mixed blessings that, all together, have taught the layman a singular lesson: the promising fruits of science and technology often come with hidden worms.

[Stem]
Which of the following is the best title of the passage?

[Types of Alternative]
①
②
③
④
⑤

- Show all the alternatives.

4 Better Questions

2. Prompt: Make a question with 5 multiple choices with the answer and explanation. Follow the Instruction.

[Instruction]
* Passage to use
The fading of this mythology is the result of Americans' gradual realization that science and technology's dreamy wonders sometimes turn out to be nightmarish blunders. Detergents that make dishes gleam may kill rivers. Dyes that prettify the food may cause cancer. Pills that make sex safe may dangerously complicate health. DDT, cyclamates, thalidomide and estrogen are but a few of the mixed blessings that, all together, have taught the layman a singular lesson: the promising fruits of science and technology often come with hidden worms.

* Stem
Which of the following is the best title of the passage?

When making the option, make sure to include idioms or symbolic expressions related to the passage, and explain them in the answer.

* Type of Alternative
①
②
③
④
⑤

- Show all the alternatives.

문제유형 ④ ▶ 빈칸 채우기 만들기

보통 수능과 내신에서 변별력이 높은 문제로 처리되는 문장 완성의 형태인 빈칸 문제를 만들어 보겠습니다. 지문은 위에서 활용한 지문을 그대로 다시 사용해 보겠습니다.

Prompt) *Make a question with 5 multiple choices along with the answer and explanation using the passage below.*

Passage

The fading of this mythology is the result of Americans' gradual realization that science and technology's dreamy wonders sometimes turn out to be nightmarish blunders. Detergents that make dishes gleam may kill rivers. Dyes that prettify the food may cause cancer. Pills that make sex safe may dangerously complicate health. DDT, cyclamates, thalidomide and estrogen are but a few of the mixed blessings that, all together, have taught the layman a singular lesson: the promising fruits of science and technology often (A)_____.

[Stem]
Which of the following best fills in the blank (A) in the passage?

[Types of Alternative]
①
②
③
④
⑤

- Show all the alternatives.

챗GPT 4 Better Questions

아래와 같은 결과값을 얻었습니다.

① come with hidden worms
② are worth the risk
③ are always beneficial
④ have predictable outcomes
⑤ are necessary for progress

The correct answer is ① come with hidden worms.

Explanation: The passage discusses how Americans are gradually realizing that the promising fruits of science and technology often come with hidden worms, meaning that even though they may have benefits, they also have negative consequences. The examples given in the passage, such as detergents that kill rivers, dyes that cause cancer, and pills that dangerously complicate health, demonstrate this point. Therefore, the best option to fill in the blank (A) in the passage is ① come with hidden worms. The other options either do not reflect the message of the passage or present a biased view of science and technology.

보기의 내용을 보면, 원문의 표현을 그대로 활용하여 구성했습니다. 여기서 주목한 chatGPT의 특징은 대화의 내용을 기억하는 내용의 연속성입니다. 원문을 기억한다는 것이죠. 만약, 원문의 표현을 고려하지 않고 순수하게 chatGPT가 만들어주는 문제를 원한다면 chatGPT를 다시 시작하고 프롬프트를 넣으시면 됩니다. 이전 대화를 기억하지 않는 상황에 프롬프트를 다시 넣어 보겠습니다.

① Come with unintended consequences
② Exceed expectations
③ Benefit society greatly
④ Are worth the risks involved
⑤ Are always successful

The answer is ① "Come with unintended consequences."

Explanation: The passage explains that Americans have realized that science and technology's benefits can often turn into negative consequences. The passage provides examples of various products that were meant to provide benefits but resulted in negative outcomes. Therefore, the best option to fill in the blank is "come with unintended consequences."

같은 말이지만, "Come with unintended consequences"의 선지를 주었습니다.

이어서 다중 빈칸 문제를 만들어 보겠습니다. 이번에는 보기의 내용을 표로 작성해 달라는 명령까지 넣어보겠습니다.

Prompt) Make a question with 5 multiple choices along with the answer and explanation using the passage below.

Passage

The fading of this mythology is the result of Americans' gradual realization that science and technology's dreamy wonders sometimes (A)_____. Detergents that make dishes gleam may kill rivers. Dyes that prettify the food may cause cancer. Pills that make sex safe may dangerously complicate health. DDT, cyclamates, thalidomide and estrogen are but a few of the mixed blessings that, all together, have taught the layman a singular lesson: the promising fruits of science and technology often (B)_____.

[Stem]
Which of the following pairs best fills in the blanks (A) and (B) in the passage?

[Types of Alternative]
①
②
③
④
⑤

- Displays all the alternatives <u>in a tabular format with numbers in vertical rows and content in horizontal rows.</u>

🔍 표의 형식으로 만들어 달라는 명령어입니다.

챗GPT 4 Better Questions

아래와 같은 결과값이 나왔습니다.

	(A)	(B)
①	come with unexpected consequences	prove to be dangerous or harmful
②	always have positive outcomes	exceed our expectations
③	are the solution to all problems	are the answer to our prayers
④	are completely safe	deliver all that they promise
⑤	are perfectly predictable	come with no drawbacks

Answer:

The best pair of choices that fills in the blanks (A) and (B) in the passage is ① and ①, respectively.

보기의 내용도 그렇고 표도 원하는 형태로 결과값이 나왔습니다. 아래와 같이 해설에 대한 상세한 내용도 함께 제공하고 있습니다.

Explanation:

The passage is discussing how Americans are gradually realizing that science and technology do not always have the positive outcomes that were expected. In fact, the passage gives examples of how some of the products of science and technology can have unintended negative consequences. The phrase "sometimes" in blank (A) suggests that there are instances where science and technology do not meet our expectations. The phrase "mixed blessings" in the passage also implies that there are both positive and negative aspects to these products. Thus, the best choice to fill in blank (A) is "come with unexpected consequences."

In blank (B), the passage is referring to the negative side of science and technology. The phrase "promising fruits" suggests that there were high hopes for these products, but the phrase "mixed blessings" implies that there are both positive and negative aspects to these products. The phrase "have taught the layman a singular lesson" suggests that there were significant and noteworthy negative consequences. Thus, the best choice to fill in blank (B) is "prove to be dangerous or harmful."

PART 2

이번에는 난이도를 조금 높여 보기를 구성할 때 특정 단어를 반드시 사용하도록 프롬프트를 짜서 결과값을 살펴보도록 하겠습니다.

Prompt) *Make a question with 5 multiple choices along with the answer and explanation according to the instruction below.*

instruction

* When making the filler question
Use the passage

* When making the options
Do NOT use the same words, phrases or sentences as they are in the passage.
Please include at least any one of the words below.
go through, objective evaluation, connect, social context, allow, public criticism, universal link with, various, academic fields

🔍 보기의 내용에 사용할 특정 단어, 구, 절을 사용하도록 조건부에 넣을 수 있습니다.

Passage

One of the key contributions of critical theorists concerns the production of knowledge. Given that the transmission of knowledge is an integral activity in schools, critical scholars in the field of education have been especially concerned with how knowledge is produced. The scholars argue that a key element of social injustice involves the claim that particular knowledge is objective, neutral, and universal. An approach based on critical theory calls into question the idea that objectivity is desirable or even possible. The term used to describe this way of thinking about knowledge is that knowledge is socially constructed. When we refer to knowledge as socially constructed we mean that knowledge is reflective of the values and interests of those who produce it. This concept captures the understanding that all knowledge and all means of knowing _____.

[Stem]
Which of the following best fills in the blank in the passage?

챗GPT 4 Better Questions

[Types of Alternative]
①
②
③
④
⑤

* Display all the options.

아래와 같은 결과값을 주었습니다. 참고로, 원문 빈칸의 정답은 are connected to a social context입니다.

> [Stem]
> Which of the following best fills in the blank in the passage?
>
> [Types of Alternative]
> ① go through a process of objective evaluation.
> ② connect people from different social contexts.
> ③ allow for public criticism from various academic fields.
> ④ establish a universal link with the scientific community.
> ⑤ vary depending on the social context in which it is produced.
>
> [Answer]
> ⑤ Vary depending on the social context in which it is produced.
>
> [Explanation]
> The passage discusses the concept of socially constructed knowledge, which means that knowledge is reflective of the values and interests of those who produce it. This idea challenges the claim that particular knowledge is objective, neutral, and universal. Therefore, the blank in the passage should be filled with an option that supports the concept of socially constructed knowledge. Option ⑤, "vary depending on the social context in which it is produced," is the best option because it reflects the idea that knowledge is not objective, neutral, or universal, but rather is influenced by the social context in which it is produced. The other options do not accurately reflect the concept of socially constructed knowledge described in the passage.

위 선지의 내용을 보시면 프롬프트에서 명령한 아래 표현을 사용해서 문제를 만든 것을 알 수 있습니다.

go through, objective evaluation, connect, social context, allow, public criticism, universal link with, various, academic fields

특히, 정답이 되는 선지의 내용이 원본보다 훨씬 더 매력적입니다.

이번에는 관용적 표현을 활용하여 선지를 구성하도록 요청해 보겠습니다.

Prompt) *Make a question with 5 multiple choices along with the answer and explanation according to the instruction below.*

instruction

* When making the filler question
Use the passage below.

* When making the options
Do NOT use the same words, phrases or sentences as they are in the passage.
- <u>Include at least a couple of idioms that are of K-5 level, and explain them in the explanation.</u>

🔍 선지를 만들 때 K-5 수준의 관용 표현을 적어도 두 개는 넣어 달라고 요청했습니다.

Passage

Jill is driving her two young sons to the movies. After the third time that the kids have quarreled, she pulls over the car, turns around, and screams at them at the top of her lungs: "ENOUGH! One more word and nobody goes to the movies!" After seeing the frightened looks on the children's faces and feeling the aftermath of the hurricane that just overtook her, she drives to the movies in a state of shock and disbelief. The kids were just being kids, she thinks. How could I have lost it and scared them so badly? Jill finds herself feeling overwhelmed, exhausted, and _____.

[Stem]
Which of the following best fills in the blank in the passage?

[Types of Alternative]
①
②

4 Better Questions

③
④
⑤

* *Display all the options.*

다음과 같은 결과값을 얻었습니다.

 [Stem]
Which of the following best fills in the blank in the passage?

[Types of Alternative]
① emotionally numb
② mentally relaxed
③ physically energetic
④ mentally drained
⑤ emotionally euphoric

빈칸에 들어갈 보기의 내용을 K-5 수준에 맞춰 너무 잘 만들었네요.

[Options]
① Emotionally numb - This option suggests that Jill has shut down emotionally as a result of her outburst. However, there is no indication in the passage that Jill is emotionally numb. Therefore, this option is incorrect.
② Mentally relaxed - This option suggests that Jill is feeling calm and at ease after her outburst. However, given the context of the passage and the fact that Jill is feeling overwhelmed and exhausted, this option is unlikely. Therefore, this option is incorrect.
③ Physically energetic - This option suggests that Jill is feeling energetic and ready to take on new challenges. However, given the context of the passage and the fact that Jill is feeling overwhelmed and exhausted, this option is unlikely. Therefore, this option is incorrect.
④ Mentally drained - This option correctly fills in the blank and aligns with the description of Jill feeling overwhelmed and exhausted after her outburst. The idiomatic expression "mentally drained" refers to feeling mentally exhausted or depleted. This is a common experience after experiencing a highly emotional event, such as Jill's outburst. Therefore, this option is the correct answer.
⑤ Emotionally euphoric - This option suggests that Jill is feeling emotionally euphoric, or extremely happy, after her outburst. However, given the context of the passage and the fact that Jill is feeling overwhelmed and exhausted, this option is unlikely. Therefore, this option is incorrect.

각 보기의 내용에 대한 상세한 설명을 해 주고 있는데, 마지막에 아래와 같이 정답에서 활용된 관용적 표현에 대한 설명을 덧붙여 주고 있습니다.

> Explanation of Idiom:
>
> - "mentally drained" - This idiom refers to feeling mentally exhausted or depleted, often as a result of a highly emotional event or experience. In the context of the passage, Jill's outburst at her children has left her feeling overwhelmed and mentally drained, which is a common response to such an event.

4 Better Questions

나도 Prompt Engineer

1. Prompt: Make a question with 5 multiple choices along with the answer and explanation using the passage below.

[Passage]
The fading of this mythology is the result of Americans' gradual realization that science and technology's dreamy wonders sometimes turn out to be nightmarish blunders. Detergents that make dishes gleam may kill rivers. Dyes that prettify the food may cause cancer. Pills that make sex safe may dangerously complicate health. DDT, cyclamates, thalidomide and estrogen are but a few of the mixed blessings that, all together, have taught the layman a singular lesson: the promising fruits of science and technology often (A)_____.

[Stem]
Which of the following best fills in the blank (A) in the passage?

[Types of Alternative]
①
②
③
④
⑤

- Show all the alternatives.

2. Prompt: Make a question with 5 multiple choices along with the answer and explanation using the passage below.

[Passage]
The fading of this mythology is the result of Americans' gradual realization that science and technology's dreamy wonders sometimes (A)_____. Detergents that make dishes gleam may kill rivers. Dyes that prettify the food may cause cancer. Pills that make sex safe may dangerously complicate health. DDT, cyclamates, thalidomide and estrogen are but a few of the mixed blessings that,
all together, have taught the layman a singular lesson: the promising fruits of science and technology often (B)_____.

[Stem]
Which of the following pairs best fills in the blanks (A) and (B) in the passage?

[Types of Alternative]
①
②
③
④
⑤

- Displays all the alternatives
in a tabular format with numbers in vertical rows and content in horizontal rows.

챗GPT 4 Better Questions

3. Prompt: Make a question with 5 multiple choices along with the answer and explanation according to the instruction below.

[Instruction]
* When making the filler question
- Use the passage

* When making the options
- Do NOT use the same words, phrases or sentences as they are in the passage.
- Please include at least any one of the words below.

go through, objective evaluation, connect, social context, allow, public criticism, universal link with, various, academic fields

[Passage]
One of the key contributions of critical theorists concerns the production of knowledge. Given that the transmission of knowledge is an integral activity in schools, critical scholars in the field of education have been especially concerned with how knowledge is produced. The scholars argue that a key element of social injustice involves the claim that particular knowledge is objective, neutral, and universal. An approach based on critical theory calls into question the idea that objectivity is desirable or even possible. The term used to describe this way of thinking about knowledge is that knowledge is socially constructed. When we refer to knowledge as socially constructed we mean that knowledge is reflective of the values and interests of those who produce it. This concept captures the understanding that all knowledge and all means of knowing _____.

[Stem]
Which of the following best fills in the blank in the passage?

[Types of Alternative]
①
②
③
④
⑤

* Display all the options.

4. Prompt: Make a question with 5 multiple choices along with the answer and explanation according to the instruction below.

[Instruction]
* When making the filler question
Use the passage below.

* When making the options
- Do NOT use the same words, phrases or sentences as they are in the passage.
-
Include at least a couple of idioms that are of K-5 level, and explain them in the explanation.

[Passage]
Jill is driving her two young sons to the movies. After the third time that the kids have quarreled, she pulls over the car, turns around, and screams at them at the top of her lungs: "ENOUGH! One more word and nobody goes to the movies!" After seeing the frightened looks on the children's faces and feeling the aftermath of the hurricane that just overtook her, she drives to the movies in a state of shock and disbelief. The kids were just being kids, she thinks. How could I have lost it and scared them so badly? Jill finds herself feeling overwhelmed, exhausted, and _____.

[Stem]
Which of the following best fills in the blank in the passage?

[Types of Alternative]
①
②
③
④
⑤

* Display all the options.

챗GPT 4 Better Questions

문제유형 5 ▶ 내용일치 / 불일치 / 추론 문제 만들기

프롬프트 하나로 좋은 문제를 만들기 위해서 그 많은 정교한 프롬프트를 짜기 위한 많은 노력이 들어갑니다. 원하는 결과값을 얻어내기 위해 프롬프트의 fine-tuning을 끊임없이 짜내는 것도 좋지만, 오히려 수동적인 작업이 질 높은 문제를 만들어주기도 합니다. 다양한 시도를 통해서 좋은 문제를 한 번 만들어 보도록 하겠습니다.

Prompt) Make a question with 5 multiple choices along with the answer and explanation using the passage below.

> **Passage**
>
> The fading of this mythology is the result of Americans' gradual realization that science and technology's dreamy wonders sometimes turn out to be nightmarish blunders. Detergents that make dishes gleam may kill rivers. Dyes that prettify the food may cause cancer. Pills that make sex safe may dangerously complicate health. DDT, cyclamates, thalidomide and estrogen are but a few of the mixed blessings that, all together, have taught the layman a singular lesson: the promising fruits of science and technology often come with hidden worms.

[Stem]
Which of the following statements is NOT correct about the passage?

[Types of Alternative]
①
②
③
④
⑤

- Show all the alternatives.

아래와 같은 결과 값이 나왔습니다.

 [Types of Alternative]

① The passage discusses the negative consequences of some products of science and technology.
② Americans have gradually realized that the promising fruits of science and technology often come with hidden worms.
③ All products of science and technology are always positive and do not have any negative outcomes.
④ Detergents that make dishes gleam may kill rivers, and dyes that prettify the food may cause cancer.
⑤ The passage mentions DDT, cyclamates, thalidomide, and estrogen as examples of the negative consequences of some products of science and technology.

Answer:
The statement that is NOT correct about the passage is ③: All products of science and technology are always positive and do not have any negative outcomes.

Explanation:
The passage is discussing the negative consequences of some products of science and technology, and it provides several examples of such negative outcomes, including how detergents that make dishes gleam can kill rivers, dyes that prettify the food can cause cancer, and pills that make sex safe can dangerously complicate health. The passage also mentions several specific products, including DDT, cyclamates, thalidomide, and estrogen, that have had negative consequences. Therefore, statement ③ is incorrect because the passage clearly states that not all products of science and technology have positive outcomes, and some can have negative outcomes

↻ Regenerate response

나름 괜찮은 보기를 만들었다고 생각은 들지만, 선지의 내용 중 ④은 본문의 내용을 거의 그대로 옮겨 놓은 보기입니다.

본문: Detergents that make dishes gleam may kill rivers. Dyes that prettify the food may cause cancer.
선지: Detergents that make dishes gleam may kill rivers, and dyes that prettify the food may cause cancer.

챗GPT 4 Better Questions

이러한 부분을 만회하기 위해서 프롬프트를 조금 바꾸어 넣어보도록 하겠습니다.

Prompt Make a question with 5 multiple choices along with the answer and explanation with the instruction below.

instruction
- When making the options, do NOT use the content of the text as it is.
- When writing the content of the options, at least one option should be attractive enough to be mistaken for an incorrect answer.

🔍 instruction에서 본문의 내용을 그대로 선택지에 옮겨 만들지 말고, 정답 중 적어도 하나는 오답으로 오인할 수 있도록 "매력적으로" 만들어 달라고 지시했습니다.

Passage

The fading of this mythology is the result of Americans' gradual realization that science and technology's dreamy wonders sometimes turn out to be nightmarish blunders. Detergents that make dishes gleam may kill rivers. Dyes that prettify the food may cause cancer. Pills that make sex safe may dangerously complicate health. DDT, cyclamates, thalidomide and estrogen are but a few of the mixed blessings that, all together, have taught the layman a singular lesson: the promising fruits of science and technology often come with hidden worms.

[Stem]
Which of the following statements is NOT stated or implied in the passage?

🔍 질문을 단순히 내용일치/불일치의 형태로 묻지 않고, 추론 문제를 함께 넣어 보았습니다.

[Types of Alternative]
①
②
③
④
⑤

- Display all the alternatives.

아래와 같은 결과값이 나왔습니다.

> [Stem]
> Which of the following statements is NOT stated or implied in the passage?
>
> [Types of Alternative]
> ① Americans have gradually come to realize that science and technology can have negative consequences.
> ② Detergents that make dishes gleam can have harmful effects on the environment.
> ③ All the benefits of science and technology are tainted by hidden risks.
> ④ Thalidomide is an example of a mixed blessing in science and technology.
> ⑤ Americans have completely lost faith in the promises of science and technology.
>
> [Answer]
> ⑤ Americans have completely lost faith in the promises of science and technology.

다른 것보다 ②, ⑤의 선지가 괜찮아 보입니다.

② Detergents that make dishes gleam can **have harmful effects on** the environment.

⑤ Americans **have completely lost faith in** the promises of science and technology.

이번에는 다소 수동적으로 본문에 대한 꼼꼼한 분석을 요구하는 프롬프트를 바탕으로 수동으로 선지의 내용을 뽑아 내 보도록 하겠습니다. 프롬프트는 아주 간단합니다.

Prompt *Display a line-by-line analysis and implication for each sentence.*

> **Passage**
>
> *The fading of this mythology is the result of Americans' gradual realization that science and technology's dreamy wonders sometimes turn out to be nightmarish blunders. Detergents that make dishes gleam may kill rivers. Dyes that prettify the food may cause cancer. Pills that make sex safe may dangerously complicate health. DDT, cyclamates, thalidomide and estrogen are but a few of the mixed blessings that, all together, have taught the layman a singular lesson: the promising fruits of science and technology often come with hidden worms.*

아래와 같은 결과값을 얻었습니다.

챗GPT **4 Better Questions**

> Sure, here's a line-by-line analysis and implication for each sentence in the passage:
>
> 1. The fading of this mythology is the result of Americans' gradual realization that science and technology's dreamy wonders sometimes turn out to be nightmarish blunders.
>
> Analysis: The author is discussing how Americans are losing their faith in the idea that science and technology will always lead to positive outcomes. They are realizing that these fields can also result in negative consequences.
>
> Implication: The author is suggesting that blind faith in science and technology can be dangerous, and that we need to be aware of the potential negative consequences of our actions.
>
> 2. Detergents that make dishes gleam may kill rivers.
>
> Analysis: The author provides an example of a product that can have negative consequences. While the detergent may make dishes look clean, it can harm the environment by polluting waterways.
>
> Implication: The author is warning readers that even seemingly harmless products can have unintended negative consequences.

각 문장에 대한 문자 그대로의 분석을 넘어 <u>함축적 의미까지 분석</u>해 주고 있습니다. 전체 결과값에서 아래와 같은 내용일치/불일치 문제를 만들어 보았습니다.

아래 본문에 대한 바른 이해 또는 추론의 <u>총 개수</u>를 고르면?

- Americans are losing their faith in the idea that science and technology will always lead to positive outcomes.
- Blind faith in science and technology can be dangerous, and that we need to be aware of the potential negative consequences of our actions.
- Even seemingly harmless products can have unintended negative consequences.
- The desire for visually appealing products can come at a cost to our health.
- Products meant to improve our health or quality of life can have negative consequences.

① 1개 ② 2개
③ 3개 ④ 4개
⑤ 5개

4도 Prompt Engineer

1. Prompt: Make a question with 5 multiple choices along with the answer and explanation using the passage below.

[Passage]
The fading of this mythology is the result of Americans' gradual realization that science and technology's dreamy wonders sometimes turn out to be nightmarish blunders. Detergents that make dishes gleam may kill rivers. Dyes that prettify the food may cause cancer. Pills that make sex safe may dangerously complicate health. DDT, cyclamates, thalidomide and estrogen are but a few of the mixed blessings that, all together, have taught the layman a singular lesson: the promising fruits of science and technology often come with hidden worms.

[Stem]
Which of the following statements is NOT correct about the passage?

[Types of Alternative]
①
②
③
④
⑤

- Show all the alternatives.

4 Better Questions

2. Prompt: Make a question with 5 multiple choices along with the answer and explanation with the instruction below.

[Instruction]
- When making the options, do NOT use the content of the text as it is.
- When writing the content of the options, at least one option should be attractive enough to be mistaken for an incorrect answer.

[Passage]
The fading of this mythology is the result of Americans' gradual realization that science and technology's dreamy wonders sometimes turn out to be nightmarish blunders. Detergents that make dishes gleam may kill rivers. Dyes that prettify the food may cause cancer. Pills that make sex safe may dangerously complicate health. DDT, cyclamates, thalidomide and estrogen are but a few of the mixed blessings that, all together, have taught the layman a singular lesson: the promising fruits of science and technology often come with hidden worms.

[Stem]
Which of the following statements is NOT stated or implied in the passage?

[Types of Alternative]
①
②
③
④
⑤

- Display all the alternatives.

3. Prompt: Display a line-by-line analysis and implication for each sentence.

[Passage]
The fading of this mythology is the result of Americans' gradual realization that science and technology's dreamy wonders sometimes turn out to be nightmarish blunders. Detergents that make dishes gleam may kill rivers. Dyes that prettify the food may cause cancer. Pills that make sex safe may dangerously complicate health. DDT, cyclamates, thalidomide and estrogen are but a few of the mixed blessings that, all together, have taught the layman a singular lesson: the promising fruits of science and technology often come with hidden worms.

챗GPT 4 Better Questions

문제유형 6 ▶ 밑줄 친 내용의 문맥 추론/의도 및 목적 파악 문제

chatGPT를 활용하여 문제를 만들 때 가장 빛을 발하는 영역이 아닐까 싶습니다.

Prompt) Make 2 questions with 5 multiple choices along with the answer and explanation using the passage below.

> **Passage**
>
> The fading of (가)this mythology is the result of Americans' gradual realization that science and technology's dreamy wonders sometimes turn out to be nightmarish blunders. Detergents that make dishes gleam may kill rivers. Dyes that prettify the food may cause cancer. Pills that make sex safe may dangerously complicate health. DDT, cyclamates, thalidomide and estrogen are but a few of the mixed blessings that, all together, have taught the layman a singular lesson: the promising fruits of science and technology often come with (나)hidden worms.

[Stem]

Question 1: Which of the following best explains the contextual meaning of "this mythology" of the underlined (가)?

Question 2: What is the purpose of the author mentioning "hidden worms" of the underlined (나)?

[Types of Alternative]
①
②
③
④
⑤

Display all alternatives.

PART 2

아래와 같은 멋진 결과값이 나왔습니다.

Question 2: What is the purpose of the author mentioning "hidden worms" of the underlined (나)?

① To emphasize that science and technology are always dangerous.
② To suggest that science and technology should be avoided altogether.
③ To highlight the unintended consequences of scientific progress.
④ To argue that science and technology are inherently flawed.
⑤ To promote alternative solutions to problems.

Answer: ③ To highlight the unintended consequences of scientific progress.

Explanation: The author mentions "hidden worms" to refer to the unintended negative consequences of scientific progress. The author does not argue that science and technology are inherently flawed or that they should be avoided altogether, but rather suggests that people should be aware of the potential negative consequences of scientific progress.

 Question 1: Which of the following best explains the contextual meaning of "this mythology" of the underlined (가)?

① The mythology of ancient Greek and Roman gods and goddesses.
② The mythology of American folktales and legends.
③ The mythology of science and technology being the solution to all problems.
④ The mythology of natural remedies and alternative medicine.
⑤ The mythology of the dangers of science and technology.

Answer: ③ The mythology of science and technology being the solution to all problems.

Explanation: The passage discusses how Americans have gradually realized that science and technology are not always the solution to all problems. The phrase "this mythology" refers to the belief that science and technology can solve all problems, which is an idea that the passage argues is fading.

위와 같이 밑줄 친 내용에 대한 적절한 문맥적 의미 추론과 특정 표현을 통해 작가가 의도한 바를 추론하는 문제를 만들어 주었습니다.

4 Better Questions

 나도 Prompt Engineer

1. Prompt: Make 2 questions with 5 multiple choices along with the answer and explanation using the passage below.

[Passage]
The fading of (가) this mythology is the result of Americans' gradual realization that science and technology's dreamy wonders sometimes turn out to be nightmarish blunders. Detergents that make dishes gleam may kill rivers. Dyes that prettify the food may cause cancer. Pills that make sex safe may dangerously complicate health. DDT, cyclamates, thalidomide and estrogen are but a few of the mixed blessings that, all together, have taught the layman a singular lesson: the promising fruits of science and technology often come with (나) hidden worms.

[Stem]
Question 1: Which of the following best explains the contextual meaning of "this mythology" of the underlined (가)?
Question 2: What is the purpose of the author mentioning "hidden worms" of the underlined (나)?

[Types of Alternative]
①
②
③
④
⑤

- Display all alternatives.

PART 2

문제유형 7 ▶ 문학 장치를 묻는 문제

창작 수준의 높은 문제로 출제가 쉽지 않은 부분입니다. 하지만, chatGPT를 활용하면 해당 문제도 출제가 가능합니다. Lucy Maud Montgomery의 "Anne of Green Gables"의 소설의 첫 문단을 활용해 보겠습니다.

Prompt) *Find all the literary devices found in the passage below, and explain them in detail.*

Passage

Mrs. Rachel Lynde lived just where the Avonlea main road dipped down into a little hollow, fringed with alders and ladies' eardrops and traversed by a brook that had its source away back in the woods of the old Cuthbert place; it was reputed to be an intricate, headlong brook in its earlier course through those woods, with dark secrets of pool and cascade; but by the time it reached Lynde's Hollow it was a quiet, well-conducted little stream, for not even a brook could run past Mrs. Rachel Lynde's door without due regard for decency and decorum; it probably was conscious that Mrs. Rachel was sitting at her window, keeping a sharp eye on everything that passed, from brooks and children up, and that if she noticed anything odd or out of place she would never rest until she had ferreted out the whys and wherefores thereof.

챗GPT 4 Better Questions

> The passage contains several literary devices, which are:
>
> 1. Alliteration: The repetition of the "l" sound in "little hollow, fringed with alders and ladies' eardrops."
> 2. Imagery: The passage uses vivid descriptions to create a mental image of the hollow, brook, and Mrs. Rachel's house. For example, the brook is described as "headlong," with "dark secrets of pool and cascade." This creates a sense of mystery and intrigue. Mrs. Rachel's house is described as a place where even a brook would show "due regard for decency and decorum." This emphasizes the strict and watchful nature of Mrs. Rachel.
> 3. Hyperbole: The passage uses exaggeration to emphasize Mrs. Rachel's strict and watchful nature. For example, the passage states that "not even a brook could run past Mrs. Rachel Lynde's door without due regard for decency and decorum."
> 4. Personification: The passage personifies the brook by suggesting that it is "probably conscious" of Mrs. Rachel's presence and her watchful eye.
> 5. Irony: The passage contains an ironic tone as it describes the brook's transformation from a wild and headlong stream to a well-behaved little stream. This transformation is attributed to Mrs. Rachel's watchful eye and her strict adherence to decency and decorum.
>
> Overall, the literary devices in this passage help to create a vivid and memorable image of Mrs. Rachel's character and her role in the community. The use of hyperbole and irony adds humor to the passage, while the use of imagery and personification helps to bring the scene to life in the reader's mind.
>
> ↻ Regenerate response

입력한 지문에서 파악할 수 있는 문학장치를 구체적인 문장을 들어 설명해 주고 있습니다. 예전에는 해당 내용을 파악하려면 다양한 온오프 소스를 통해서 많은 시간을 할애하고, 애초에 해당 문학작품에 대한 이해가 없이는 출제가 불가능했습니다. It's literally one click away now.

이제 좀 구체적인 프롬프트와 함께 앞서 연습한 문제들도 함께 만들어 보도록 하겠습니다.

- 문학장치
- 지칭대상
- 작가의 목적 / 의도

Prompt) *Make three questions with 5 multiple choices along with the answer and explanation using the passage below.*

🔍 3개의 문제를 창작할 경우 아래 내용에 구체적 문제를 따로 언급해야 원하는 문제가 만들어 집니다.

PART 2

Passage

Mrs. Rachel Lynde lived just where the Avonlea main road dipped down into a little hollow, fringed with alders and ladies' eardrops and traversed by a brook that had its source away back in the woods of the old Cuthbert place; it was reputed to be an intricate, headlong brook in its earlier course through those woods, with dark secrets of pool and cascade; but (가)<u>by the time it reached Lynde's Hollow it was a quiet, well-conducted little stream, for not even a brook could run past Mrs. Rachel Lynde's door without due regard for decency and decorum</u>; (나)<u>it</u> probably was conscious that (다)<u>Mrs. Rachel was sitting at her window, keeping a sharp eye on everything that passed, from brooks and children up, and that if she noticed anything odd or out of place she would never rest until she had ferreted out the whys and wherefores thereof</u>.

[Types of Stem]

Question 1: Which literary device is found in the underlined expression "by the time it reached Lynde's Hollow it was a quiet, well-conducted little stream, for not even a brook could run past Mrs. Rachel Lynde's door without due regard for decency and decorum" in the passage?

Question 2: Which of the following refers to the pround "it" in (가)?

Question 3: What is the author's purpose of mentioning the underline expression "Mrs. Rachel was sitting at her window, keeping a sharp eye on everything that passed, from brooks and children up, and that if she noticed anything odd or out of place she would never rest until she had ferreted out the whys and wherefores thereof" in (다)?

[Types of Alternative]
①
②
③
④
⑤

- Show all the alternatives.

챗GPT 4 Better Questions

결과물은 다음과 같습니다.

Question 1: Which literary device is found in the underlined expression "by the time it reached Lynde's Hollow it was a quiet, well-conducted little stream, for not even a brook could run past Mrs. Rachel Lynde's door without due regard for decency and decorum" in the passage?

> Question 1: Which literary device is found in the underlined expression "by the time it reached Lynde's Hollow it was a quiet, well-conducted little stream, for not even a brook could run past Mrs. Rachel Lynde's door without due regard for decency and decorum" in the passage?
> ① Simile
> ② Metaphor
> ③ Personification
> ④ Hyperbole
> ⑤ Irony
> Answer: ③ Personification
>
> Explanation: Personification is a literary device that gives human qualities, characteristics, or emotions to non-human entities. In this sentence, the brook is given human-like qualities, as if it is aware of Mrs. Rachel Lynde's presence and behaves accordingly.

Question 2: Which of the following refers to the pround "it" in (가)?

> Question 2: Which of the following refers to the pround "it" in (가)?
> ① The Avonlea main road
> ② A little hollow
> ③ A brook
> ④ The woods of the old Cuthbert place
> ⑤ Mrs. Rachel Lynde's door
> Answer: ③ A brook
>
> Explanation: The pronoun "it" refers to the closest preceding noun, which in this case is "brook."

PART 2

Question 3: What is the author's purpose of mentioning the underline expression "Mrs. Rachel was sitting at her window, keeping a sharp eye on everything that passed, from brooks and children up, and that if she noticed anything odd or out of place she would never rest until she had ferreted out the whys and wherefores thereof" in (다)?

> Question 3: What is the author's purpose of mentioning the underlined expression "Mrs. Rachel was sitting at her window, keeping a sharp eye on everything that passed, from brooks and children up, and that if she noticed anything odd or out of place she would never rest until she had ferreted out the whys and wherefores thereof" in (다)?
> ① To describe Mrs. Rachel's physical appearance
> ② To explain the history of Lynde's Hollow
> ③ To emphasize the beauty of the alders and ladies' eardrops
> ④ To illustrate the brook's behavior
> ⑤ To characterize Mrs. Rachel's personality
> Answer: ⑤ To characterize Mrs. Rachel's personality
>
> Explanation: The author uses this sentence to describe Mrs. Rachel's character and her role in the community. She is depicted as a vigilant and nosy person who keeps a watchful eye on everything that goes on in her surroundings. This characterization is important in understanding her later actions and interactions with the other characters in the story.

챗GPT 4 Better Questions

나도 Prompt Engineer

1. Prompt: Find all the literary devices found in the passage below, and explain them in detail.

[Passage]
Mrs. Rachel Lynde lived just where the Avonlea main road dipped down into a little hollow, fringed with alders and ladies' eardrops and traversed by a brook that had its source away back in the woods of the old Cuthbert place; it was reputed to be an intricate, headlong brook in its earlier course through those woods, with dark secrets of pool and cascade; but by the time it reached Lynde's Hollow it was a quiet, well-conducted little stream, for not even a brook could run past Mrs. Rachel Lynde's door without due regard for decency and decorum; it probably was conscious that Mrs. Rachel was sitting at her window, keeping a sharp eye on everything that passed, from brooks and children up, and that if she noticed anything odd or out of place she would never rest until she had ferreted out the whys and wherefores thereof.

2. Prompt: Make three questions with 5 multiple choices along with the answer and explanation using the passage below.

[Passage]
Mrs. Rachel Lynde lived just where the Avonlea main road dipped down into a little hollow, fringed with alders and ladies' eardrops and traversed by a brook that had its source away back in the woods of the old Cuthbert place; it was reputed to be an intricate, headlong brook in its earlier course through those woods, with dark secrets of pool and cascade; but (가)by the time it reached Lynde's Hollow it was a quiet, well-conducted little stream, for not even a brook could run past Mrs. Rachel Lynde's door without due regard for decency and decorum; (나)it probably was conscious that (다)Mrs. Rachel was sitting at her window, keeping a sharp eye on everything that passed, from brooks and children up, and that if she noticed anything odd or out of place she would never rest until she had ferreted out the whys and wherefores thereof.

PART 2

[Types of Stem]
Question 1: Which literary device is found in the underlined expression "by the time it reached Lynde's Hollow it was a quiet, well-conducted little stream, for not even a brook could run past Mrs. Rachel Lynde's door without due regard for decency and decorum" in the passage?
Question 2: Which of the following refers to the pround "it" in (가)?
Question 3: What is the author's purpose of mentioning the underline expression "Mrs. Rachel was sitting at her window, keeping a sharp eye on everything that passed, from brooks and children up, and that if she noticed anything odd or out of place she would never rest until she had ferreted out the whys and wherefores thereof" in (다)?

[Types of Alternative]
①
②
③
④
⑤

- Show all the alternatives.

챗GPT 4 Better Questions

문제유형 ⑧ ▶ 지문의 형태를 변형하여 문제만들기

이번에는 지문의 형태를 변형하여 문제를 출제해 보도록 하겠습니다.

Prompt *Transform the passage below into a dialogue between a flight attendant and a passenger.*

Passage

"In case you're wondering," I said as I approached her again, "your husband is sound asleep, and your darling little boy is wide awake, watching everything that is going on." "Oh man," she said with a laugh, "That little guy is always so good for his dad!" Just a few minutes before we were preparing to land, I noticed the dad was awake. I also noticed that the seat next to him was empty, as it had been the entire flight.

"I told your wife that you had a good nap," I said, goodheartedly.

He laughed and then added, "Is she okay?"

"Oh, she's fine. But… If you don't mind my asking… why isn't she sitting next to you?" His eyes lit up, and with such love in his voice, he said, "Oh, this is my gift for her." I knew just what he meant. She was going to have two hours… two full hours… to sit alone. She could sleep. She could read. She could do nothing, but she did not have to worry about her son.

아래와 같은 결과값이 나왔습니다.

PART 2

Flight Attendant: Excuse me, sir. Can I help you with anything?
Passenger: No, thank you. I'm fine.
Flight Attendant: Alright. By the way, I just want to let you know that your husband is sound asleep, and your little boy is wide awake, watching everything that is going on.
Passenger: (surprised) Oh, really? That little guy is always so good for his dad!
Flight Attendant: Yes, he is. Just a few minutes before we land, I noticed your husband was awake. And, I also noticed that the seat next to him was empty, as it has been the entire flight.
Passenger: (curious) I see. What did you say to my wife?
Flight Attendant: I told her that your husband had a good nap. And, your husband asked if she is okay.
Passenger: (concerned) Is she okay?
Flight Attendant: (reassuring) Yes, she is. But, if you don't mind my asking, why isn't she sitting next to you?
Passenger: (smiling) Oh, this is my gift for her. She's going to have two hours to sit alone, sleep, read, or do nothing without worrying about our son.
Flight Attendant: (impressed) That's so sweet. You're a thoughtful husband.

원문과 대화체를 바탕으로 프롬프트를 만들어 결과값을 얻어 보겠습니다.

Prompt *Make a question with 5 multiple choices along with the answer and explanation using the passage below.*

Passage [A]

"In case you're wondering," I said as I approached her again, "your husband is sound asleep, and your darling little boy is wide awake, watching everything that is going on." "Oh man," she said with a laugh, "That little guy is always so good for his dad!" Just a few minutes before we were preparing to land, I noticed the dad was awake. I also noticed that the seat next to him was empty, as it had been the entire flight.

"I told your wife that you had a good nap," I said, goodheartedly.

He laughed and then added, "Is she okay?"

"Oh, she's fine. But… If you don't mind my asking… why isn't she sitting next to you?" His eyes lit up, and with such love in his voice, he said, "Oh, this is my gift for her." I knew just what he meant. She was going to have two hours… two full hours… to sit alone. She could sleep. She could read. She could do nothing,

4 Better Questions

but she did not have to worry about her son.

🔍 Passage [B]

Flight Attendant: Excuse me, sir. Can I help you with anything?

Passenger: No, thank you. I'm fine.

Flight Attendant: Alright. By the way, I just want to let you know that your husband is sound asleep, and your little boy is wide awake, watching everything that is going on.

Passenger: (surprised) Oh, really? That little guy is always so good for his dad!

Flight Attendant: Yes, he is. Just a few minutes before we land, I noticed your husband was awake. And, I also noticed that the seat next to him was empty, as it has been the entire flight.

Passenger: (curious) I see. What did you say to my wife?

Flight Attendant: I told her that your husband had a good nap. And, your husband asked if she is okay.

Passenger: (concerned) Is she okay?

Flight Attendant: (reassuring) Yes, she is. But, if you don't mind my asking, why isn't she sitting next to you?

Passenger: (smiling) Oh, this is my gift for her. She's going to have two hours to sit alone, sleep, read, or do nothing without worrying about our son.

Flight Attendant: (impressed) That's so sweet. _____.

[Stem]
Considering the passage [A], which of the following best fills in the blank in the passage [B]?

[Types of Alternative]
①
②
③
④
⑤

- Show all the alternatives.

아래와 같은 결과값이 나왔습니다.

① "I'm glad to hear that."
② "I hope she enjoys her alone time."
③ "I didn't expect that from a father."
④ "I should do that for my spouse sometime."
⑤ "I will make sure to mention that in my report."

Answer: ② "I hope she enjoys her alone time."

Explanation: The passenger's husband gave his wife the gift of sitting alone for two hours, which impressed the flight attendant. As a response, saying "I hope she enjoys her alone time" would be the most appropriate and polite comment. The other options are either unrelated or not appropriate in this situation.

원문 대화의 빈칸에 있던 "You are a thoughtful husband."로 변형하여 아주 기본적이지만 나름 괜찮은 문제를 만들어 주었습니다.

이번에는 제시된 지문의 내용을 바탕으로 시를 써 달라고 요청한 후 문제를 만들어 보겠습니다.

Prompt *Transform the passage below into a poem*

Six minutes to six, said the great round clock over the information booth in Grand Central Station. The tall, young Army lieutenant who had just come from the direction of the tracks lifted his sunburned face, and his eyes narrowed to note the exact time. His heart was pounding with a beat that shocked him because he could not control it. In six minutes, he would see the woman who had filled such a special place in his life for the past thirteen months, the woman he had never seen, yet whose written words had been with him and sustained him unfailingly.

결과값은 다음과 같습니다.

챗GPT 4 Better Questions

> Tick-tock, the clock
> Proclaimed with might
> Six minutes left
> 'Til a special sight
>
> A young lieutenant
> With face sun-kissed
> Observed the time
> His heart clenched, missed
>
> For in mere moments
> He'd finally meet
> The woman who'd written
> Words oh so sweet
>
> For thirteen months
> She'd been by his side
> Though never met
> Her words did provide
>
> A sustaining force
> In his time of need
> And now at last
> Their paths would finally meet.

Prompt) Make a question with 5 multiple choices along with the answer and explanation using the intruction below.

instruction

* Use the passages A and B provided below.

Passage A

Six minutes to six, said the great round clock over the information booth in Grand Central Station. The tall, young Army lieutenant who had just come from the direction of the tracks lifted his sunburned face, and his eyes narrowed to note the exact time. His heart was pounding with a beat that shocked him because he could not control it. In six minutes, he would see the woman who had filled such a special place in his life for the past thirteen months, the woman he had never seen, yet whose written words had been with him and sustained him unfailingly.

Passage B
Tick-tock, the clock
Proclaimed with might
Six minutes left
'Til a special sight

A young lieutenant
With face (A)_____
Observed the time
His heart (B)_____, missed

For in mere moments
He'd finally meet
The woman who'd written
Words oh so sweet

For thirteen months
She'd been by his side
Though never met
Her words did provide

A sustaining force
In his time of (C)_____
And now at last
Their paths would finally meet.

* Stem
Given the passage A, which of the pairs best fill in the blanks (A), (B), (C) in passage B?

* Type of Alternative
①

챗GPT 4 Better Questions

②
③
④
⑤

- *When making the options, make them in the form of table.*

다음과 같은 결과값을 얻었습니다.

Option	(A)	(B)	(C)
①	pounding	beat	pain
②	sunburned	aching	excitement
③	sweating	racing	sorrow
④	flushed	missing	struggle
⑤	darkened	skipping	desperation

Answer:

The correct pair of words to fill in the blanks (A), (B), and (C) respectively are "sunburned", "missed", and "struggle" which can be found in option ④.

명령대로 정갈하게 표로 보기를 만들어 주었습니다. 답에 대한 설명이 잘 되어 있습니다. 원문만큼이나 좋은 보기를 만들어 주었습니다. 물론, 원문의 단어를 활용하셔도 되겠습니다.

해설까지 꼼꼼하게 제공하고 있습니다.

> Explanation:
>
> In passage A, the young Army lieutenant lifted his sunburned face to note the exact time. This is consistent with the word "flushed" in option ④, but the lieutenant's face is not described as flushed in the passage. The young lieutenant's heart was pounding and he could not control it, which is consistent with the word "racing" in option ④. Finally, the passage mentions that the woman's written words had sustained him unfailingly for the past thirteen months, implying that he was struggling, which is consistent with the word "struggle" in option ④. Therefore, the correct pair of words to fill in the blanks (A), (B), and (C) respectively are "sunburned", "missed", and "struggle" which can be found in option ④.

4 Better Questions

나도 Prompt Engineer

1. Prompt: Transform the passage below into a dialogue between a flight attendant and a passenger.

[Passage]
"In case you're wondering," I said as I approached her again, "your husband is sound asleep, and your darling little boy is wide awake, watching everything that is going on." "Oh man," she said with a laugh, "That little guy is always so good for his dad!" Just a few minutes before we were preparing to land, I noticed the dad was awake. I also noticed that the seat next to him was empty, as it had been the entire flight.
"I told your wife that you had a good nap," I said, goodheartedly.
He laughed and then added, "Is she okay?"
"Oh, she's fine. But… If you don't mind my asking… why isn't she sitting next to you?" His eyes lit up, and with such love in his voice, he said, "Oh, this is my gift for her." I knew just what he meant. She was going to have two hours… two full hours… to sit alone. She could sleep. She could read. She could do nothing, but she did not have to worry about her son.

2. Prompt: Make a question with 5 multiple choices along with the answer and explanation using the passage below.

[Passage]
Passage [A]
"In case you're wondering," I said as I approached her again, "your husband is sound asleep, and your darling little boy is wide awake, watching everything that is going on." "Oh man," she said with a laugh, "That little guy is always so good for his dad!" Just a few minutes before we were preparing to land, I noticed the dad was awake. I also noticed that the seat next to him was empty, as it had been the entire flight.
"I told your wife that you had a good nap," I said, goodheartedly.
He laughed and then added, "Is she okay?"
"Oh, she's fine. But… If you don't mind my asking… why isn't she sitting next to you?"

His eyes lit up, and with such love in his voice, he said, "Oh, this is my gift for her." I knew just what he meant. She was going to have two hours··· two full hours··· to sit alone. She could sleep. She could read. She could do nothing, but she did not have to worry about her son.

Passage [B]
Flight Attendant: Excuse me, sir. Can I help you with anything?
Passenger: No, thank you. I'm fine.
Flight Attendant: Alright. By the way, I just want to let you know that your husband is sound asleep, and your little boy is wide awake, watching everything that is going on.
Passenger: (surprised) Oh, really? That little guy is always so good for his dad!
Flight Attendant: Yes, he is. Just a few minutes before we land, I noticed your husband was awake. And, I also noticed that the seat next to him was empty, as it has been the entire flight.
Passenger: (curious) I see. What did you say to my wife?
Flight Attendant: I told her that your husband had a good nap. And, your husband asked if she is okay.
Passenger: (concerned) Is she okay?
Flight Attendant: (reassuring) Yes, she is. But, if you don't mind my asking, why isn't she sitting next to you?
Passenger: (smiling) Oh, this is my gift for her. She's going to have two hours to sit alone, sleep, read, or do nothing without worrying about our son.
Flight Attendant: (impressed) That's so sweet. _____.

[Stem]
Considering the passage [A], which of the following best fills in the blank in the passage [B]?
[Types of Alternative]
①
②
③
④
⑤

- Show all the alternatives.

4 Better Questions

3. Prompt: Transform the passage below into a poem

Six minutes to six, said the great round clock over the information booth in Grand Central Station. The tall, young Army lieutenant who had just come from the direction of the tracks lifted his sunburned face, and his eyes narrowed to note the exact time. His heart was pounding with a beat that shocked him because he could not control it. In six minutes, he would see the woman who had filled such a special place in his life for the past thirteen months, the woman he had never seen, yet whose written words had been with him and sustained him unfailingly.

4. Prompt: Make a question with 5 multiple choices along with the answer and explanation using the intruction below.

[Instruction]
* Use the passages A and B provided below.
Passage A
Six minutes to six, said the great round clock over the information booth in Grand Central Station. The tall, young Army lieutenant who had just come from the direction of the tracks lifted his sunburned face, and his eyes narrowed to note the exact time. His heart was pounding with a beat that shocked him because he could not control it. In six minutes, he would see the woman who had filled such a special place in his life for the past thirteen months, the woman he had never seen, yet whose written words had been with him and sustained him unfailingly.

Passage B
Tick-tock, the clock
Proclaimed with might
Six minutes left
'Til a special sight

A young lieutenant
With face (A)_____
Observed the time
His heart (B)_____, missed

For in mere moments
He'd finally meet
The woman who'd written
Words oh so sweet

For thirteen months
She'd been by his side
Though never met
Her words did provide

A sustaining force
In his time of (C)_____
And now at last
Their paths would finally meet.

* Stem
Given the passage A, which of the pairs best fill in the blanks (A), (B), (C) in passage B?

* Type of Alternative
①
②
③
④
⑤

- When making the options, make them in the form of table.

🔍 보기를 표로 만들어 달라고 해 보았습니다.

챗GPT 4 Better Questions

문제유형 9 ▶ 사례를 활용한 응용문제

아래는 본문에 언급된 Apple사의 marketing 전략을 바탕으로 동일한 사례를 골라내는 응용문제를 만들어 보도록 하겠습니다. 프롬프트는 아래와 같습니다.

Prompt) Make a question with 5 multiple choices along with the answer and explanation using passage below.

🔍 Passage

Let me give you an example. I use Apple because they're easy to understand and everybody gets it. If Apple were like everyone else, a marketing message from them might sound like this: "We make great computers. They're beautifully designed, simple to use and user friendly. Want to buy one?" "Meh." And that's how most of us communicate. That's how most marketing is done, that's how most sales is done and that's how most of us communicate interpersonally. We say what we do, we say how we're different or how we're better and we expect some sort of a behavior, a purchase, a vote, something like that. Here's our new law firm: We have the best lawyers with the biggest clients, we always perform for our clients who do business with us. Here's our new car: It gets great gas mileage, it has leather seats, buy our car. But it is just uinspiring.

Here's how Apple actually communicates. "Everything we do, we believe in challenging the status quo." We believe in thinking differently. The way we challenge the status quo is by making our products beautifully designed, simple to use and user friendly. We just happen to make great computers. Want to buy one?" Totally different right? You are happy to buy a computer from me.. All I did was reverse the order of the information. What it proves to us is that people don't buy what you do; people buy why you do it. People don't buy what you do they buy why you do it.

[Stem]
Which of the marketing strategies most resembles how Apple actually communicates mentioned in the passage?

PART 2

> 해당 질문은 지문의 종류에 따라 변경해서 사용 가능합니다.

[Types of Alternative]
①
②
③
④
⑤

* Make the options using concrete examples.

아래는 결과값이다.

 Which of the marketing strategies most resembles how Apple actually communicates mentioned in the passage?

① "Our hotel has the best amenities and luxurious accommodations. Book now for your next vacation."
② "Our restaurant serves delicious food made with the freshest ingredients. Come and dine with us today."
③ "Our fashion brand creates unique and innovative designs. Be bold and express yourself with our clothing."
④ "Our fitness program focuses on holistic wellness, helping you achieve balance and a healthier lifestyle. Join us now."
⑤ "Our nonprofit organization believes in empowering communities to make a positive impact. We do this by providing education and resources to those in need."

Answer: ⑤ "Our nonprofit organization believes in empowering communities to make a positive impact. We do this by providing education and resources to those in need."

Explanation: The marketing strategy of the nonprofit organization in option ⑤ most resembles how Apple communicates because it focuses on why the organization exists rather than what it does. Like Apple, the organization communicates its belief and purpose first and then describes how it achieves that purpose. Apple communicates its belief in challenging the status quo and thinking differently, while the nonprofit organization communicates its belief in empowering communities to make a positive impact. Both use this belief as the basis for their products and services, which is more inspiring and memorable than simply listing features and benefits.

챗GPT 4 Better Questions

이번에는 역사적 사례를 응용한 문제를 만들어 보겠습니다.

우선, 앞선 프롬프트와 같이 입력해 보겠습니다.

Prompt) *Make a question with 5 multiple choices along with the answer and explanation using the passage below.*

> **Passage**
>
> *Fearmongering is a method used historically by many people in positions of power to control their population. They do this by intimidating their peoples with ideas of death, disease, or violence. They might try to assure their audience that the worst will come to pass if they refuse to join them or do what the person in power wants them to. Normal everyday people can also often use fearmongering against other people, often threatening someone with social exclusion or being shunned from a group. This style of social engineering, using fear and shame to control whoever you want in whatever way you need, has been used to control and keep down the public for many years. Although the way that some people use this kind of manipulation has evolved to fit the narrative of our modern lives over the years, the core values of the methods remain the same: you either persuade an audience by being open about your values and trying to get them to side with you, or you can get under that person's skin.*

<Stem>

Which of the following historical events is most appropriate as an example of the method mentioned in the passage?

<Type of Alternative>

①
②
③
④
⑤

* Show all the alternatives.

아래와 같은 결과값을 얻었습니다.

 Sure, here are the complete options for the multiple-choice question:

① Using the threat of disease to control a population during a pandemic.
② Encouraging people to join a political movement by offering them free food and drinks.
③ Persuading people to donate money to charity by telling them heart-wrenching stories of people in need.
④ Convincing a friend to come to a party by telling them that everyone else will be there.
⑤ Telling a group of students that they will fail the course if they don't do exactly what the teacher says.

하지만, 좀 더 <u>구체적인 역사적 사건을 바탕으로 선지의 내용을 구성했으면</u> 해서 아래와 같은 프롬프트를 주었습니다.

Prompt *Upgrade the question using more specific historical events.*

 Sure, here is an upgraded version of the question:
<Stem>
Which of the following historical events is most appropriate as an example of the method mentioned in the passage, where fearmongering was used to control the population?
<Types of Alternatives>
① The Salem Witch Trials of 1692, where people were accused of practicing witchcraft and were executed based on flimsy evidence.
② The Cuban Missile Crisis of 1962, where the threat of a nuclear war between the United States and the Soviet Union caused panic among the American population.
③ The Vietnam War protests of the 1960s and 1970s, where government officials used fearmongering tactics to label anti-war protesters as unpatriotic and dangerous.
④ The Rwandan Genocide of 1994, where the Hutu majority government used propaganda to dehumanize and vilify the Tutsi minority population, leading to mass killings.
⑤ The COVID-19 pandemic of 2020, where government officials and media outlets used fearmongering to encourage people to follow public health guidelines and get vaccinated.

위와 같이 구체적 연도까지 언급된 선지로 구성된 문제를 만들어 주었습니다. 하지만 앞서 언급했듯이 chatGPT가 만들어 주는 문제와 선지의 내용을 반드시 검토해야 합니다. 위 문제의 경우 정답을 다시 물어보면 매번 다른 답을 제시해 주는 경우가 많아 수작업을 통해서 문제를 다시 작성해야 합니다. chatGPT를 활용해서 문제를 만들 경우 2차 가공이 필요한 문제가 있음을 기억해 두어야 합니다.

챗GPT 4 Better Questions

💬 나도 Prompt Engineer

1. Prompt: Make a question with 5 multiple choices along with the answer and explanation using passage below.

[Passage]
Let me give you an example. I use Apple because they're easy to understand and everybody gets it. If Apple were like everyone else, a marketing message from them might sound like this: 'We make great computers. They're beautifully designed, simple to use and user friendly. Want to buy one?" "Meh." And that's how most of us communicate. That's how most marketing is done, that's how most sales is done and that's how most of us communicate interpersonally. We say what we do, we say how we're different or how we're better and we expect some sort of a behavior, a purchase, a vote, something like that. Here's our new law firm: We have the best lawyers with the biggest clients, we always perform for our clients who do business with us. Here's our new car: It gets great gas mileage, it has leather seats, buy our car. But it is just uinspiring.
Here's how Apple actually communicates. "Everything we do, we believe in challenging the status quo." We believe in thinking differently. The way we challenge the status quo is by making our products beautifully designed, simple to use and user friendly. We just happen to make great computers. Want to buy one?" Totally different right? You are happy to buy a computer from me.. All I did was reverse the order of the information. What it proves to us is that people don't buy what you do; people buy why you do it. People don't buy what you do they buy why you do it.

[Stem]
Which of the marketing strategies most resembles how Apple actually communicates mentioned in the passage?

[Types of Alternative]
①
②
③
④
⑤

* Make the options using concrete examples.

2. Prompt: Make a question with 5 multiple choices along with the answer and explanation using the passage below.

⟨Passage⟩
Fearmongering is a method used historically by many people in positions of power to control their population. They do this by intimidating their peoples with ideas of death, disease, or violence. They might try to assure their audience that the worst will come to pass if they refuse to join them or do what the person in power wants them to. Normal everyday people can also often use fearmongering against other people, often threatening someone with social exclusion or being shunned from a group. This style of social engineering, using fear and shame to control whoever you want in whatever way you need, has been used to control and keep down the public for many years.
Although the way that some people use this kind of manipulation has evolved to fit the narrative of our modern lives over the years, the core values of the methods remain the same: you either persuade an audience by being open about your values and trying to get them to side with you, or you can get under that person's skin.

⟨Stem⟩
Which of the following historical events is most appropriate as an example of the method mentioned in the passage?

⟨Type of Alternative⟩
①
②
③
④
⑤
* Show all the alternatives.

chatGPT를 활용한 영어문제 창작

Version 2.0

PART 3

학교별 특화 내신유형 문제

챗GPT 4 Better Questions

해당 파트에서는 학교별 특화 유형의 문제를 살펴보기 전에 객관식 선지의 보기내용을 만드는 방법을 다룬 후 실전 문제를 만드는 프롬프트를 살펴보겠습니다. 그리고 실전문제 제작을 위한 프롬프트와 관련하여 chatGPT의 속성을 좀 더 심도깊게 이해하는 의미에서 복잡한 단일의 프롬프트 보다는 다소 아나로그식의 수작업을 병행하는 방식으로 문제를 함께 만들어 보겠습니다. 참고로, 복잡한 프롬프트일수록 일관된 결과값을 얻기가 쉽지 않기에 프롬프트 제작 전문가 수준이 아니라면 다중의 프롬프트와 해당 결과값을 활용한 문제제작이 좀 더 정교한, 그러면서도 일관된 결과값을 얻을 수 있습니다.

1 문장전환을 활용한 객관식/주관식 문제응용

chatGPT의 활용이 일반화되면서 학교 내신 시험에서도 큰 변화들이 나타나고 있다. 특히, 서술형 문제 뿐 아니라 chatGPT를 활용한 다양한 객관식 문제가 출제되고, 내용일치와 추론문제의 선지 문장 길이가 길어지는 동시에 내용의 난이도 또한 상당히 높아졌다. 그런 의미에서 내신문제 출제를 할 때 주어진 지문에 대한 객관식 선지 제작에 애를 써야 함은 당연하다.

1) 구와 절의 전환

모든 문제유형 제작의 기본적 원리가 패러프레이징이라는 점에서 창작자의 능력 중 구를 절로, 절을 구로 전환이 가능한 표현을 찾고, 해당 표현을 전환하는 능력을 기르는 것이 중요하다. chatGPT를 이용하면 손쉽게 구를 절로, 절을 구로 전환 가능한 표현을 찾아 전환이 가능하다.

활용할 지문은 다음과 같다.

[샘플 Passage]
Fromm distinguishes between 'freedom from' (negative freedom) and 'freedom to' (positive freedom). The former refers to emancipation from restrictions such as social conventions placed on individuals by other people or institutions. This is the kind of freedom typified by the existentialism of Sartre, and has often been fought for historically but, according to Fromm, on its own it can be a destructive force unless accompanied by a creative element – 'freedom to' – the use of freedom to employ the total integrated personality in creative acts. This, he argues, necessarily implies a true connectedness with others that goes beyond the superficial bonds of conventional social intercourse: "...in the spontaneous realization of the self, man unites himself anew with the world..."

PART 3

해당 지문을 바탕으로 다음과 같은 프롬프트를 넣으면 됩니다.

Prompt) *Please find as many expressions in the following text as possible where a phrase can be changed into a clause or a clause into a phrase, and then change each expression into the respective clause or phrase.*

Fromm distinguishes between 'freedom from' (negative freedom) and 'freedom to' (positive freedom). The former refers to emancipation from restrictions such as social conventions placed on individuals by other people or institutions. This is the kind of freedom typified by the existentialism of Sartre, and has often been fought for historically but, according to Fromm, on its own it can be a destructive force unless accompanied by a creative element – 'freedom to' – the use of freedom to employ the total integrated personality in creative acts. This, he argues, necessarily implies a true connectedness with others that goes beyond the superficial bonds of conventional social intercourse: "...in the spontaneous realization of the self, man unites himself anew with the world..."

다음과 같은 결과값을 얻을 수 있다.

1. **"freedom from restrictions such as social conventions placed on individuals"**
   - *Phrase*: "freedom from restrictions like social conventions"
   - *Clause*: "freedom from restrictions that are placed on individuals, such as social conventions"

2. **"the use of freedom to employ the total integrated personality in creative acts"**
   - *Phrase*: "using freedom to engage one's integrated personality in creative acts"
   - *Clause*: "freedom that allows individuals to employ their entire integrated personality creatively"

3. **"in the spontaneous realization of the self"**
   - *Phrase*: "through spontaneously realizing the self"
   - *Clause*: "when one spontaneously realizes the self"

4. **"a true connectedness with others that goes beyond the superficial bonds"**
   - *Phrase*: "true connection with others beyond superficial bonds"
   - *Clause*: "a true connectedness with others which transcends superficial social bonds"

챗GPT 4 Better Questions

위 결과값 중 3을 살펴보면 원문의 "in the spontaneous realizatino of the self"를 아래와 같이 구와 절로 모두 패러프레이징을 해 주고 있다.

구: through spontaneously **realizing** the self
절: when one spontaneously **realizes** the self

해당 결과값을 통해서 변형 없이 객관식 문제 선택지로 활용할 수도 있고, 어휘의 추가적 변형을 가미한 내용을 활용할 수 있다. 특히, 패러프레이징된 구와 절의 밑줄 친 단어에 주목해서 **동명사를 활용하는 능력과 구를 절로 바꾸었을 때 품사의 적절한 활용을 묻는 다음과 같은 서술형 문제 제작**도 가능한다.

[샘플문제]

Fromm distinguishes between 'freedom from' (negative freedom) and 'freedom to' (positive freedom). The former refers to emancipation from restrictions such as social conventions placed on individuals by other people or institutions. This is the kind of freedom typified by the existentialism of Sartre, and has often been fought for historically but, according to Fromm, on its own it can be a destructive force unless accompanied by a creative element – 'freedom to' – the use of freedom to employ the total integrated personality in creative acts. This, he argues, necessarily implies a true connectedness with others that goes beyond the superficial bonds of conventional social intercourse: "...(가)in the spontaneous realization of the self, man unites himself anew with the world..."

문제. 본문의 밑줄 친 구의 표현을 아래 제시어를 활용하여 절로 전환하시오.
　　　(단, 추가단어 있음)
제시어: man / realizes / self / spontaneously / the / a

구: in the spontaneous realization of the self, man unites himself anew with the world..."
절: _____, he unites himself anew with the world..."

정답: When a man spontaneously realizes the self

제시어에 모든 단어를 줄 수도 있지만, 문제의 난이도를 조절하기 위해 추가단어의 조건을 제시하면서 절의 형태와 활용을 묻는 동시에 전치사 in의 의미가 when으로 전환 될 수 있음을 함께 묻는 중상급 문제로 출제했다.

2) 특정 구문을 활용한 문장 뽑기

객관식 선택지를 만들 때 특정 구문을 활용한 선지를 만들고 싶을 때가 있다. 특히, 내신 시험 범위에 해당하는 문법 사항을 적용한 선지를 만들고 싶을 때 chatGPT를 활용면 된다.

활용할 지문은 다음과 같다.

[샘플 Passage]
When we see something, we naturally and automatically break it up into shapes, colors, and concepts that we have learned through education. We recode what we see through the lens of everything we know. We reconstruct memories rather than retrieving the video from memory. This is a useful trait. It's a more efficient way to store information — a bit like an optimal image compression algorithm such as JPG, rather than storing a raw bitmap image file. People who lack this ability and remember everything in perfect detail struggle to generalize, learn, and make connections between what they have learned. But representing the world as abstract ideas and features comes at a cost of seeing the world as it is. Instead, we see the world through our assumptions, motivations, and past experiences. The discovery that our memories are reconstructed through abstract representations rather than played back like a movie completely undermined the legal primacy of eyewitness testimony. Seeing is not believing.

해당 지문을 바탕으로 아래와 같이 내용일치 문제를 만들어 보겠습니다.

Prompt *Make a multiple choice question with 5 options with the answer and explanation at the bottom.*

챗GPT 4 Better Questions

Passage

When we see something, we naturally and automatically break it up into shapes, colors, and concepts that we have learned through education. We recode what we see through the lens of everything we know. We reconstruct memories rather than retrieving the video from memory. This is a useful trait. It's a more efficient way to store information — a bit like an optimal image compression algorithm such as JPG, rather than storing a raw bitmap image file. People who lack this ability and remember everything in perfect detail struggle to generalize, learn, and make connections between what they have learned. But representing the world as abstract ideas and features comes at a cost of seeing the world as it is. Instead, we see the world through our assumptions, motivations, and past experiences. The discovery that our memories are reconstructed through abstract representations rather than played back like a movie completely undermined the legal primacy of eyewitness testimony. Seeing is not believing.

[Stem]

Which of the following is NOT correct about the passage?

[Type of Alternative]

①
②
③
④
⑤

답

*Show the contents of all the options.

다음과 같은 결과값을 얻었습니다.

> **Question:**
> Which of the following is NOT correct about the passage?
>
> **Options:**
> ① When we see things, we process them based on shapes, colors, and concepts we have learned.
> ② Memories are reconstructed rather than retrieved like a video playback.
> ③ Remembering everything in perfect detail is advantageous for learning and making connections.
> ④ Representing the world as abstract ideas affects our ability to see it as it truly is.
> ⑤ The reliability of eyewitness testimony has been questioned due to the nature of memory reconstruction.
>
> **Answer:**
> ③ Remembering everything in perfect detail is advantageous for learning and making connections.

선택지의 내용을 살펴보면,

① When we see things, we process them based on shapes, colors, and concepts we have learned.
② Memories are reconstructed rather than retrieved like a video playback.
③ Remember**ing** everything in perfect detail is **advantageous** for learning and making connections.
④ Representing the world as abstract ideas **affects our ability to see it as it truly is**.
⑤ The reliability of eyewitness testimony **has been questioned** due to the nature of memory reconstruction.

위의 밑줄 친 부분에서 확인할 수 있는 바와 같이 패러프레이징이 된 것을 볼 수 있다. 하지만, 내신시험 범위에 다양한 강조용법이 포함된다면 다음과 같이 업그레이드가 가능하다.

Prompt *Please paraphrase each of the following sentences using the conditions.*

챗GPT 4 Better Questions

💡 **Condition**

* Cleft Sentences: These split the sentence to highlight a specific part.
  Example: It was Sarah who completed the project.
* Inversion: Changing the usual word order to stress a particular element.
  Example: Never have I seen such beautiful artwork.
* Do/Does/Did Emphasis: Using "do," "does," or "did" in statements to emphasize action.
  Example: I do believe in their ability to succeed.

① When we see things, we process them based on shapes, colors, and concepts we have learned.
② Memories are reconstructed rather than retrieved like a video playback.
③ Remembering everything in perfect detail is advantageous for learning and making connections.
④ Representing the world as abstract ideas affects our ability to see it as it truly is.
⑤ The reliability of eyewitness testimony has been questioned due to the nature of memory reconstruction.

다음과 같은 결과값을 얻었습니다.

① Original: When we see things, we process them based on shapes, colors, and concepts we have learned.
Cleft Sentence: **It** is based on shapes, colors, and concepts we have learned **that** we process things when we see them.
Inversion: Only through shapes, colors, and learned concepts **do we process** what we see.
Do/Does/Did Emphasis: We **do** process things based on shapes, colors, and learned concepts when we see them.

② Original: Memories are reconstructed rather than retrieved like a video playback.
Cleft Sentence: **It** is through reconstruction, not playback, **that** memories are recalled.
Inversion: Only through reconstruction **are memories recalled**, not as a video playback.
Do/Does/Did Emphasis: Memories **do** undergo reconstruction rather than being retrieved like a video.

③ Original: Remembering everything in perfect detail is advantageous for learning and making connections.

Cleft Sentence: **It** is the act of remembering everything in perfect detail **that** benefits learning and making connections.

Inversion: Advantageous for learning and connections **is remembering** everything in perfect detail.

Do/Does/Did Emphasis: Remembering everything in perfect detail **does** provide advantages for learning and connections.

④ Original: Representing the world as abstract ideas affects our ability to see it as it truly is.

Cleft Sentence: **It** is our ability to see the world as it truly is **that** is affected by representing it as abstract ideas.

Inversion: **Affected is our ability** to see the world as it truly is when we represent it through abstract ideas.

Do/Does/Did Emphasis: Representing the world as abstract ideas **does** impact our ability to see it as it truly is.

⑤ Original: The reliability of eyewitness testimony has been questioned due to the nature of memory reconstruction.

Cleft Sentence: **It** is due to the nature of memory reconstruction **that** the reliability of eyewitness testimony has been questioned.

Inversion: **Questioned has been the reliability** of eyewitness testimony due to memory reconstruction.

Do/Does/Did Emphasis: The reliability of eyewitness testimony **does** come into question because of memory reconstruction.

각 선택지의 내용을 세 가지 강조용법에 맞춰 재진술 해 주었습니다. 1차 프롬프트로 만든 문제에 원하는 문장으로 대체해서 문제를 업그레이드하면 됩니다. 이번에는 다음과 같이 프롬프트를 수정하나 한 개의 프롬프트로 동일한 결과값을 얻어 보도록 하겠습니다.

Prompt) *Make a multiple choice question with 5 options with the answer and explanation at the bottom according to the following condtions.*

챗GPT 4 Better Questions

💡 Condition

When making options, make sure each options has one of the following's structures.
* Cleft Sentences: These split the sentence to highlight a specific part.
  Example: It was Sarah who completed the project.
* Inversion: Changing the usual word order to stress a particular element. Example: Never have I seen such beautiful artwork.
* Do/Does/Did Emphasis: Using "do," "does," or "did" in statements to emphasize action.
  Example: I do believe in their ability to succeed.

🔍 Passage

When we see something, we naturally and automatically break it up into shapes, colors, and concepts that we have learned through education. We recode what we see through the lens of everything we know. We reconstruct memories rather than retrieving the video from memory. This is a useful trait. It's a more efficient way to store information — a bit like an optimal image compression algorithm such as JPG, rather than storing a raw bitmap image file. People who lack this ability and remember everything in perfect detail struggle to generalize, learn, and make connections between what they have learned. But representing the world as abstract ideas and features comes at a cost of seeing the world as it is. Instead, we see the world through our assumptions, motivations, and past experiences. The discovery that our memories are reconstructed through abstract representations rather than played back like a movie completely undermined the legal primacy of eyewitness testimony. Seeing is not believing.

[Stem]
Which of the following is NOT correct about the passage?

[Type of Alternative]
①
②
③
④
⑤

답
*Show the contents of all the options.

다음과 같이 멋진 결과값을 제시해 주네요.

> **Question:**
> Which of the following is NOT correct about the passage?
>
> **Options:**
> ① It is through shapes, colors, and learned concepts that we process things we see.
> ② Never are memories retrieved in the same way as video playback.
> ③ People do benefit from remembering every detail perfectly for generalizing, learning, and connecting ideas.
> ④ It is the nature of abstract representation that affects how we see the world as it is.
> ⑤ Questioned has been the reliability of eyewitness testimony due to the reconstructive nature of memory.

강조용법 외 다양한 구문을 활용한 선지를 위의 프롬프트를 활용해서 만들 수 있습니다.

3) 문법을 활용한 심화응용
앞서 살펴본 구와 절의 전환에 이어 문법을 활용한 좀 더 심화된 내신 문제들을 만들어 보겠습니다.

① 관계사가 없는 문장을 관계사를 포함한 문장으로 전환
아래 지문을 활용해서 문제를 만들어 보겠습니다.

챗GPT 4 Better Questions

[샘플지문]
Healthcare workers have been dressing up like clowns to help patients relax and reduce the stress staying in the hospital can cause. Evidence suggests the laughter these medical clowns create is as effective as some medication. In one experiment, researchers sent clowns to entertain children being prepared for surgery. One group of kids spent about half an hour with a clown, while a second group of children received a sedative instead. The kids who met with clowns showed the same reduction in anxiety as those who were given the sedative. It is believed that medical clowns could also be used to help kids with autism and young burn victims in need of painful bandage-changing.

지문의 첫 번째 문장 바탕으로 관계대명사를 포함한 문장으로 전환해 보도록 하겠습니다.

Prompt *Rewrite the following sentence using the relative clause.*

Healthcare workers have been dressing up like clowns to help patients relax and reduce the stress staying in the hospital can cause.

아래와 같은 결과값을 주었습니다.

 Healthcare workers, who have been dressing up like clowns, help patients relax and reduce the stress staying in the hospital can cause.

아래와 같이 계속적 용법의 관계대명사 who가 활용된 문장으로 전환되었습니다.
Healthcare workers, **who** dress up like clowns, have been helping patients relax and reduce the stress that staying in the hospital can cause.

위 내용을 바탕으로 아래와 같이 **관계대명사**와 **동사의 시제 관련 문법 문제**를 만들어 보도록 하겠습니다.

문제. 아래 문장을 재진술하려고 한다. 빈칸에 들어갈 적절한 표현을 넣으시오.
Healthcare workers have been dressing up like clowns to help patients relax and reduce the stress staying in the hospital can cause.
= Healthcare workers, _____ dress up like clowns, _____ _____ _____ patients relax and reduce the stress that staying in the hospital can cause.

답 who, have been helping

② 분사가 포함된 문장으로 전환
①에서 활용한 샘플지문의 두 번째 문장은 다음과 같습니다.

Healthcare workers have been dressing up like clowns to help patients relax and reduce the stress staying in the hospital can cause. <u>Evidence suggests the laughter these medical clowns create is as effective as some medication</u>.

두 번째 문장의 경우 아래와 같이 목적격 관계대명사가 생략된 구문이 포함되어 있습니다.

Evidence suggests the laughter (that) these medical clowns create is as effective as some medication.

해당 문장을 아래와 같은 프롬프트를 넣어 재진술해 보겠습니다.

 Prompt *Paraphrase the following sentence.*

Evidence suggests the laughter (that) these medical clowns create is as effective as some medication

아래와 같은 결과값을 얻었습니다.

 Research indicates that the laughter induced by these medical clowns is equally efficacious to certain medications, according to the evidence.

챗GPT 4 Better Questions

원문에 비추어 아래와 같이 단어를 수정을 하였습니다. 물론, 위 결과값에서 활용된 어휘를 그대로 사용하셔도 됩니다.

Evidence suggests <u>the laughter created by these medical clowns</u> is as effective as some medication.

원문에서는 관계대명사가 활용되었는데, 이를 과거분사가 활용된 문장으로 전환했습니다. 아래와 같이 서술형 문제 출제가 가능합니다.

문제. 아래 지문에서 밑줄 친 문장을 관계대명사가 활용된 문장으로 전환하려고 한다. 빈칸에 알맞은 표현을 써넣으시오.

> Healthcare workers have been dressing up like clowns to help patients relax and reduce the stress staying in the hospital can cause. Evidence suggests <u>the laughter created by these medical clowns is as effective as some medication</u>. In one experiment, researchers sent clowns to entertain children being prepared for surgery. One group of kids spent about half an hour with a clown, while a second group of children received a sedative instead. The kids who met with clowns showed the same reduction in anxiety as those who were given the sedative. It is believed that medical clowns could also be used to help kids with autism and young burn victims in need of painful bandage-changing.

the laughter created by these medical clowns is as effective as some medication.
= Evidence suggests the laughter _____ _____ _____ _____ _____ is as effective as some medication

답 that these medical clowns create
또는 which these medical clowns create

관계대명사가 활용된 문장을 과거분사가 활용된 문장으로 전환하는 문제도 물론 가능합니다. 난이도를 조절하기 위해 아래와 같이 <조건>을 제시해 줄 수 있을 겁니다.

─〈조건〉─
- 관계대명사 that은 사용하지 말 것.
- 아래 제시된 단어만을 사용할 것.
- 빈칸 하나에 한 단어만 넣을 것.

제시어: create / clowns / which / medical / these

③ 전치사가 포함된 문장의 전환
앞서 활용한 지문 중 아래 문장을 활용해서 문장전환을 바탕으로 한 문제를 만들어 보겠습니다.

It is believed that medical clowns could also be used to help kids with autism and young burn victims in need of painful bandage-changing.

우선, 아래와 같은 프롬프트를 작성해서 chatGPT가 제공하는 결과값을 통해 아이디어를 한 번 얻을 수 있을지 보겠습니다.

Prompt) *Paraphrase the following sentence.*

It is believed that medical clowns could also be used to help kids with autism and young burn victims in need of painful bandage-changing.

아래와 같은 결과값이 나왔습니다.

Medical clowns are thought to have the potential to assist <u>children diagnosed with autism</u> and <u>young individuals who have experienced</u> painful burns requiring bandage changes.

원문과 재진술된 부분을 살펴보면 다음과 같다.

원문: kids with autism
변형: <u>children diagnosed with autism</u>

원문: young burn victims in need of painful bandage-changing
변형: <u>young individuals who have experienced</u> painful burns requiring bandage changes

챗GPT 4 Better Questions

위 내용을 종합해서 원문을 아래와 같이 수정한 후 문제를 창작해 보겠습니다. 특히, 본문의 내용을 바탕으로 어휘력을 평가하는 문제도 함께 출제해 보도록 하겠습니다.

※ 다음을 읽고, 물음에 답하시오.

It is believed that medical clowns could also be used to help Ⓐ(자폐증 진단을 받은 아이) and Ⓑyoung individuals who have experienced painful burns requiring bandage changes.

1. 괄호 Ⓐ 안의 우리말의 동의표현을 작성하려고 한다. 각 빈칸에 들어갈 단어를 쓰시오. (단, 제시된 단어는 한 번만 사용하고, 문맥에 맞게 변형할 것)

제시어: diagnose

kids _____ autism
children _____ _____ autism

답 wit, diagnosed with

2. 밑줄 친 Ⓑ를 아래와 같이 바꾸어 표현할 때 빈칸에 들어갈 단어를 쓰시오. (단, 제시된 철자로 시작하는 단어를 문맥에 맞게 쓸 것)

young individuals who have experienced painful burns
= young burn v_____

답 victims

두 번째 문제의 경우 역으로 chatGPT를 통해 얻은 재진술문을 활용하여 본문에서 정의되는 대상의 영어표현을 묻는 어휘문제로 출제했습니다.

참고로, 동일한 프롬프트라도 **재부팅후** 다시 질문을 하면 다른 답변을 제공하기에 더 많은 문제를 만들어 낼 수 있습니다.

> Medical clowns are thought to have the potential to assist children with autism and young burn victims who require painful bandage changes.

해당 답변에서는 아래의 밑줄 친 표현을 바탕으로 관계대명사를 활용한 문제를 만들 수 있을 것입니다.

Medical clowns are thought to have the potential to assist children with autism and <u>young burn victims who require painful bandage changes</u>.

④ 관계대명사를 이용하여 두 문장을 한 문장으로 전환

두 문장의 내용을 전체 또는 부분적으로 결합하여 응용한 문제를 만들어 보겠습니다. 물론, 특정 지문 내용에서 별개의 두 문장을 관계대명사를 이용하여 결합할 수 있는지, 한 문장을 두 문장으로 나눌 수 있는지에 대한 이해가 선행되어야 하겠지만, 이 또한 chatGPT를 통해서 도움을 받을 수 있습니다.

아래 지문을 활용하여 다소 난이도 높은 응용문제까지 chatGPT를 활용하여 만들어 보도록 하겠습니다.

[샘플지문]
The Honeynet Project is an international project aimed at improving internet security by studying the behavior of hackers. It does this by creating fake versions of the files that tempt hackers and observing how the hackers break into and use the files. <u>It then teaches organizations about the kinds of measures they can take to protect their computer networks from hackers</u>. While information provided by previous security systems has traditionally been limited to the tools hackers use, the Honeynet Project provides more detailed information about hacking, such as when and why hackers hack, and how they communicate. Plus, for organizations interested in starting their own research into hacking behavior, the Honeynet Project offers the tools and techniques it has already developed at no charge.

챗GPT 4 Better Questions

chatGPT를 사용하지 않더라도, 본문의 밑줄 친 문장으로 다음과 같은 관계대명사의 활용을 묻는 문제를 만들 수 있습니다.

먼저 밑줄 친 원문을 아래와 같이 두 문장으로 바꾸었습니다.

It then teaches organizations about the kinds of measures they can take to protect their computer networks from hackers.
→ It then teaches organizations about certain kinds of measures. The organizations can take the measures to protect their computer networks from hackers.

해당 문장을 원문에 넣어 다음과 같은 문제를 만들어 볼 수 있습니다.

문제. 본문의 밑줄 친 두 문장을 관계대명사 that을 활용하여 하나의 문장으로 만드시오. (단, 대명사의 활용에 주의할 것)

The Honeynet Project is an international project aimed at improving internet security by studying the behavior of hackers. It does this by creating fake versions of the files that tempt hackers and observing how the hackers break into and use the files. It then teaches organizations about certain kinds of measures. The organizations can take the measures to protect their computer networks from hackers. While information provided by previous security systems has traditionally been limited to the tools hackers use, the Honeynet Project provides more detailed information about hacking, such as when and why hackers hack, and how they communicate. Plus, for organizations interested in starting their own research into hacking behavior, the Honeynet Project offers the tools and techniques it has already developed at no charge.

It then teaches organizations about certain kinds of measures. The organizations can take the measures to protect their computer networks from hackers.
= It then teaches organizations about the kinds of measures ___ ___ ___ ___ ___ ___ their computer networks from hackers.

답 that they can take to protect

위 문제의 경우 반복어구의 생략 뿐 아니라 관계대명사에 걸리는 주어를 대명사로 사용해야 한다는 점에서 다소 난이도가 높아졌다고 볼 수 있습니다.

이번에는 동일한 문장 아래와 같은 프롬프트를 이용하여 두 문장으로 나눠보도록 시켜 보겠습니다.

Prompt) *Break the following sentence into two without changing the meaning of it.*

It then teaches organizations about the kinds of measures they can take to protect their computer networks from hackers.

아래와 같은 결과값을 얻었습니다.

 It teaches organizations about the types of measures that can be taken to protect their computer networks from hackers. Additionally, it provides information on how to protect their computer networks from hackers.

It teaches organizations about the types of measures <u>that can be taken to protect their computer networks from hackers</u>. *Additionally, it provides information on how to protect their computer networks from hackers.*

목적격 관계대명사를 주격관계대명사로 표현하면서 수동태의 활용까지 묻는 문제로 응용할 수 있게 되었습니다.

챗GPT 4 Better Questions

문제. 밑줄 친 표현을 아래 조건에 맞게 동일한 의미를 전달하는 표현으로 전환하시오.

The Honeynet Project is an international project aimed at improving internet security by studying the behavior of hackers. It does this by creating fake versions of the files that tempt hackers and observing how the hackers break into and use the files. It then teaches organizations about the kinds of measures they can take to protect their computer networks from hackers. While information provided by previous security systems has traditionally been limited to the tools hackers use, the Honeynet Project provides more detailed information about hacking, such as when and why hackers hack, and how they communicate. Plus, for organizations interested in starting their own research into hacking behavior, the Honeynet Project offers the tools and techniques it has already developed at no charge.

―――――――〈조건〉―――――――
- 적절한 관계대명사를 넣을 것.
- 수동태의 표현을 반드시 활용하고, 행위의 주체를 표현하는 [by + 대명사]는 생략할 것.

It then teaches organizations about the kinds of measures they can take to protect their computer networks from hackers.
= It then teaches organizations about the kinds of measures ____ ____ ____ ____ to protect their computer networks from hackers.

답 that(which) can be taken

위와 같이 목적격관계대명사를 주격관계대명사로 전환하면서 수동태의 활용까지 묻는 문제가 출제 가능합니다.

이번에는 [전치사 + 관계대명사]를 활용하여 두 문장을 한 문장으로 연결하는 문제를 만들어 보겠습니다.

[샘플지문]
The basin of the Amazon River is noted for its mudflats. Other well-known mudflats around the world include the Atlantic coastal regions of both Canada and the United States and the coastal area along the North Sea in Germany. <u>The Korean peninsula itself is also remarkably rich in mudflats. Those found along its west coast are considered impressive mudflats.</u>

해당 지문에서 밑줄 친 부분을 아래와 같이 프롬프트를 작성해 넣어 보았습니다.

Prompt *combine the following two sentences into one using "among which."*

The Korean peninsula itself is also remarkably rich in mudflats. Those found along its west coast are considered impressive mudflats.

결과값은 다음과 같습니다.

The Korean peninsula itself is remarkably rich in mudflats, <u>among which those found along its west coast are considered particularly impressive</u>.

among which를 활용한 문장으로 패러프레이징 되었습니다. 그리고 considered 뒤의 구조가 바뀌었음을 알 수 있습니다.

The Korean peninsula itself is also remarkably rich in mudflats. Those found along its west coast <u>are considered impressive mudflats</u>.
The Korean peninsula itself is remarkably rich in mudflats, among which those found along its west coast <u>are considered particularly impressive</u>.

해당 부분에 주의해서 다음과 같이 문제를 창작해 보았습니다.

챗GPT 4 Better Questions

> [고난도] 밑줄 친 (가)의 두 문장을 관계대명사를 사용하여 한 문장으로 만들 때 빈 칸에 들어갈 단어를 쓰시오.
>
> The Korean peninsula itself is also remarkably rich in mudflats. Those found along its west coast are considered impressive mudflats.
> The Korean peninsula itself is remarkably rich in mudflats, _____ _____ those found along its west coast are considered particularly _____.
>
> 답 among which, impressive

⑤ 본문에 언급된 부분적 내용을 바탕으로 관계대명사를 활용한 문장 만들기

이번에는 본문에 나온 부분적인 내용을 바탕으로 관계대명사를 활용한 문장으로 전환하는 문제를 만들어 보겠습니다. 앞 선 지문의 내용에서 아래 밑줄 친 두 부분을 활용한 문제입니다.

> 문제. 본문의 첫 번째 문장의 밑줄 친 부분을 <u>관계대명사</u>를 이용하여 하나의 문장으로 영작하시오.
>
> <u>The Honeynet Project is an international project</u> aimed at improving internet security by <u>studying the behavior of hackers</u>. It does this by creating fake versions of the files that tempt hackers and observing how the hackers break into and use the files.
>
> <u>The Honeynet Project is an international project</u> aimed at improving internet security by <u>studying the behavior of hackers</u>.
> → _____.
>
> 답 The Honeynet Project is an international project <u>which studies</u> the behavior of hackers.

지칭추론 문제와 연계해서 관계대명사의 활용을 묻는 문제를 만들 수 있습니다.

문제. 본문에서 밑줄 친 The former group이 문맥상 지칭하는 대상을 영어로 작성하려고 한다. 제시어를 활용하여 빈칸을 채우시오. (단, 추가단어 있고, 필요시 문맥에 맞게 단어의 형태를 변형할 것)

In one experiment, researchers sent clowns to entertain children being prepared for surgery. One group of kids spent about half an hour with a clown, while a second group of children received a sedative instead. The former group showed the same reduction in anxiety as those who were given the sedative.

제시어: meet, clowns, kids, the

_____ _____ _____ _____ _____ _____

답 The kids who met with clowns

2 최신 유형의 독해 문제

chatGPT의 활용이 일반화되면서 다양한 유형의 독해 문제가 출제되고 있습니다. 1.0 Version에서 소개한 문제에 추가적으로 신유형과 함께 다양한 어휘문제도 함께 출제하는 프롬프트를 살펴보겠습니다.

1) 적절한 질문 찾기
본문 전체 또는 특정 내용을 바탕으로 할 수 있는 가장 적절한 질문을 고르는 문제를 만드는 프롬프트는 다음과 같다.

Prompt *Make a multiple choice question with 5 options with the answer and explanation at the bottom.*

챗GPT 4 Better Questions

> **Passage**
>
> IN THE PREVIOUS CHAPTER WE SAW THAT although Sapiens had already populated East Africa 150,000 years ago, they began to overrun the rest of planet Earth and drive the other human species to extinction only about 70,000 years ago. In the intervening millennia, even though these archaic Sapiens looked just like us and their brains were as big as ours, they did not enjoy any marked advantage over other human species, did not produce particularly sophisticated tools, and did not accomplish any other special feats.
>
> <u>In fact, in the first recorded encounter between Sapiens and Neanderthals, the Neanderthals won</u>. About 100,000 years ago, some Sapiens groups migrated north to the Levant, which was Neanderthal territory, but failed to secure a firm footing. It might have been due to nasty natives, an inclement climate, or unfamiliar local parasites. Whatever the reason, the Sapiens eventually retreated, leaving the Neanderthals as masters of the Middle East.

[Stem]
Based on the sentence "In fact, in the first recorded encounter between Sapiens and Neanderthals, the Neanderthals won." from the passage, which of the following is the most appropriate question to ask?

[Type of Alternative]
①
②
③
④
⑤

*Show the contents of all the options.

결과값은 다음과 같다.

[Options]
1. ① Why did the Sapiens fail to secure a foothold in the Levant?
2. ② How did the Sapiens differ from the Neanderthals in physical appearance?
3. ③ What were the tools used by the Neanderthals in the Levant?
4. ④ When did the Sapiens first reach East Africa?
5. ⑤ Why did the Sapiens eventually drive Neanderthals to extinction?

Answer:
① Why did the Sapiens fail to secure a foothold in the Levant?

Explanation:
The passage mentions that the Neanderthals won the first encounter with the Sapiens, who were unable to establish themselves in the Levant. This directly leads to the question of *why* the Sapiens failed, as it is the central topic of the sentence. The other options do not address this specific interaction between the Sapiens and Neanderthals.

본문 전체의 내용을 고려하면서 특정 정보를 바탕으로 던질 수 있는 가장 논리적 질문을 묻는 참신한 문제 제작이 가능하다.

2) 요약정리 문제

글의 요약문을 바탕으로 빈칸 문제를 만들고 싶으면 다음과 같은 프롬프트를 사용하면 된다. 먼저 주어진 지문에 대한 요약문을 작성해 보자.

Prompt *Summarize the passage within no more than 3 sentences.*

Self-control has been an important factor in Western civilization. In his recent economic history, Clark contended that it played a decisive role in the Industrial Revolution and the economic and cultural dominance of Western civilization. Noting that the Industrial Revolution occurred in England rather than other countries with similar governmental and other structures, Clark proposed that the key difference was that in England, the upper classes reproduced far more than the lower ones, and given the limited opportunities in the social structure, this entailed substantial downward mobility. As a result, the lower classes gradually filled up with people who

챗GPT 4 Better Questions

had the genetic and environmental benefits of the upper classes, including self-control. This created the potential for a working class that could be relied on to be punctual, diligent, and effective at the factory work required for the Industrial Revolution — something Clark notes that many third world countries have been still unable to achieve centuries after the British showed the way.

결과값은 다음과 같습니다.

> By examining the connection between self-control, social mobility, and industrialization, the author implies that the cultural and genetic factors influencing self-control played a significant role in shaping Western civilization's economic and technological advancements. The ability to exercise self-control was crucial in driving productivity and progress during the Industrial Revolution, contributing to the dominance of Western nations in that era.

해당 결과값을 바탕으로 아래와 같은 프롬프트를 만들어 보았습니다.

Prompt) Make a multiple choice question with 5 options with the answer and explanation at the bottom.

Passage

Self-control has been an important factor in Western civilization. In his recent economic history, Clark contended that it played a decisive role in the Industrial Revolution and the economic and cultural dominance of Western civilization. Noting that the Industrial Revolution occurred in England rather than other countries with similar governmental and other structures, Clark proposed that the key difference was that in England, the upper classes reproduced far more than the lower ones, and given the limited opportunities in the social structure, this entailed substantial downward mobility. As a result, the lower classes gradually filled up with people who had the genetic and environmental benefits of the upper classes, including self-control. This created the potential for a working class that could be relied on to be punctual, diligent, and effective at the factory work required for the Industrial Revolution — something Clark notes that many third world countries have been still unable to achieve centuries after the British showed the way.

PART 3

[Stem]

Below is the summary of the passage. Which of the following pairs best fills the blanks Ⓐ and Ⓑ?

By examining the connection between self-control, social mobility, and industrialization, the author implies that the cultural and Ⓐ_____ factors influencing self-control played a significant role in shaping Western civilization's economic and technological advancements. The ability to exercise self-control was crucial in driving productivity and progress during the Industrial Revolution, contributing to the Ⓑ_____ of Western nations in that era.

[Type of Alternative]
①
②
③
④
⑤

*Show the contents of all the options.

결과값은 다음과 같습니다.

[Options]

1. ① Ⓐ economic / Ⓑ authority
2. ② Ⓐ environmental / Ⓑ supremacy
3. ③ Ⓐ genetic / Ⓑ dominance
4. ④ Ⓐ economic / Ⓑ improvement
5. ⑤ Ⓐ political / Ⓑ stability

Answer:
③ Ⓐ genetic / Ⓑ dominance

Explanation:
The passage discusses how genetic factors, combined with social mobility, influenced the development of self-control in England's working class, which played a decisive role in the country's dominance during the Industrial Revolution. The other options do not accurately capture the specific focus on "genetic" factors and "dominance" of Western civilization as presented in the passage.

챗GPT 4 Better Questions

3 요지 문제의 응용

요지문제의 응용으로 역사적 인물의 이론/주장을 활용한 문제 출제가 가능하다.

Prompt) Make a multiple choice question with 5 options with the answer ans explanation at the bottom.

> **Passage**
>
> *The influence that empathy has on our daily lives is easy to recognize. It's the reason we love to be immersed in a good novel or get hooked on a new TV drama. Aside from being entertaining, their stories provide opportunities for us to feel what the characters are going through. We imagine being in their situation and find ourselves laughing or crying along with them. Empathy also plays an important role in our personal relationships. By empathizing with the experiences of our friends and loved ones, as opposed to just playing armchair quarterback to their struggles, we can understand them better and provide more meaningful support. Not only is this helpful for them, but it's also beneficial for us. Studies have shown that being empathetic can have a variety of positive effects, such as improving communication skills and reducing stress levels.*

[Stem]
Followings are the explanations for the philosopher and his views about empathy. Which philosopher's view best represents the main idea of the passage?

[Type of Alternative]
①
②
③
④
⑤
* *show the contents of the options.*

결과값은 다음과 같다.

[Options]

1. ① **Aristotle:**
Believed that empathy helps us understand the emotions of others, which can enhance moral development and social harmony.

2. ② **David Hume:**
Argued that empathy is a fundamental aspect of human nature that enables us to connect with others' feelings and experiences.

3. ③ **Friedrich Nietzsche:**
Claimed that empathy is a weakness that can hinder personal growth and success by diverting focus from self-interest.

4. ④ **Jean-Paul Sartre:**
Proposed that empathy can lead to a loss of individuality, as one may overly identify with the experiences of others.

5. ⑤ **Martin Heidegger:**
Suggested that empathy arises from our shared existence but cautioned against it being a means of escape from personal responsibility.

다음은 정답과 해설이다.

Answer:
② David Hume

Explanation:
The passage highlights the positive effects of empathy in understanding and supporting others, which aligns with David Hume's view that empathy is essential for connecting with others' feelings and experiences. The other philosophers either focus on a more negative interpretation of empathy or discuss its implications in ways that do not align with the main idea presented in the passage.

해당 유형은 본문의 특정 정보와 관련하여 응용출제도 가능하다.

챗GPT 4 Better Questions

Prompt) Make a question with 5 multiple choices along with the answer and explantion.

Passage

Today, with the advent of the internet and new technology for editing digital material, more people than ever before can produce artistic creations and share them with the world. Many critics, though, have expressed concern that this is causing us to lose our sense of what makes truly great art. (가)Great art challenges our perceptions of the world and forever changes the ways that we think and feel. Artists ought to remember that new technologies are nothing more than tools that can be used in the creative process. In other words, the goal of the modern artist should not be simply to utilize technology for its own sake. Rather, it should be to produce unique creations that will allow the public to have new, eye-opening experiences.

[Stem]

Which of the following scholar carries the contextual meaning of the sentence "Great art challenges our perceptions of the world and forever changes the ways that we think and feel." in the passage?

[Type of Alternative]
① Scholar A:
② Scholar B:
③ Scholar C:
④ Scholar D:
⑤ Scholar E:

* Display all alternatives.

4 속담을 활용한 문제응용

요지 문제의 응용으로 속담을 고르는 문제를 창작할 수 있다.

Prompt) *Make a multiple choice question with 5 options with the answer and explantion at the bottom.*

Passage

People believe that they are a product of their surroundings, but it is actually the opposite. People's surroundings are largely shaped by their decisions and the circumstances they create for themselves. Therefore, it is important to approach life actively rather than passively. It is more likely that seeking happiness will lead you to success than it is that success will bring happiness to you. So don't allow the storms that life sends your way to push you around and decide your path. Instead, find your own way out of the stormy weather by facing any problems or conflicts you have directly and looking for ways to solve them. By dealing with your issues, you will contribute to a more peaceful and sunny environment around you. If you allow them to remain unresolved, you'll be lost in the cold, miserable storm. Remember, this creates that, not the other way around.

[Stem]
Which of the following proverbs is at odds with the perspective implied in the phrase "People's surroundings are largely shaped by their decisions and the circumstances they create for themselves." in the passage?

[Type of Alternative]
①
②
③
④
⑤

* Show the contents of all the alternatives.

챗GPT 4 Better Questions

결과값은 다음과 같다.

> [Options]
>
> 1. ① "You can't control the weather, but you can change your umbrella."
>   This implies that external factors are beyond our control, but we can adapt.
>
> 2. ② "Every cloud has a silver lining."
>   This suggests that positive outcomes can arise from difficult situations, reinforcing an active approach to challenges.
>
> 3. ③ "Life is what happens to you while you're busy making other plans."
>   This implies that life's circumstances shape our reality more than our decisions do.
>
> 4. ④ "When it rains, it pours."
>   This suggests that misfortunes come in groups and can overpower personal efforts to change circumstances.
>
> 5. ⑤ "Where there's a will, there's a way."
>   This reinforces the idea that determination and effort can shape outcomes and environments.

선택지의 내용 아래 설명이 덧붙여진 형태로 나왔다. 답과 해설은 다음과 같다.

> **Answer:**
> ③ "Life is what happens to you while you're busy making other plans."
>
> **Explanation:**
> This proverb suggests that external circumstances have a greater influence on our lives than our decisions, which contradicts the passage's main idea that individuals shape their surroundings through their choices and actions. The other proverbs either support an active approach to dealing with life's challenges or emphasize personal agency, aligning more closely with the passage's perspective.

5 "질문-답변" 응용문제

내신 문제에 단골로 등장하는 문제 중 하나인 "본문을 통해서 답할 수 없는 질문은?"은 다음과 같은 프롬프트를 통해서 쉽게 창작이 가능하다.

Prompt) Make a multiple choice question with 5 options with the answer and explanation at the bottom.

Passage

When we see something, we naturally and automatically break it up into shapes, colors, and concepts that we have learned through education. We recode what we see through the lens of everything we know. We reconstruct memories rather than retrieving the video from memory. This is a useful trait. It's a more efficient way to store information — a bit like an optimal image compression algorithm such as JPG, rather than storing a raw bitmap image file. People who lack this ability and remember everything in perfect detail struggle to generalize, learn, and make connections between what they have learned. But representing the world as abstract ideas and features comes at a cost of seeing the world as it is. Instead, we see the world through our assumptions, motivations, and past experiences. The discovery that our memories are reconstructed through abstract representations rather than played back like a movie completely undermined the legal primacy of eyewitness testimony. Seeing is not believing.

[Stem]
Which of the following questions can NOT be answered by the passage?

[Type of Alternative]
①
②
③
④
⑤

답
*Show the contents of all the options.

결과값은 다음과 같다.

챗GPT 4 Better Questions

> **Question** Which of the following questions can NOT be answered by the passage?
>
> ① Why do people naturally break what they see into shapes, colors, and concepts?
> ② How does the way we store information in memory resemble an image compression algorithm?
> ③ Why might people who remember everything in perfect detail struggle to generalize?
> ④ What is one drawback of reconstructing memories instead of storing them like a video?
> ⑤ What specific brain regions are responsible for reconstructing memories?
>
> **Answer and Explanation**
> Answer: ⑤
> The passage explains the general process of how people reconstruct memories and why this is efficient and beneficial in certain ways. However, it does not address the specific brain regions responsible for memory reconstruction. Therefore, question ⑤ cannot be answered by the information provided in the passage.

해당 유형의 문제를 만들 때 오답에 해당하는 질문은 지문을 달리해도 다음과 같은 질문의 형태로만 제시된다는 점은 주의해야 한다.

⑤ **What specific** brain regions are responsible for reconstructing memories?

지문을 달리해도 위의 밑줄 친 표현을 중심으로 오답을 만들기에 오답에 해당하는 내용은 본문의 내용에 맞춰 수정을 하는 것이 좋다. 본인은 해당 프롬프트를 사용하는 경우도 있지만, 아래 프롬프트를 통해서 수동적으로 선택지를 선택하고, 해당 과정에서 내용을 수정해서 눈에 보이는 답이 되지 않도록 2차 가공을 한다.

Prompt *Please create even questions based on the text with their corresponding answers.*

When we see something, we naturally and automatically break it up into shapes, colors, and concepts that we have learned through education. We recode what we see through the lens of everything we know. We reconstruct memories rather than retrieving the video from memory. This is a useful trait. It's a more efficient way to store information — a bit like an optimal image compression algorithm such as JPG, *rather than storing a raw bitmap image file. People who lack this ability and remember everything in perfect detail struggle to generalize, learn, and make connections between what they have learned. But representing the world as abstract ideas and features comes at a cost of seeing the world as it is. Instead, we see the world through our assumptions, motivations, and past experiences. The discovery that our memories are reconstructed through abstract representations rather than played back like a movie completely undermined the legal primacy of eyewitness testimony. Seeing is not believing.*

결과값은 다음과 같다.

Question 1:
What process occurs automatically when we see something?

Answer:
We naturally and automatically break what we see into shapes, colors, and concepts that we have learned through education.

Question 2:
How do we interpret or recode what we see?

Answer:
We interpret or recode what we see through the lens of everything we know, including our past knowledge and experiences.

공간의 제약으로 두 개의 질문만 담았지만, 이렇게 만들어진 질문을 바탕으로 상황에 따라 수정하면 일관된 유형의 질문만 오답이 되는 것을 피할 수 있다.

아래와 같은 응용문제도 출제 가능하다.

---

* 다음을 읽고, 물음에 답하시오.

One aspect in which virtual relationships are different from other more tangible forms is that, because the interaction is mediated and abstracted away from the

4 Better Questions

physical person, people may experiment with different aspects of their personas in a manner not easily executed in face-to-face interaction. For example, there are instances of gender inversion, whereby a man may use a female avatar to participate in an online community and vice versa. Also, depending on the application or game, age, weight, skin color, and other phenotypes can be altered so that the player may try out a different look and see how he or she is accepted by the community. Although there is evidence that many people will adapt their virtual selves to look a lot like themselves offline, there is an understanding among those in the virtual community where it is acceptable practice to experiment. Thus, virtual communities provide spaces for some networked individuals to connect, interact, play, and experiment, and for their participants they are a source of meaningful interaction and purposeful relationships.

[주관식] 아래는 본문을 바탕으로 한 "질문-답변"의 내용이다. 밑줄 친 ⓐ~ⓔ 중 틀린 내용이 있는 부분의 기호 <u>두 개</u>를 쓰시오.

① Question: In what ways do virtual relationships differ from face-to-face interactions regarding personal experimentation?
   Answer: Virtual relationships offer people the opportunity to experiment with different aspects of their identity, such as gender, age, and appearance, ⓐ<u>in ways that are not easily achievable in face-to-face interactions</u>.

② Question: Can you provide an example of how individuals might change their personas in virtual communities?
   Answer: One example is gender inversion, ⓑ<u>where a man might use a female avatar to engage in an online community, and vice versa</u>.

③ Question: Why would someone choose to change their appearance in a virtual community?
   Answer: They might change their appearance ⓒ<u>to manipulate how the community think of them or to experience life from a different perspective</u>.

④ Question: Do people always create virtual identities that are very different from their real-life selves, according to the passage?
   Answer: No, the passage indicates that ⓓ<u>many people design their virtual selves to fake their real-life selves, although experimentation is also a common practice</u>.

⑤ Question: What are some advantages of virtual communities mentioned in the passage?
Answer: Virtual communities provide spaces ⓔwhere networked individuals can connect, interact, play, experiment, and establish meaningful interactions and purposeful relationships.

답

ⓒto manipulate how the community think of them or to experience life from a different perspective.

ⓓmany people design their virtual selves to fake their real-life selves, although experimentation is also a common practice.

6 외부지문의 활용

chatGPT를 활용하면 굳이 외부지문을 찾는 수고를 줄여준다. 다음의 프롬프트와 절차를 확인해 보도록 하자.

Prompt) 아래 지문에 대한 "행동주의학자의 분석"을 작성해 주세요.

My wife had just told our daughters to listen at the door, promising that I would whistle shortly before I departed. Apparently I had. I say apparently, because I certainly wasn't aware of it. Having no recollection of whistling, I concluded that they were just having fun with me. Several days later, lost in deep thought in the washroom, I reached for the toilet paper. I heard myself whistle. Shocked, I started to laugh. What was going on? Upon reflection I determined the origin of such odd behavior. During my toilet-training, my mother would often leave me seated on the toilet while she went about her housework. I was to alert her when I finished. I would signal my readiness with a whistle — a behavior that became unconsciously ingrained.

챗GPT 4 Better Questions

아래는 위의 프롬프트의 결과값을 이용한 응용문제이다.

---

* 다음을 읽고, 물음에 답하시오.

My wife had just told our daughters to listen at the door, promising that I would whistle shortly before I departed. Apparently I had. I say apparently, because I certainly wasn't aware of it. Having no recollection of whistling, I concluded that they were just having fun with me. Several days later, lost in deep thought in the washroom, I reached for the toilet paper. I heard myself whistle. Shocked, I started to laugh. What was going on? Upon reflection I determined the origin of such odd behavior. During my toilet-training, my mother would often leave me seated on the toilet while she went about her housework. I was to alert her when I finished. I would signal my readiness with a whistle — a behavior that became unconsciously ingrained.

다음은 본문에서 다뤄진 내용에 대한 <u>행동심리학자의 분석</u>이다. 밑줄 친 내용 중 가장 설득력이 떨어지는 것은?

The incident described is ①<u>a classic example of conditioned behavior and the power of early childhood training on later life actions</u>. The individual's whistling behavior in the washroom can be understood through the lens of operant conditioning, a concept introduced by B.F. Skinner. During toilet training, ②<u>the individual was conditioned to whistle as a signal for his mother, who would then respond by attending to him</u>. ③<u>This behavior, reinforced repeatedly during a formative period, became an conditional response</u> — a learned behavior that persisted into adulthood ④<u>despite the original context no longer being relevant</u>.
From a psychological perspective, this scenario demonstrates ⑤<u>how deeply ingrained habits and behaviors can form through early experiences</u>. *The individual's mother, by responding to his whistle, provided positive reinforcement, thus strengthening the behavior. Over time, the act of whistling became an unconscious response triggered by the situational context of being in the washroom.*

답 ③This behavior, reinforced repeatedly during a formative period, became an ~~conditional~~(-> automatic or unconditional) response

7 어휘문제

어휘문제를 위한 두 종류의 프롬프트를 살펴보자.

첫 번째는 빈칸에 들어갈 단어에 대한 영영풀이를 활용한 문제다.

Prompt) Make a multiple choice question with 5 options with the answer and explanation at the bottom.

> **Passage**
> * A person will tend to feel guilty when his or her conduct ___(a)___ that principle.
> * They ___(b)___ laws that kept black people separate from white people.
> * All money raised will be donated to ___(c)___.
> * Borrowers are ___(d)___ for returning items on time and in good condition.
> * Using the laundry machines late at night can ___(e)___ others' sleep.

[Stem]
각 문장의 빈칸에 들어갈 낱말의 문장 내의 영어정의로 적절하지 않는 것은?
① (a):
② (b):
③ (c):
④ (d):
⑤ (e):

빈칸에 들어갈 단어는 순서대로 다음과 같다.
violates
implemented
charity
responsible
disturb

여기서 한 개의 영어정의는 적절하지 않게 해 주세요.

챗GPT 4 Better Questions

답
*Show the contents of all the options.

결과값은 다음과 같다.

[Stem]
각 문장의 빈칸에 들어갈 낱말의 문장 내의 영어 정의로 적절하지 않은 것은?

Options:
① (a): violates – acts against or goes against (a principle or rule)
② (b): implemented – put (a decision, plan, or agreement) into effect
③ (c): charity – an organization set up to provide help and raise money for those in need
④ (d): responsible – having a duty to deal with something or being accountable for something
⑤ (e): disturb – to make (someone) feel peaceful or to reassure

Answer and Explanation
Answer: ⑤ (e)
The word "disturb" in this context means to interrupt or bother someone, especially by causing noise. However, the definition given here, "to make (someone) feel peaceful or to reassure," is incorrect as it does not match the intended meaning in the sentence about disturbing others' sleep.

두 번째 프롬프트는 영영과 예문을 함께 다루는 문제이다.

Prompt *Make a multiple choice question with 5 options with the answer and explanation at the bottom.*

Passage

14 The predators—insects that kill and consume other insects—are of many kinds. Some are quick and with the speed of swallows snatch their prey from the air. Others plod ⓐmethodically along a stem, plucking off and devouring ⓑsedentary insects like the aphids. The yellowjackets capture soft-bodied insects and feed the juices to their young. Muddauber wasps build columned nests of mud under the

caves of houses and ⓒstock them with insects on which their young will feed. The horseguard wasp hovers above herds of grazing cattle, destroying the bloodsucking flies that torment them. The loudly buzzing syrphid fly, often ⓓmistaken for a bee, lays its eggs on leaves of aphis-infested plants; the hatching larvae then consume immense numbers of aphids. Ladybugs or lady beetles are among the most effective destroyers of aphids, scale insects, and other plant-eating insects. Literally hundreds of aphids are consumed by a single ladybug to ⓔstoke the little fires of energy which she requires to produce even a single batch of eggs.

[Stem]
본문에 나온 각 단어의 문맥적 영영풀이와 예문이 모두 옳지 <u>않은</u> 것을 하나 고르시오.

[Type of Alternative]
① ⓐ*methodically*:
Example sentence:
② ⓑ*sedentary*:
Example sentence:
③ ⓒ*stock*:
Example sentence:
④ ⓓ*mistaken for*:
Example sentence:
⑤ ⓔ*stoke*:
Example sentence:

답

*Show the contents of all the options.

결과값은 다음과 같다.

챗GPT 4 Better Questions

> [Options]
>
> 1. ⓐ **methodically:**
>   *Definition:* in a systematic or organized way.
>   *Example sentence:* He works methodically, following a set routine every day.
>
> 2. ⓑ **sedentary:**
>   *Definition:* remaining in one place; not moving much.
>   *Example sentence:* Aphids are sedentary insects, often staying on a single plant for long periods.
>
> 3. ⓒ **stock:**
>   *Definition:* to supply or fill with something.
>   *Example sentence:* The squirrel stocks its den with nuts for the winter.
>
> 4. ⓓ **mistaken for:**
>   *Definition:* to be incorrectly identified as something else.
>   *Example sentence:* The flower was often mistaken for a wild rose, even though it was different.
>
> 5. ⓔ **stoke:**
>   *Definition:* to fuel or add to a fire or energy source.
>   *Example sentence:* She stokes her motivation by listening to inspiring speeches.

정의와 함께 예문이 함께 들어간 선택지의 내용을 확인할 수 있고, 아래는 정답과 해설이다.

> **Answer:**
> ⑤ ⓔstoke
>
> **Explanation:**
> In the passage, "stoke" refers to fueling the energy needs of the ladybug to produce eggs. The example sentence provided, however, describes "stoke" in a figurative sense related to motivation, which is not consistent with the literal meaning in the context of the passage.

나도 Prompt Engineer

1. Prompt: Please find as many expressions in the following text as possible where a phrase can be changed into a clause or a clause into a phrase, and then change each expression into the respective clause or phrase.

Fromm distinguishes between 'freedom from' (negative freedom) and 'freedom to' (positive freedom). The former refers to emancipation from restrictions such as social conventions placed on individuals by other people or institutions. This is the kind of freedom typified by the existentialism of Sartre, and has often been fought for historically but, according to Fromm, on its own it can be a destructive force unless accompanied by a creative element – 'freedom to' – the use of freedom to employ the total integrated personality in creative acts. This, he argues, necessarily implies a true connectedness with others that goes beyond the superficial bonds of conventional social intercourse: "...in the spontaneous realization of the self, man unites himself anew with the world..."

2. Prompt: Make a multiple choice question with 5 options with the answer and explanation at the bottom.

[Passage]
When we see something, we naturally and automatically break it up into shapes, colors, and concepts that we have learned through education. We recode what we see through the lens of everything we know. We reconstruct memories rather than retrieving the video from memory. This is a useful trait. It's a more efficient way to store information — a bit like an optimal image compression algorithm such as JPG, rather than storing a raw bitmap image file. People who lack this ability and remember everything in perfect detail struggle to generalize, learn, and make connections between what they have learned. But representing the world as abstract ideas and features comes at a cost of seeing the world as it is. Instead, we see the world through our assumptions, motivations, and past experiences. The discovery that our memories are reconstructed through abstract representations rather than played back like a movie completely undermined the legal primacy of eyewitness testimony. Seeing is not believing.

4 Better Questions

[Stem]
Which of the following is NOT correct about the passage?

[Type of Alternative]
①
②
③
④
⑤

- Show the contents of all the options.

3. Prompt: Please paraphrase each of the following sentences using the conditions.

[Conditions]
* Cleft Sentences: These split the sentence to highlight a specific part.
  Example: It was Sarah who completed the project.
* Inversion: Changing the usual word order to stress a particular element.
  Example: Never have I seen such beautiful artwork.
* Do/Does/Did Emphasis: Using "do," "does," or "did" in statements to emphasize action.
  Example: I do believe in their ability to succeed.

① When we see things, we process them based on shapes, colors, and concepts we have learned.
② Memories are reconstructed rather than retrieved like a video playback.
③ Remembering everything in perfect detail is advantageous for learning and making connections.
④ Representing the world as abstract ideas affects our ability to see it as it truly is.
⑤ The reliability of eyewitness testimony has been questioned due to the nature of memory reconstruction.

4. Prompt: Make a multiple choice question with 5 options with the answer and explanation at the bottom according to the following condtions.

[conditions]
When making options, make sure each options has one of the following's structures.
* Cleft Sentences: These split the sentence to highlight a specific part.
  Example: It was Sarah who completed the project.
* Inversion: Changing the usual word order to stress a particular element.
  Example: Never have I seen such beautiful artwork.
* Do/Does/Did Emphasis: Using "do," "does," or "did" in statements to emphasize action.
  Example: I do believe in their ability to succeed.

[Passage]
When we see something, we naturally and automatically break it up into shapes, colors, and concepts that we have learned through education. We recode what we see through the lens of everything we know. We reconstruct memories rather than retrieving the video from memory. This is a useful trait. It's a more efficient way to store information — a bit like an optimal image compression algorithm such as JPG, rather than storing a raw bitmap image file. People who lack this ability and remember everything in perfect detail struggle to generalize, learn, and make connections between what they have learned. But representing the world as abstract ideas and features comes at a cost of seeing the world as it is. Instead, we see the world through our assumptions, motivations, and past experiences. The discovery that our memories are reconstructed through abstract representations rather than played back like a movie completely undermined the legal primacy of eyewitness testimony. Seeing is not believing.

[Stem]
Which of the following is NOT correct about the passage?

4 Better Questions

[Type of Alternative]
①
②
③
④
⑤

– Show the contents of all the options.

5. Prompt: Rewrite the following sentence using the relative clause.
   Healthcare workers have been dressing up like clowns to help patients relax and reduce the stress staying in the hospital can cause.

6. Prmopt: Paraphrase the following sentence.
   It is believed that medical clowns could also be used to help kids with autism and young burn victims in need of painful bandage-changing.

7. Prompt: Break the following sentence into two without changing the meaning of it.
   It then teaches organizations about the kinds of measures they can take to protect their computer networks from hackers.

8. Prompt: combine the following two sentences into one using "among which."
   The Korean peninsula itself is also remarkably rich in mudflats. Those found along its west coast are considered impressive mudflats.

9. Prompt: Make a multiple choice question with 5 options with the answer and explanation at the bottom.

[Passage]
IN THE PREVIOUS CHAPTER WE SAW THAT although Sapiens had already populated East Africa 150,000 years ago, they began to overrun the rest of planet Earth and drive the other human species to extinction only about 70,000 years ago. In the intervening millennia, even though these archaic Sapiens looked just like us and their brains were as big as ours, they did not enjoy any marked advantage over other human species, did not produce particularly sophisticated tools, and did not accomplish any other special feats.

<u>In fact, in the first recorded encounter between Sapiens and Neanderthals, the Neanderthals won</u>. About 100,000 years ago, some Sapiens groups migrated north to the Levant, which was Neanderthal territory, but failed to secure a firm footing. It might have been due to nasty natives, an inclement climate, or unfamiliar local parasites. Whatever the reason, the Sapiens eventually retreated, leaving the Neanderthals as masters of the Middle East.

[Stem]
Based on the sentence "In fact, in the first recorded encounter between Sapiens and Neanderthals, the Neanderthals won." from the passage, which of the following is the most appropriate question to ask?

[Type of Alternative]
①
②
③
④
⑤

* Show the contents of all the options.

4 Better Questions

10. Prompt: Summarize the passage within no more than 3 sentences.

Self-control has been an important factor in Western civilization. In his recent economic history, Clark contended that it played a decisive role in the Industrial Revolution and the economic and cultural dominance of Western civilization. Noting that the Industrial Revolution occurred in England rather than other countries with similar governmental and other structures, Clark proposed that the key difference was that in England, the upper classes reproduced far more than the lower ones, and given the limited opportunities in the social structure, this entailed substantial downward mobility. As a result, the lower classes gradually filled up with people who had the genetic and environmental benefits of the upper classes, including self-control. This created the potential for a working class that could be relied on to be punctual, diligent, and effective at the factory work required for the Industrial Revolution — something Clark notes that many third world countries have been still unable to achieve centuries after the British showed the way.

11. Prompt: Make a multiple choice question with 5 options with the answer and explanation at the bottom.

[Passage]
Self-control has been an important factor in Western civilization. In his recent economic history, Clark contended that it played a decisive role in the Industrial Revolution and the economic and cultural dominance of Western civilization. Noting that the Industrial Revolution occurred in England rather than other countries with similar governmental and other structures, Clark proposed that the key difference was that in England, the upper classes reproduced far more than the lower ones, and given the limited opportunities in the social structure, this entailed substantial downward mobility. As a result, the lower classes gradually filled up with people who had the genetic and environmental benefits of the upper classes, including self-control. This created the potential for a working class that could be relied on to be punctual, diligent, and effective at the factory work required for the Industrial Revolution — something Clark notes that many third world countries have been still unable to achieve centuries after the British showed the way.

[Stem]
Below is the summary of the passage. Which of the following pairs best fills the blanks Ⓐ and Ⓑ?
By examining the connection between self-control, social mobility, and industrialization, the author implies that the cultural and Ⓐ_____ factors influencing self-control played a significant role in shaping Western civilization's economic and technological advancements. The ability to exercise self-control was crucial in driving productivity and progress during the Industrial Revolution, contributing to the Ⓑ_____ of Western nations in that era.

[Type of Alternative]
①
②
③
④
⑤

*Show the contents of all the options.

12. Prompt: Make a multiple choice question with 5 options with the answer ans explanation at the bottom.

[Passage]
The influence that empathy has on our daily lives is easy to recognize. It's the reason we love to be immersed in a good novel or get hooked on a new TV drama. Aside from being entertaining, their stories provide opportunities for us to feel what the characters are going through. We imagine being in their situation and find ourselves laughing or crying along with them. Empathy also plays an important role in our personal relationships. By empathizing with the experiences of our friends and loved ones, as opposed to just playing armchair quarterback to their struggles, we can understand them better and provide more meaningful support. Not only is this helpful for them, but it's also beneficial for us. Studies have shown that being empathetic can have a variety of positive effects, such as improving communication skills and reducing stress levels.

4 Better Questions

[Stem]
Followings are the explanations for the philosopher and his views about empathy. Which philosopher's view best represents the main idea of the passage?

[Type of Alternative]
①
②
③
④
⑤

*show the contents of the options.

13. Prompt: Make a question with 5 multiple choices along with the answer and explantion.

[Passage]
Today, with the advent of the internet and new technology for editing digital material, more people than ever before can produce artistic creations and share them with the world. Many critics, though, have expressed concern that this is causing us to lose our sense of what makes truly great art. (가)Great art challenges our perceptions of the world and forever changes the ways that we think and feel. Artists ought to remember that new technologies are nothing more than tools that can be used in the creative process. In other words, the goal of the modern artist should not be simply to utilize technology for its own sake. Rather, it should be to produce unique creations that will allow the public to have new, eye-opening experiences.

[Stem]
Which of the following scholar carries the contextual meaning of the sentence "Great art challenges our perceptions of the world and forever changes the ways that we think and feel." in the passage?

[Type of Alternative]
① Scholar A:
② Scholar B:
③ Scholar C:
④ Scholar D:
⑤ Scholar E:

* Display all alternatives.

14. Prompt: Make a multiple choice question with 5 options with the answer and explantion at the bottom.

[Passage]
People believe that they are a product of their surroundings, but it is actually the opposite. People's surroundings are largely shaped by their decisions and the circumstances they create for themselves. Therefore, it is important to approach life actively rather than passively. It is more likely that seeking happiness will lead you to success than it is that success will bring happiness to you. So don't allow the storms that life sends your way to push you around and decide your path. Instead, find your own way out of the stormy weather by facing any problems or conflicts you have directly and looking for ways to solve them. By dealing with your issues, you will contribute to a more peaceful and sunny environment around you. If you allow them to remain unresolved, you'll be lost in the cold, miserable storm. Remember, this creates that, not the other way around.

[Stem]
Which of the following proverbs is at odds with the perspective implied in the phrase "People's surroundings are largely shaped by their decisions and the circumstances they create for themselves." in the passage?

4 Better Questions

[Type of Alternative]
①
②
③
④
⑤

* Show the contents of all the alternatives.

15. Prompt: Make a multiple choice question with 5 options with the answer and explanation at the bottom.

[Passage]
When we see something, we naturally and automatically break it up into shapes, colors, and concepts that we have learned through education. We recode what we see through the lens of everything we know. We reconstruct memories rather than retrieving the video from memory. This is a useful trait. It's a more efficient way to store information — a bit like an optimal image compression algorithm such as JPG, rather than storing a raw bitmap image file. People who lack this ability and remember everything in perfect detail struggle to generalize, learn, and make connections between what they have learned. But representing the world as abstract ideas and features comes at a cost of seeing the world as it is. Instead, we see the world through our assumptions, motivations, and past experiences. The discovery that our memories are reconstructed through abstract representations rather than played back like a movie completely undermined the legal primacy of eyewitness testimony. Seeing is not believing.

[Stem]
Which of the following questions can NOT be answered by the passage?

[Type of Alternative]
①
②
③
④
⑤

답
*Show the contents of all the options.

16. Prompt: Please create even questions based on the text with their corresponding answers.

When we see something, we naturally and automatically break it up into shapes, colors, and concepts that we have learned through education. We recode what we see through the lens of everything we know. We reconstruct memories rather than retrieving the video from memory. This is a useful trait. It's a more efficient way to store information — a bit like an optimal image compression algorithm such as JPG, rather than storing a raw bitmap image file. People who lack this ability and remember everything in perfect detail struggle to generalize, learn, and make connections between what they have learned. But representing the world as abstract ideas and features comes at a cost of seeing the world as it is. Instead, we see the world through our assumptions, motivations, and past experiences. The discovery that our memories are reconstructed through abstract representations rather than played back like a movie completely undermined the legal primacy of eyewitness testimony. Seeing is not believing.

챗GPT 4 Better Questions

17. Prompt: 아래 지문에 대한 "행동주의학자의 분석"을 작성해 주세요.

My wife had just told our daughters to listen at the door, promising that I would whistle shortly before I departed. Apparently I had. I say apparently, because I certainly wasn't aware of it. Having no recollection of whistling, I concluded that they were just having fun with me. Several days later, lost in deep thought in the washroom, I reached for the toilet paper. I heard myself whistle. Shocked, I started to laugh. What was going on? Upon reflection I determined the origin of such odd behavior. During my toilet-training, my mother would often leave me seated on the toilet while she went about her housework. I was to alert her when I finished. I would signal my readiness with a whistle — a behavior that became unconsciously ingrained.

18. Prompt: Make a multiple choice question with 5 options with the answer and explanation at the bottom.

[Passage]

* A person will tend to feel guilty when his or her conduct ___(a)___ that principle.
* They ___(b)___ laws that kept black people separate from white people.
* All money raised will be donated to ___(c)___.
* Borrowers are ___(d)___ for returning items on time and in good condition.
* Using the laundry machines late at night can ___(e)___ others' sleep.

[Stem]
각 문장의 빈칸에 들어갈 낱말의 문장 내의 영어정의로 적절하지 않은 것은?
① (a):
② (b):
③ (c):
④ (d):
⑤ (e):

빈칸에 들어갈 단어는 순서대로 다음과 같다.
violates
implemented
charity
responsible
disturb

여기서 한 개의 영어정의는 적절하지 않게 해 주세요.

답
*Show the contents of all the options.

19. Prompt: Make a multiple choice question with 5 options with the answer and explanation at the bottom.

[Passage]
14 The predators—insects that kill and consume other insects—are of many kinds. Some are quick and with the speed of swallows snatch their prey from the air. Others plod ⓐmethodically along a stem, plucking off and devouring ⓑsedentary insects like the aphids. The yellowjackets capture soft-bodied insects and feed the juices to their young. Muddauber wasps build columned nests of mud under the caves of houses and ⓒstock them with insects on which their young will feed. The horseguard wasp hovers above herds of grazing cattle, destroying the bloodsucking flies that torment them. The loudly buzzing syrphid fly, often ⓓmistaken for a bee, lays its eggs on leaves of aphis-infested plants; the hatching larvae then consume immense numbers of aphids. Ladybugs or lady beetles are among the most effective destroyers of aphids, scale insects, and other plant-eating insects. Literally hundreds of aphids are consumed by a single ladybug to ⓔstoke the little fires of energy which she requires to produce even a single batch of eggs.

챗GPT 4 Better Questions

[Stem]
본문에 나온 각 단어의 문맥적 영영풀이와 예문이 모두 옳지 않은 것을 하나 고르시오.

[Type of Alternative]
① ⓐmethodically:
   Example sentence:
② ⓑsedentary:
   Example sentence:
③ ⓒstock:
   Example sentence:
④ ⓓmistaken for:
   Example sentence:
⑤ ⓔstoke:
   Example sentence:

답
*Show the contents of all the options.

M·E·M·O

chatGPT를 활용한 영어문제 창작

Version 2.0

PART 4
chatGPT를 활용한 실전문제 소개

이번 장에선 chatGPT를 활용하여 창작한 실전문제를 살펴보겠습니다.
해당 문제들을 보면서 더 좋은 아이디어로 참신한 문제를 만들어 보세요.

4 Better Questions

[1-4] 다음을 읽고, 물음에 답하시오.

"It is approaching one in the morning, and I am ⓐ_____ my phone. The TV is on, the laptop is whirring away, and I have even got the radio ⓑ_____. If anyone asked, I would tell them I am a night person. The truth, though, is that I am suffering from FOMO, a condition whose acronymic name stands for the Fear of Missing Out."

This is the experience of worrying that other people have more friends than you, are doing more interesting things than you, and are just all around living a better and cooler life. It is actually not something new — diverse forms of this condition have been around for ages. Yet its ⓒ_____ and intensity in our modern age are ⓓ_____.

One of the prime sources of FOMO, ㉠as you may have guessed, is social media, which allows you to check out what is happening in other people's lives. Imagine you are spending a quiet night at home and you see pictures online of your friends having fun together. Or maybe you are still ⓔ_____ at your homework and you catch some of your fellow classmates enjoying their day out at the amusement park.

Just scroll through the mountains of pictures and comments on social media and ㉡you will get the idea. However, FOMO-inducing media is hardly limited to the Internet. Simply take a look at the TV and you are faced with reality shows that tend to glorify the fabulous lifestyles of the rich and famous and advertisements that are populated only by gorgeous young people at beach parties or on fantastic road trips.

What might be some of your first reactions to such visual stimuli? The symptoms of an onset of FOMO include nervousness, sudden restlessness, and a general feeling of anxiety that starts to impair your brain function. ㉢Allowed to fester, it sucks you into living and judging other people's lives instead of enjoying your own, and it turns what could be motivation for ㉣taking life by the horns into extreme envy and depression. In order to remedy the situation once you feel an attack of FOMO coming on, make efforts to ward it off by asking yourself the following simple questions.

PART 4

01 빈칸 ⓐ~ⓔ에 들어갈 표현과 문맥적 의미, 그리고 그 활용이 <u>적절하지 않을 것을 두 개</u> 고르면?

①	ⓐ glued to
	to be completely engrossed or absorbed in something, often to the point of being unable to divert one's attention.
	I was so **glued to** my book that I didn't even notice when my friend walked into the room.
②	ⓑ on standby
	to be ready and waiting to act or be called upon if needed.
	The ambulance drivers were **on standby** in case of any emergencies during the concert.
③	ⓒ prevalence
	the state or condition of being widespread or in general use or acceptance
	The **prevalence** of social media has dramatically changed the way people communicate and interact with one another.
④	ⓓ precedented
	something that has never been done before, or has never happened before in history
	The COVID-19 pandemic was an **precedented** global event that affected people all over the world.
⑤	ⓔ toiling away
	to work hard, often for a long period of time, in a laborious or repetitive manner
	After a long week of work, it's nice to spend the weekend **tailing away** and taking it easy instead of toiling away on more projects.

02 Which of the following can <u>NOT</u> be answered from the passage?

① What is FOMO and how is it experienced?
② How has social media contributed to the prevalence of FOMO?
③ What are the symptoms of FOMO?
④ What is the remedy for FOMO?
⑤ How many people in the world suffer from FOMO?

챗GPT 4 Better Questions

03 밑줄 친 ㉠~㉣에 대한 설명 중 <u>옳은 것만으로</u> 짝지어진 것은?

> I. The purpose of saying ㉠ is that the author believes the reader has already guessed or assumed that social media is one of the prime sources of FOMO. The phrase serves to introduce the topic of social media as a source of FOMO in a more casual or conversational manner.
>
> II. What the phrase in ㉡ means is that by looking at social media, you will be able to see examples of what people are doing and how they are having fun, which may make you feel like you are missing out on something.
>
> III. The contextual meaning of ㉢ is "if the feelings of FOMO are not addressed and dealt with."
>
> IV. The contextual meaning of ㉣ is "constantly comparing oneself to others."

① I, and III only
② I and IV only
③ II, III and IV only
④ III and IV only
⑤ I, II, and III only

04 아래는 본문의 내용을 바탕으로 작성한 논문이다. 본문의 내용에 비추어 <u>어색한 부분을</u> 포함한 것을 <u>한 개</u> 고르시오.

> ### Introduction
>
> In today's digital age, many of us are glued to our screens and constantly connected to social media. However, this has led to a phenomenon called FOMO or the Fear of Missing Out. ⓐ<u>This is the experience of worrying that other people have more friends than you, are doing more interesting things than you, and are just all around living a better and cooler life.</u> This paper will explore the causes and effects of FOMO and provide some solutions to combat it.
>
> ### Body:
>
> FOMO is not a new phenomenon. ⓑ<u>Diverse forms of this condition have been around for ages.</u> However, its prevalence and intensity in our modern age are unprecedented. ⓒ<u>One of the prime sources of FOMO is social media, which allows you to check out what is happening in other people's lives.</u> The constant scrolling through pictures and comments on social media can induce FOMO. ⓓ<u>However, FOMO-inducing media is fairly limited to the Internet except in TV shows and advertisements where the fabulous</u>

lifestyles of the rich and famous are glorified, resulting only in making us feel inadequate.

The symptoms of an onset of FOMO include nervousness, sudden restlessness, and a general feeling of anxiety that starts to impair your brain function. ⓔFOMO can turn what could be motivation for taking life by the horns into extreme envy and depression. To remedy the situation, it is important to ward off FOMO by asking yourself some simple questions. Do you really want to be doing what the other person is doing? Are you just trying to fit in? Are you missing out on your own life by comparing it to others?

Conclusion

In conclusion, FOMO is a common condition that can have negative effects on our mental health. The prevalence of social media and other media sources can induce FOMO and make us feel inadequate. However, by asking ourselves some simple questions and focusing on our own lives, we can combat FOMO and lead a more fulfilling life.

① ⓐ
② ⓑ
③ ⓒ
④ ⓓ
⑤ ⓔ

[5-7] 다음을 읽고, 물음에 답하시오.

Well, Ethan is only five feet tall, and his legs unnaturally bend away from each other. It is difficult for him to walk, run, or move around. Because of his condition, he decided to leave his crowded high school in the big city. He moved to our school in the middle of his first year in high school. That following summer, he asked the coach if he could join the football team as a sophomore. The coach wasn't sure at first, but in the end he allowed Ethan to come to practice. Regardless of his physical difficulties, Ethan worked just as hard as every other player on the team. Although (A)_____, he poured his heart and soul into practice every day.

Over time, however, Ethan became valuable to the team in different ways. His passion for the game was an inspiration to all his teammates. Because Ethan motivated and encouraged them, they became his most passionate fans. Day in and day out, seeing Ethan's smile,

챗GPT 4 Better Questions

positive attitude, and hard work lifted everyone's spirits. Right before every game, Ethan would always be in the middle of the group offering motivational words. He had a special talent for calming people down and bringing out the best in them. Ethan was also Winston High's loudest supporter. He always observed each play carefully from the sidelines. Although he wasn't the one making the actual plays on the field, (B)_____. Everyone could sense his love for football, and the coaches admired his commitment.

For the past three years, Ethan has been schooling us all in the game of life. He always reminds us that everyone is important to a team's success, though their role on the team may be small. Instead of putting all his efforts into trying to be the team's best player, he has done everything he can to make the team better. As Ethan has shown us, lifting up those around us is also of great worth. When we help others shine, their light will shine on us in return. Yes, sometimes there is something better than being the best.

05 윗글의 밑줄 (A), (B)에 들어갈 문장으로 바르게 짝지은 것은?

①	(A)	he had a more comprehensive knowledge of the game than any other player on the team
	(B)	Ethan was always mentally present with his teammates
②	(A)	he knew he would never be a valuable player in any of the team's games
	(B)	Ethan's mind was always right there with his teammates
③	(A)	Ethan's physical challenges were an obvious obstacle to his performances on the field
	(B)	he constantly reassured himself that he would eventually get the opportunity to showcase his abilities.
④	(A)	he was "a pain in the neck" on the team
	(B)	Ethan was always mentally present with his teammates
⑤	(A)	he knew more than any other person that he was physically limited
	(B)	he constantly reassured himself that he would eventually get the opportunity to showcase his abilities.

06 본문의 이해로 부적절한 사람을 모두 고르시오.

① 한영: Despite facing challenges in his everyday life, he showed a remarkable work ethic and determination to improve.

② 배재: Ethan's story serves as a reminder that with hard work and dedication, anyone can overcome their obstacles and make a meaningful contribution to their community."

③ 송파: The coach never had any doubts that, despite Ethan's physical limitations, he would be a real contributor on and off the field, and that eventually proved to be true on the pitch.

④ 고덕: Ethan's physical condition may have limited his ability to play football, but it didn't stop him from becoming a valuable member of the team.

⑤ 명일: Although Ethan's physical limitations were present, his mental toughness enabled him to score crucial goals during games, proving that his physical flaws did not hinder his ability to contribute to the team's success.

07 Below is a literary review on the passage. Among the underlined sentences ⓐ~ⓔ, which of the following is NOT consistent with the passage?

The passage tells the inspiring story of Ethan, a high school student with physical limitations who overcomes his challenges to become a valuable member of his school's football team. ⓐThe narrative is powerful, with vivid descriptions of Ethan's physical struggles and his unwavering dedication to the sport. The author masterfully portrays Ethan's transformation from a new kid in school to a respected leader on the team.

The narrative is expertly crafted to highlight the universal themes of perseverance and the importance of teamwork. ⓑThe author's use of figurative language and powerful euphemism effectively conveys the emotional impact of Ethan's journey. For instance, the phrase "Ethan poured his heart and soul into practice every day" captures the intensity and commitment of his efforts to succeed.

Furthermore, the author adeptly conveys the message that everyone can contribute to the success of a team, regardless of their physical abilities. Ethan's passion and positive attitude inspire his teammates to give their best and support each other. ⓒHis journey shows that one can make a significant impact through kindness, encouragement, and commitment.

ⓓThe passage is a remarkable testament to the human spirit and a valuable

챗GPT 4 Better Questions

> lesson in the power of perseverance and teamwork. It inspires readers to believe in their potential and the potential of others, to embrace challenges and work hard towards their goals, and to appreciate the value of lifting up others around us. ⓔThe narrative is a powerful reminder that sometimes, being the best is not the most important thing.

① ⓐ ② ⓑ
③ ⓒ ④ ⓓ
⑤ ⓔ

[8-9] 아래 [B]는 글 [A]를 읽고, 작성한 시이다. 물음에 답하시오.

[A]

With only two minutes to play, both teams were fighting for the football. It was the last home game for the seniors of Winston High, and they were determined to win. Since it had been a close game the whole evening, the best players of each team hadn't left the field. Once Winston High's coach finally knew that victory was theirs, all the seniors on the sidelines were allowed to play for the last few seconds. One of the seniors, Ethan, was especially happy. He had never played in any of the games before. Now, Ethan was finally getting the chance to step onto the grass. When the rival team dropped the ball, one of our players recovered it and quickly ran down the field with it. Ethan ran right after him to catch up. As our player got closer to the end zone, he saw Ethan behind him on his left. Instead of running straight ahead, the player kindly passed the ball to Ethan so that he could score a touchdown.

All eyes were on Ethan. With the ball in his hands, everything seemed to be moving in slow motion, like in a Hollywood movie. People kept their eyes on him as he made his way to the end zone. They saw him cross the goal line right before the clock ran out. Unexpectedly, everyone in the crowd leapt to their feet with their hands in the air. They were bursting with excited shouts and unending cheers for Ethan. In this moment, all of Ethan's hard work and dedication was being rewarded with glory. Ethan's touchdown didn't win the game, but it will be worth remembering. By now you're probably wondering why.

[B]

With two minutes ⓐ_____ on the clock
Both teams were giving it their all

Winston High's seniors were determined
To win, and not to fall

It had been a ⓑ_____ game all evening
The best players never left the field
And then, the coach knew victory was theirs
(가)The seniors could finally yield

Ethan was especially happy
He had never played before
But now, he was getting his chance
To step onto the field's ⓒ_____

The rival team dropped the ball
One of our players quickly recovered
Ethan ran right after him to catch up
And the goal line was then discovered

The player saw Ethan behind him
And passed the ball with kindness and grace
All eyes were on Ethan as he made his way
To score the touchdown, (나)the final embrace

People watched in slow motion
As Ethan crossed the goal line with ⓓ_____
The crowd leapt to their feet with excitement
Their cheers echoed far and wide

It was a moment of glory
For Ethan's hard work and dedication
Though the touchdown didn't win the game
It will be remembered with ⓔ_____.

08 빈칸 ⓐ~ⓔ에 대한 들어갈 표현이 문맥적으로 <u>어색한</u> 것은?

① ⓐ left
② ⓑ neck-and-neck
③ ⓒ green floor
④ ⓓ humiliation
⑤ ⓔ admiration

09 Which of the following best interprets the <u>CONTEXTUAL</u> meanings of the underlined (A) and (B)?

①	(A)	The seniors could finally rest after a tough game
	(B)	the last tackle before the touchdown.
②	(A)	The seniors were able to surrender
	(B)	the moment when Ethan scores the touchdown
③	(A)	The seniors could finally win
	(B)	the last score before the end of the game
④	(A)	the senior players could finally get the chance to play in the game
	(B)	the final celebration after the touchdown
⑤	(A)	The seniors were finally able to pass the responsibility to the younger players
	(B)	the final run towards the touchdown

[10-11] 다음을 읽고, 물음에 답하시오.

> For years, I've been working in the historically African-American neighborhood of Bayview Hunters Point in San Francisco, on a plot of land that once held a power plant. Back in the '90s, a community group led by mothers who lived in the public housing on the hill above the plant fought for its closure. They won. <u>The utility company</u> finally tore it down, cleaned the soil and capped most of the site with asphalt so that the clean soil wouldn't blow away. Sounds like a success story, right? (A)<u>Well, not so fast</u>. You see, because of various issues

like land entitlements, lease agreements, etc., the land actually couldn't be redeveloped for at least five to 10 years. What that meant is that this community that had been living near a power plant for decades, now had 30 acres of asphalt in their backyard. (B)To put that in context for you, 30 acres is equal to about 30 football fields. Now, the utility company didn't want to be the bad guy here. Recognizing that they owed the community, (C)they actually put out a call for designers to propose temporary uses for this site, hoping to turn it into a community benefit rather than blight.

I'm part of the diverse team of designers that responded to that call, and for the last four years, we've been collaborating with those mothers and other residents, as well as local organizations and the utility company. We've been experimenting with all types of events to try and address issues of spatial justice. Everything from job training workshops to an annual circus to even a beautiful, new shoreline trail. In the four years that we've been operational, over 12,000 people have come and done something on this site (D)that we hope has transformed their relationship to it. But lately, I'm starting to realize that events are not enough.

A few months ago, there was a community meeting in this neighborhood. The utility company was finally ready to talk concretely about long-term redevelopment. That meeting was kind of a disaster. There was a lot of yelling and anger. People asked things like, (E)"If you're going to sell it to a developer, wouldn't they just build luxury condos like everyone else?" And "Where has the city been?" "Why aren't there more jobs and resources in this neighborhood?"

It was not that our events had failed to bring joy. But in spite of that, there was still pain here. Pain from a history of environmental injustice that left many industrial uses in this neighborhood, leaving residents living near toxic waste and, literally, shit. There's pain from the fact that this zip code still has one of the lowest per capita income, highest unemployment and highest incarceration rates in a city which tech giants like Twitter, Airbnb and Uber call home. And those tech companies -- hm -- they've actually helped to trigger a gentrification push that is rapidly redefining this neighborhood, both in terms of identity and population.

챗GPT 4 Better Questions

+10 밑줄 친 the utility company와 관련된 내용과 거리가 먼 것을 두 개 고르시오.

(1) The power plant operating in Bayview Hunters Point had to be demolished due to backlash from a group of local residents.

(2) The company covered the site of the plant with asphalt to prevent the soil from flying.

(3) The company undertook a project to transform a former plant site covered with asphalt into one that would benefit the community.

(4) When the former site used as a power plant became obsolete, the company issued a notice seeking a new site for the plant.

(5) Residents' reactions to the long-term redevelopment for industrial uses proposed by the company were divided into different opinions.

11 글 전체의 내용을 바탕으로 밑줄 친 (A) ~ (E) 각 문장에 대한 설명으로 옳지 않은 것을 고르시오.

(1) (A) : The phrase carries the meaning that one disagrees with what someone has said.

(2) (B) : Figurative expression is used to help the reader better understand.

(3) (C) : As the first step toward the company's long-term goal for coexistence with the community, it shows the company's short-term efforts to dispel the dissatisfaction of the residents.

(4) (D) : Grammatically speaking, the phrase 'we hope' is inserted between the relative pronoun and the verb. The word 'it' at the end refers to 'this site'.

(5) (E) : It can be inferred that what local people really want is 'spatial justice', which emphasizes industrial development that is aligned with the benefit of the community.

12 본문을 읽고, 핵심내용을 요약한 내용이다. 아래 빈칸 어디에도 들어갈 수 없는 단어는?

> The world has become a nation of laws and governance that has introduced a system of public administration and management to keep order. With this administrative management system, urban institutions of government have evolved to offer increasing levels of services to their citizenry, provided through a taxation process and/or fee for services (e.g., police and fire, street maintenance, utilities, waste management, etc.). Frequently this has displaced citizen involvement. Money for services is not a replacement for citizen responsibility and public participation. Responsibility of the

citizen is slowly being supplanted by government being the substitute provider. Consequentially, there is a philosophical and social change in attitude and sense of responsibility of our urban-based society to become involved. The sense of community and associated responsibility of all citizens to be active participants is therefore diminishing. Governmental substitution for citizen duty and involvement can have serious implications. This impedes the nations of the world to be responsive to natural and man-made disasters as part of global preparedness.

The _____ of the government with _____, which has increased the level of providing public services based on public taxes, has _____ the responsibility and role of citizens in public participation. This governmental _____ for citizen duty and involvement has an adverse effect on the role of citizens in preparing for natural and man-made _____ that may occur across the board.

(1) substitution
(2) responsibility
(3) emergence
(4) weakened
(5) "a fat wallet"

[13-14] 다음을 읽고, 물음에 답하시오.

Q. You've been quoted as saying, "You may never touch the ocean, but the ocean touches you." What do you mean by this?

[A] Dr. Earle: The vast majority of the earth's water, about 97%, is contained in oceans. What's more, ⓐthe water vapor that's in the air and the water that falls from the sky in the form of precipitation originates in the oceans. The ocean powers the constant flow of water that has been cycling around our planet for ages, and thus it can be thought of, in a way, as the heart of our planet's circulatory system.

[B] That's why I like to say the ocean is where the action is, but its significance doesn't stop there. ⓑIt is also where oxygen comes from, so if you took away the ocean, you have a planet much like Mars. ⓒThe ocean governs planetary chemistry, regulates temperature, and has the power to directly affect many of the things in life we care

챗GPT 4 Better Questions

about most, such as the economy, our health, our security, and above all else, our basic ability to survive on this planet. Ultimately, that is the most essential thing we take out of the ocean—our very existence.

[C] ⓓI was inspired by a number of great scientists who understood that the ocean and the atmosphere are a single, continuous, interacting system, inextricably linked and worked together in concert. Many people consider the atmosphere and the ocean to be completely separate, but ⓔwhen you view them from a distance, it seems obvious that they make up one interacting system. We may never touch the ocean, but the ocean touches us with every breath we take and every drop of water we drink.

13 밑줄 친 ⓐ~ⓔ 중 어법 상 어색한 것이 포함된 것을 모두 고르시오.

① ⓐ
② ⓑ
③ ⓒ
④ ⓓ
⑤ ⓔ

14 아래는 위 본문을 쓰기 전의 개요에 작성한 것이다. 밑줄 친 부분 중 본문과 일치하지 않는 부분은?

I. Introduction

①Quotation from Dr. Earle: "You may never touch the ocean, but the ocean touches you."

The passage will explore the meaning behind this statement.

II. Body

- ②The significance of the ocean

The majority of the earth's water is contained in the oceans

The ocean is the source of water vapor and precipitation

The ocean powers the water cycle and can be thought of as the heart of the planet's circulatory system

- ③The ocean's impact on life

The ocean is where oxygen comes from and is essential for life on earth

The ocean regulates planetary chemistry and temperature

The ocean directly affects important aspects of life such as the economy, health, and security

- ④The ocean and the atmosphere
Explanation that the ocean and atmosphere are interconnected systems
Contrary to the popular belief, the ocean and atmosphere don't work together in concert
The ocean touches us with every breath we take and every drop of water we drink

III. Conclusion
⑤Restate the significance of the ocean and its impact on life
Reiterate the quote from Dr. Earle and its meaning.

[15-16] 다음을 읽고, 물음에 답하시오.

Q. How do problems such as overfishing affect our oceans?
Dr. Earle: The chemistry of the ocean is also shaped by life in the ocean and its vast, interconnected food webs. Let me give you an example. A whale eats krill, and after the digestion process, it puts back into the ocean nutrients that promote the growth of phytoplankton, which are consumed by krill, which in turn are ⓐconsumed by more whales, and so on. That's a simple example of these chains of events that have been taking place for over hundreds of millions of years.

Nothing has ever happened to ocean wildlife that equals to what occurred in the latter part of the 20th century. Now, in the 21st century, humans are equipped with technology capable of ⓑextracting hundreds of millions of tons of ocean wildlife, and in the process of doing so, we are destroying the ⓒintegrity of the wild ocean's natural systems, which have taken all of ⓓpreceding history to be established. In all of our planet's history, never has there been a predator as powerful, as ⓔcomprehensive, and as destructive as humans.

챗GPT 4 Better Questions

15 밑줄 친 ⓐ~ⓔ의 문맥적 의미와 그 예문으로 적절하지 <u>않은</u> 것을 <u>모두</u> 고르면?

①	ⓐ consumed
	to eat or use up
	It's important to <u>consume</u> a balanced diet in order to maintain good health.
②	ⓑ extracting
	to remove or take out
	The dentist had to <u>extract</u> my wisdom teeth because they were causing me a lot of pain.
③	ⓒ integrity
	the quality of being whole and undivided
	A modern extension on the old building would ruin its architectural <u>integrity</u>.
④	ⓓ preceding
	entirely new or unique, without any comparable previous examples
	The <u>preceding</u> chapter in the book provided important background information for the current one.
⑤	ⓔ comprehensive
	affecting all levels of the food chain and causing widespread and significant damage
	He explained a complex topic in a way that is <u>comprehensive</u> to their students by using simple language and providing clear examples.

16 아래는 윗글을 읽고 <u>해양생태계 보호 방안</u>에 대한 <u>토론</u>한 내용이다. 흐름상 적절하지 <u>않</u>은 발언을 한 학생은?

① 수지: We should Implement sustainable fishing practices that regulate the amount and type of fish that can be caught.
② 지성: We must create marine protected areas where fishing is prohibited or restricted to allow fish populations to recover.
③ 준성: We should promote education and awareness about the importance of healthy oceans and the impact of overfishing on marine ecosystems.
④ 지현: It is important to encourage the use of alternative protein sources, such as

plant-based or lab-grown alternatives, to put a complete end to the consumption of seafood.

⑤ 기찬: It is time to develop new technologies that allow for more precise and selective fishing to reduce bycatch and minimize harm to non-target species.

* bycatch: fish or other sea creatures that are caught unintentionally by people who are trying to catch other types of fish

[17-20] 다음을 읽고, 물음에 답하시오.

> Pesticides of various types are used in most sectors of the U.S. economy. In general terms, a pesticide is any agent (use) to kill or control undesired insects, weeds, rodents, fungi, bacteria, or other organisms. Thus, the term "pesticides" includes insecticides, herbicides, rodenticides, fungicides, nematicides, and acaricides as well as disinfectants, fumigants, wood preservatives, and plant growth regulators. Pesticides play a vital role in (control) agricultural, industrial, home/garden, and public health pests. Many crops, commodities, and services in the United States could not (supply) in an economic fashion without controlling pests using chemicals or other means. As a result, goods and services can be supplied at lower costs and/or with better quality. These economic benefits from pesticide use are not achieved without potential risks to human health and the environment due to the toxicity of pesticide chemicals. For this reason, these chemicals are regulated under federal or state pesticide laws (avoid) unacceptable risks.

17 괄호 안의 단어의 바른 형태를 적으시오. (필요시, 단어 추가할 것)

18 본문에 대한 이해 또는 추론으로 <u>가장 부적절한 것</u>은?

① Pesticides are an essential tool in managing pests that can damage crops, products, and public health.
② The term "pesticide" is a generic term that encompasses various agents used to manage and control undesired organisms, including insects, weeds, rodents, fungi, bacteria, and other organisms.
③ There are various forms of pesticides that serve different purposes.

④ Without pesticides, the cost of production could be much lower, and the quality of goods and services could also be lower.

⑤ The benefits of pesticide use come at a cost, which should be thoroughly assessed and managed at the federal or state level.

19 본문과 관련하여 Pesticide의 활용에 대한 수행평가로 찬반의 견해를 나누었다. 각각의 항목이 바르게 연결되지 <u>않은</u> 짝은?

①	Pros	Pesticides are effective in controlling pests that damage crops, thus leading to higher yields and better quality produce.
	Cons	Pesticides can have adverse effects on human health, such as causing cancer, birth defects, and neurological disorders.
②	Pros	Pesticides can be used in a variety of sectors such as agriculture, industry, and public health to control pests that pose a threat to human health and the environment.
	Cons	Pesticides can harm non-target organisms such as beneficial insects, birds, and mammals, leading to a decline in biodiversity.
③	Pros	Pesticides help to reduce the cost of producing goods and services, making them more accessible to consumers.
	Cons	Pesticides can contaminate soil, water, and air, leading to environmental pollution and ecosystem degradation.
④	Pros	Pesticides can lead to the development of pesticide-resistant pests, making them less effective over time.
	Cons	Pesticides are easy to use and can quickly control pest outbreaks, preventing further damage.
⑤	Pros	Pesticides can help to control the spread of diseases carried by insects and rodents, which is crucial for public health.
	Cons	Pesticide use can have long-term effects on soil health, leading to a decline in soil fertility and nutrient depletion.

20 밑줄 친 ⓐ~ⓗ에 대한 설명 중 옳은 것의 총 개수는?

Archaeologists have long discussed the motives that ⓐcompelled people to begin growing crops and raising animals: Was it overpopulation or climate change that made them do so? Or was it a desire to settle down? It is likely that in many parts of the world, Mesolithic foragers had filled up the landscape, so when ⓑa hunting-gathering band had ⓒdepleted its local resources, it could not simply move into a new unoccupied territory. If, in addition, the carrying capacity of the land was ⓓincreased, the need for new resources was even more urgent. The search for security might have been a strong motive as well. In many places, ⓔsharp seasonal variations provided an incentive for people to ⓕput aside food for the ⓖlean months of the year by storing grains and nuts or by capturing and confining animals to be eaten later. Besides, even the richest natural environments went through cycles of abundance and scarcity and seasons of plenty and ⓗwant. Certain food sources, such as nut-bearing trees, varied their yields from year to year, even in a steady climate.   *Mesolithic 중석기 시대의 **forager 수렵 채집인

* ⓐ can be replaced with 'pressured.'
* A hunting-gathering band in ⓑ is the same entity with the Mesolithic foragers mentioned in the same sentence.
* A synonym for "depleted" in ⓓ could be "exhausted" or 'drained'.
* The term "increased" used in ⓓ is not suitable for the context and should be replaced with "reduced."
* Given the context, 'sharp' in ⓔ means that the seasonal variations were noticeable and distinct. Some possible replacements could be 'marked' 'significant,' or 'pronounced.'
* Given the context, 'put aside' in ⓕ means to save or reserve something for future use.
* The word 'lean' in ⓖ refers to a time when food or resources are in short supply.
* Given the context, 'want' in ⓗ means a desire to stay filled with food.

① 4개 ② 5개
③ 6개 ④ 7개
⑤ 8개

챗GPT 4 Better Questions

[21-22] 다음을 읽고, 물음에 답하시오.

Along with small everyday items, much bigger things can also be upcycled—even old buildings that cannot be used for their original purpose anymore. The German Government showed us an excellent example of this with a former steel plant that closed in 1985. Rather than destroy the plant's buildings or abandon the entire facility, they decided to give it new meaning as a series of useful public structures. Many of the buildings kept their original shapes, but received extra equipment and new designs in their surrounding areas. For instance, old gas tanks became pools for divers. Concrete walls of iron storage towers were turned into ideal training fields for rock climbers. Can you believe a building for melting metal is now a viewing platform with a gorgeous 360-degree view? The final result is the Landscape Park Duisburg Nord. It has almost 570 acres of land filled with gardens, cycling paths, and pretty lights at night, in addition to its creatively repurposed buildings.

21 Which is the topic of the passage?

① Repurposing old industrial sites for public use
② The history of a former steel plant in Germany
③ The importance of preserving heritage buildings
④ The development of Landscape Park Duisburg Nord
⑤ The environmental impact of demolishing old buildings

22 본문의 내용을 바탕으로 세 사람이 나눈 대화이다. 박스 안의 단어를 사용하여 대화를 완성하시오. (단, 박스안의 단어 외 추가단어 있음. 필요 시 문맥에 맞게 단어형태를 변형할 것)

Person 1: Have you heard of upcycling?
Person 2: Yeah, it's when you give something old or ㉠_____ a new purpose, right?
Person 1: Exactly! And it's not just for small items. The German Government did an amazing job of upcycling an entire old steel plant.
Person 3: Really? What did they do with it?
Person 1: Instead of ㉡_____ _____ _____, they turned the buildings into useful public structures. They even ㉢_____ old gas tanks into pools for divers and the walls of iron storage towers into training fields for rock climbers.

Person 2: And get this, they turned a building for melting metal into a viewing platform with a 360-degree view!

Person 3: That's incredible! What's it like now?

Person 1: It's now called the Landscape Park Duisburg Nord, and it has almost 570 acres of land filled with gardens, cycling paths, and pretty lights at night. It's a great example of preserving the environment and the ㉣_____ of a place.

sustain	into	original
innovative	develop	down
discard	anticipate	upcycle
facilitate	receive	up
tear	repurpose	heritage

㉠ _____

㉡ _____ _____ _____

㉢ _____

㉣ _____

저 자 약 력

박지성

고려대학교 영어영문/언어학과 졸업

[현] 오목교역 스피디업 특목고/수능/내신
[현] 대치 다원교육 내신 용인외대부고 2학년
[현] 대치 메카학원 한영외고 내신 1학년
[현] 해커스 편입강사

[저서]
"chat GPT를 활용한 영어문제 창작하기" Version 1.0 (오스틴북스)
"실전대비 내신 서술형 고등영어" 기본편 (오스틴북스)
"실전대비 내신 서술형 고등영어" 실전편 (오스틴북스)
"서술형 잡는 중학 영문법" 레벨4. 동사편 (오스틴북스)
"서술형 잡는 중학 영문법" 레벨5. 품사편 (오스틴북스)
수능영어독해 정공법: 수능독해 단락독해 (종합EnG)
영어독해 개념이해 (종합EnG)
영어독해 문제원리 및 풀이 이해 (종합EnG)
수능독해 히든카드 (종합EnG)
단락독해의 정석 리딩 이노베이터 기본편 (종합EnG)
단락독해의 정석 리딩 이노베이터 실전편 (종합EnG)
자신만만 영문독해 (반석출판사)
세계 여성 명연설 30인 (반석출판사)
김용의 감성영어스피치 (종합EnG)
외 다수

"chat GPT를 활용한 영어문제 창작하기" Version 2.0

2024년 11월 20일 초판 발행

저　　자　박지성
발 행 인　김은영
발 행 처　오스틴북스
주　　소　경기도 고양시 일산동구 백석동 1351번지
전　　화　070)4123-5716
팩　　스　031)902-5716
등 록 번 호　제396-2010-000009호
e - m a i l　ssung7805@hanmail.net
홈 페 이 지　www.austinbooks.co.kr
ISBN　979-11-93806-48-7 (53740)
정　가　20,000원

* 이 책은 저작권법에 따라 보호받는 저작물이므로 무단 전재와 무단 복제를 금합니다.
* 파본이나 잘못된 책은 교환해 드립니다.
※ 저자와의 협의에 따라 인지 첩부를 생략함.